Living in Villages, Visiting in Palaces

ONE THOUSAND MEMORIES ... AND MORE

By Myrtle V. Thompson

To Roger,
& your Laura –

Myrtle Thompson
age 94+
Proverbs 3: 5, 6 –
Take the journey with me &
enjoy God's blessings!

Unless noted, all Scripture is from the NEW AMERICAN STANDARD BIBLE® (NASB). Scripture taken from the NASB Copyright © 1960, 1962, 1963, 1971, 1972, 1973, 1975, 1977, 1995 by The Lockman Foundation. Used by permission.

Scripture marked KJV is from the King James Version of the Holy Bible, Pure Cambridge Edition. Public Domain.

Maps on pages 65, 84, 213 and 242 are public domain and were accessed from Mapsland.com and published under Creative Commons Attribution-ShareAlike 3.0 Licence.

Cover photos by Thompson Family

Published by Faithful Sojourner Press
Suffolk, Virginia
ISBN 9798474514697

This book is a legacy of love, dedicated with heartfelt thanks to a long list of names and faces, all a part of who I am. It is the people who share in our lives which help shape and mold us:

My parents, my children, my extended family.

My friends and the churches which provided our prayer and financial needs as we served under TEAM -The Evangelical Alliance Mission, Wheaton, Illinois.

Candice Shelton, a retired Air Force officer who worked tirelessly, going through my collection of notebooks, journals and letters dating back to the 1950s. The book would never have become a reality without her part. We met when she and her husband were doing ministry in the same Assisted Living Facility where I was teaching Bible.

I also wish to thank Sandra Barker, a friend and author who has self-published her books and graciously gave of her time to help us do the same.

Myrtle V. "Jenny" Thompson

"I will extol You, my God, O King,
And I will bless Your name forever and ever.
Every day I will bless You,
And I will praise Your name forever and ever.
Great is the Lord, and highly to be praised,
And His greatness is unsearchable.
One generation shall praise Your works to another,
And shall declare Your mighty acts." (Psalm 145:1-4)

Contents

Preface

When my mom realized she was pregnant again, the eighth time, she struggled, not wanting to have another child, not knowing how they could care for the ones they already had. It was a painful time in the life of my parents. Mom would have been happy if her pregnancy had been terminated naturally.

Sixteen months earlier, they had lost a little daughter ten years old. This precious, lively, little girl had been loved by the whole community, who also felt the loss. She had fallen at school, hit her head on a cement slab, and was brought home with a headache. She died soon after, no one ever learning the cause. Mom was still grieving.

In desperation, she told me, she went outside one morning where no one could hear her, and lifting her hands to the sky, cried out, "Oh, God, if You will make me love this baby, I will give it back to You for whatever you want." A few months later, I was born, number eight in nine children, four others still at home. My oldest brother had joined the Navy, the second oldest had found a job away from home.

I first opened my eyes on a snowy day, February 25, 1928, delivered by a dear African American midwife. Everyone in the community called her "ol' Aunt Ella." She was known to be a very good midwife, adept and able to handle difficult situations she encountered. She was thought to be something of a mystic, with a bit of a superstitious nature.

When my head emerged, it was covered in a part of the amniotic sac. As she removed the membrane, she had said to Mom, "This young'un will cross the waters many times but never drown," a kind of prophetic utterance which none would have believed would come to pass, unless it meant swimming across the Deep Creek canal and back many times in my childhood.

But it did come to pass. At last count, I believe I have crossed the Atlantic Ocean nineteen times, and the Pacific, once. I have crossed rivers, lakes, seas, in many parts of the world, along with the Deep Creek Canal.

I am here now to tell my sojourn story.

Passing through the Valley, Our Personal Sojourn

Exodus 12:1-And the Lord spoke unto Moses and Aaron in the land of Egypt, saying, "This month shall be unto you the beginning of months, it shall be the first month of the year..."

The children of Israel were getting ready to leave the land of Egypt. They were going out by faith. God had made a way for their needs to be freely provided. In a somewhat humorous fashion those who sent them out were glad to see them go.

Theirs is not a missionary story but they were being taken out of Egypt to fulfill God's plan first put in place from Abraham's day. Jesus told His disciples to "go into all the world and preach the Gospel." Psalms 65 and 105 have similarities that speak to us, telling us what we are to do. We were going out to Pakistan, believing we were fulfilling that "great commission."

Our preparations were made. We would be leaving America on our way to a whole new land, expecting to arrive in the first month of the year, 1951. We would be faced with some of the same that Moses and his people faced in their day There was one difference. Moses was leading the sons of Abraham, Isaac, and Jacob. It was to this special group God had given the promises in Genesis 12.

Abraham had another son he dearly loved, Ishmael, but he was not the son of promise, Isaac was. Ishmael was born of an Egyptian mother. They were sent away when he was still young.

The Islamic faith still believes he has first rights because he was the firstborn, but it was human intervention, not God's plan.

What was the message which had so gripped us we wanted to share it with the sons of Ishmael? That man has no way to get to God in his own righteousness. We come to God in faith. Jesus Christ is our Mediator, the only Substitute between God and man. No Muslim denies we are sinners, only the way to go to Heaven and what will be awaiting us there.

Muslims observe some of the Old Testament traditions, prayer, fasting, giving of alms. They also say they believe in certain parts of the Scriptures, some from the Old Testament and some from the *Injil,* the New Testament. They understand we are sinners. The difference is in how to handle the sin question. They believe it is by good works. Paul quotes from the Psalms and the Old Testament prophets to remind us in the face of a Holy God we are all an unclean thing, but the blood of Jesus Christ can cleanse us from sin. it is not by good works. The narrative changes when we understand what we must do about our sin before we die.

We came to love the other son of Abraham and the people who came through him, the millions around the world, a growing number. There are many who strongly believe and propagate their faith more readily than do many Christians.

Our message would be the same for our Muslim friends and any others willing to listen, some of whom had already professed the Name of Christ but wanted teaching. We would seek to be faithful in prayer and in sharing God's Word.

Introduction

LIVING IN VILLAGES, VISITING IN PALACES
A Missionary Mother's Sojourn into the Life of Faith

"My frame was not hidden from You,
When I was made in secret ...
How precious also are Your thoughts to me, O God!
How vast is the sum of them!" (Psalm 139: 15, 17)

"Where did you come from, little one?
Who brought you here, to this small place?
How came your birth?
Can you tell us your worth?

Will you share the memories of a life lived long?
And tell us the things that have made you strong?

"I came from Him Who gave me life
He placed me here, ~ ~ and then, there
In villages, small
In palaces tall
I have seen where the great KING reigns!
(MVT, 2009)

"Go home to your people and report to them what great things
the Lord has done for you, and how He had mercy on you."
(Mark 5:19)

Mine is the life story of a missionary mother who came to
know the King of Kings, to hear a voice many others do not hear,

9

a call to a life which would place her in villages where physical poverty had a grip on the lives of the people, and in palaces where there was wealth and worth beyond her human imagination.

At the end, she came to see that whether in village or palace, it is the spiritual wealth of God's wonderful Grace which changes people and prepares them for living in the presence of the Holy God.

****

My name is Myrtle Virginia Williams Thompson. In the same house by two parents who both loved me, I was called Myrtle (my mom's choice; she and my siblings called me that) Virginia (my dad never called me by any other name) Williams, my family name. When I married Richard, that was changed to Thompson.

I grew up being teased about the name Myrtle and I came to dislike it intensely. When I was only six or seven years old, I had been teased by some kids who had called out, "Moidle's got a toidle in her goidle!" I went running into the house and asked my mom why she named me that, saying "I hate that name; when I leave home, I will never tell anyone that is my name!" She took me by the arm, led me to the hall window and pointed out the beautiful crepe myrtle trees which my dad had planted on our property line. They were all in bloom. She said, "See, aren't they beautiful? That is why I named you Myrtle!" It did not help my feelings.

In college, my roommates shortened Virginia to Jenny, so I am MVT, aka Jenny Thompson. My husband had never called me anything but Jenny. It was after I began studying and teaching Bible that I discovered one of my favorite people, Queen Esther, had the Jewish name Hadassah, translated Myrtle. It comes from the name of a tree or bush. I saw it as a time-honored name of worth, and I let those childhood memories go by me. More important was to believe God's Word.

"How blessed is the man who does not walk in the counsel of the wicked ...
He will be like a tree firmly planted by streams of water,
Which yields its fruit in its season
And its leaf does not wither;
And in whatever he does, he prospers." (Psalm 1:1,3)

I began to relate those verses to the meaning of faith in my life. Jesus pointed out how His Father cared for the flowers of the field and the birds of the air. I knew if God is that trustworthy, I should trust Him. With the help of our beloved pastor and his wife, as well as family and friends, I completed college, but along the way, I learned God does not spoil His children. I have sometimes cried out to God for something and found myself hurting because He was not answering.

How can I explain this? But I must, and the best way to say it is that the words *wait, waited, and waiting* occur over and over in the Scripture, reminding us to wait on the Lord, to have patience, to wait for His answers. He is rarely in a hurry. In our younger days, waiting is a trial we find difficult to endure! Perhaps waiting has the same effect on us that marinade has on meat: it tenderizes us and makes us more palatable for those to whom we want to minister. Although it is still hard to do, I think I have learned in a large measure to wait. At times, it was all that I could do!

****

From one small rural village in the US to small villages in other parts of the world, I have moved about from place to place, not *in faith*, but rather *into faith*. Along the way, it was my privilege to sit with some of the poor in villages and meet those who live in palaces. In the large cities, I saw the monuments which dedicated men with brilliant artistic minds and talent have created.

This was my sojourn. That is, there was no stopping place for very long. In spite of where I might have liked to have stayed, and what I might have liked to have done, I had to keep moving. The great King of Kings was leading in another direction. There were lessons of faith to be learned at each stopping point, lessons about God, about His Word, lessons about people, lessons about myself. There was sometimes a faltering, even a lapse in faith, as the road traveled upward, but God's Word always proved to be true and His promises as real as they were to men of old.

What does the Scripture teach us about faith?

There is much about faithfulness in the Old Testament, but only two writers personalize it as a part of the belief system. Deuteronomy 32 speaks of "children in whom is no faith, or "faithfulness" and Habakkuk 2:4 says, "the just shall live by his faith." St. Paul reaches back to Habakkuk's admonition and repeats it in Romans and Galatians, "the just shall live by faith."

What do we understand and what should we do with what we understand?

In short, what is faith?

What is faith? It is not anything tangible. We can't hold it in our hands. Is it something we can trust? Put into a savings account as we would put money into a bank? For an answer, the writer of Hebrews says,

"... faith is the assurance of things hoped for, the conviction of things not seen ...
By faith we understand ..." (Hebrews 11:1, 3)

When the curtains are drawn back, we are shown the reason for their moving around. It is given in Hebrews 11; they were all "looking for a city whose builder and ruler is God." They were said to be sojourners. They, like the desert Bedouins of today, moved their tents from place to place over the desert, looking for better pastureland. When they pitched their tents, they did not expect to remain in one place. God was directing the moves.

Abraham sojourned when he went down into Egypt because of a famine. Jacob sojourned with Laban's family. The children of Israel may have thought they were only going for a short stay when Joseph arranged for them to go down to Egypt. They remained there over 400 years, but the record in Scripture called it a sojourn. Because of a famine, Naomi sojourned with her husband and sons to Moab. When the curtains are drawn back and the reason for the moving around is given in Hebrews 11, we read about the sojourn of all these people.

In 1 Chronicles 29, King David is praying, praising, and thanking God. He says of himself and his people,

*"We are sojourners before You ... our days on earth
are like a shadow...all that we have is from Your Hand..."*

All these people knew the place where they were was not their final home. They saw themselves on a journey, just passing through this world, not expecting to remain on earth forever. They were looking for a world to come in which righteousness would reign.

The Bible builds a pyramid from the events surrounding their circumstances. They went through trials and tribulations as they moved from one place to another, often facing terrible situations, sometimes living in caves, at other times, being bound and imprisoned. They were beaten, and sometimes wandered about, hungry and destitute. How did it look in God's eyes? Were they delivered from difficulties? No. Instead, from God's perspective "out of weakness they were made strong." They did not get what was promised them, but they did obtain a good report through faith. They faced challenges few of us can understand. What does God say about it? It seems God is waiting to perfect both the Old and New Testament saints together. We are reminded earth is not a playground; it is a battleground and has been from the beginning of time.

Each new experience dug a well of faith from which they drew the Water of life. It would have to be the same with me if I expected to learn the lessons faith teaches. My human heart longed for something more, something only faith could bring about, faith in believing God is Who He said He is in the Bible.

My Sojourn into Faith

The calling to the simplicity of a life in villages where physical harshness often brought poverty was contrasted with visits to palaces, castles and monuments like Shah Jehan's Taj Mahal. The magnificent Taj, built by a Shah, or king, as a memorial to his wife, was done by the labor of men's hands in a day when there was no modern machinery. Expensive gemstones lined the walls. There were European Cathedrals and Westminster Abbey, edifices built extravagantly, splendor and elegance unequalled in today's world, beautiful workmanship of men's minds and hands which has lasted for posterity. It was the labor of the heart and soul of dedicated men like Michelangelo.

Sadly, both time and man have wreaked destruction on some famous places like the Parthenon in Athens, considered the "greatest masterpiece of ancient Greek architecture" and Persepolis, the magnificent palace of Xerxes in Iran, both built in the 400s BC, and ravaged in later times, one because the Turks in the 1600s had stored munitions in it and the other when Alexander the Great moved through Persia in the 330s B.C. A wise Solomon wrote:

"Vanity of vanities! All is vanity."
What advantage does man have in all his work
Which he does under the sun?
A generation goes and a generation comes,
But the earth remains forever." (Ecclesiastes 1:2-4)

For me, a new discovery was taking place. I was finding out more about my own sojourn and found myself plunging into the world of faith. Neither would be something I would understand immediately; instead, I would be indoctrinated as I passed through the experiences in the years to come. The Scripture does not fully clarify the meaning of faith. Instead, we are told it is through faith we understand what faith is. The easiest way to understand is to recognize faith is God's agenda when there is the triumph of answered prayer.

In my own sojourn, I met people who had wealth beyond my human imagination, but I gained insight into the human heart which longs for something more. I believe that **something more** is faith in a life beyond this one we have on earth. I had thought I knew all about faith; I had acted in faith through much of my early Christian experience, doing things like going to college with no money and praying for funds to go to Pakistan. I was a missionary with many different jobs to do, had prayed for the ability to do them well and I believed God had answered those prayers. However, my higher calling was always to represent Christ. In what ways had I exercised my faith?

"He has told you, O man, what is good;
And what does the Lord require of you
But to do justice, to love kindness,
And to walk humbly with your God?"
(Micah 6:8)

It seemed too little that this was really all God required of me. But that last phrase made an imprint in my mind. What did it mean to "walk humbly with (my) God?" I came to believe faith is trusting God to do His work in His own way, not asking Him to go my way, but allowing Him to lead me. I saw it is then that faith becomes the substance of things hoped for, the evidence which may not immediately be seen, but is promised to us.

To be able to trust God and not be disappointed when the answer does not come, or when the answer is not what I wanted,

I believed that to be true faith. On many occasions I have poured out my heart to Him for something that seemed right, but God did not answer prayer the way I wanted. At other times, He has answered in a unique and wonderful way, sometimes "beyond all I could ask or think."

For the past decades of my "sojourn," in exercising faith and obedience, I have seen what an unlimited God can do for His people. This book is not like many others. It is not a book about what I have accomplished, which would barely fill a page. Instead, it is the story of how at each step, I have had to dig into the bank of faith to find how real are God's promises. It is my hope that in writing this, the reader will understand the Awesome God we know and have served who can do the seemingly impossible when we trust Him.

My Early Life

"But by the grace of God, I am what I am ..." (1 Corinthians 15:10)

Village life around the world has certain things in common. We call it culture. It is the sum total of all that people do, think, and feel, along with their language. Life takes on a rural flavor in the village; people are committed to what they have to do and do it. Among them are those who rise early, work hard, earn their own way and for the most part, raise their families to do the same. There is usually a place of worship and neighbors know neighbors. The village where I was born, Deep Creek, Virginia, near the Dismal Swamp, was no different.

My First Village

Although I would not know how it would have an effect on me, my first insight into village life began when I was born. It was a preparation for God's design on my life. At age fifteen, I came to know Christ as Savior; at age sixteen, I knew God was calling me to be a missionary in a foreign land. There I would live in a village and find people whose lifestyle was not totally unlike some things I had experienced in my early years.

My parents lived in a village called Deep Creek, amidst a sprawling settlement of farms and a cluster of a few small stores which sold most anything one needed in the days before marketing took an edge on the demands of the buyers. It provided the environment in which I learned lessons which would prepare me for what lay ahead, even though I had no idea what that would be. One lesson has stayed with me; it was primarily from my parents, who proved what it meant to endure in the face of almost impossible odds without feeling sorry for oneself and without expecting others to take care of them. I do not recall hearing many complaints, except about politics! Life was lived day by day with the wisdom of an old saying, "Use it up, wear it out, make it do or do without." They overcame in the face of struggles.

I had an unusually carefree and happy life, I think, with a few times of discipline, of course, both in school and at home. I was a "strong natured" child, almost fearless, and willing to try most anything dangerous, especially if I saw someone else doing it. There is no doubt in my mind today that God had to appoint a special guardian angel to watch over me.

My sister Evelyn, almost three years my senior, was different. She was a "scaredy cat." She was afraid of the dark and would wake me if she heard a noise in the night. We were probably in our very early teens when we were wakened a couple summer nights with someone scratching on the screen of our bedroom window. We decided it was a neighbor boy who was trying to frighten us. After a night or two of that, I devised a plan. We would pretend to have a gun. In a somewhat loud whisper, I said, "Quick, get the gun!" We never heard another scratching after that. The funny thing was, we would not have known how to shoot a gun!

My parents had nine children in all. Two boys, two girls, two boys, two girls and a boy, each child 2 ½ -3 years apart. I did not know my older siblings very well until we were all grown; I never knew my second oldest sister who died from a school accident before I was born. My sister Evelyn and I benefited from our older brothers Woodie and Jack. When I was in college and had to have an appendectomy, it was Woodie who came and paid on the bill so I could be released. Jack was already driving by the time he was fifteen. No license in those days. He drove the ice truck for "Mr. Johnny," the man who owned the lumber yard and also delivered ice. Later, Jack was the first in our family to have a car. He was engaged to Mildred when he took us roller skating one night. Evelyn and I laughed to ourselves because Mildred wore hose to go skating! I don't think she knew how to skate, but we did.

I don't think we had sibling rivalry, but we did have some sibling arguing, which my parents did not tolerate. Dad took care of the older boys and Mom took care of my sister and me. They both thought it good and proper to "clear the air." When the punishment was over, it was never referred to again. I don't ever recall a word about "remember last time."

Mom's discipline when my sister and I did not do what we were told to do, or argued over who was to do it, was to "go get me a switch." That meant going out to one of the poplar trees in our yard and breaking off a small branch. We dared not break one too small, and we had to leave on a few leaves at the end. We got three or four licks with the "switching." It was never harsh; the worst part was having to bring in the right length and properly prepared switch. It was not acceptable to disobey that order. Looking back, I have often wondered why those leaves were important. They certainly did not hurt us.

Some of my very earliest memories were when I was three, and then, four. Brother Willie and his new wife Patricia came to visit. They brought Evelyn and me a children's table and chairs. I recall, but just barely—what does a three-year-old remember, except having something so special? —being given a plate of food to eat at "our table."

"Miz" Laura Culpepper lived across the road from us. She and her husband had a big, beautiful house, set back like a colonial home, with a white fence across the front of the property. They owned a large farm. I became Miz Laura's "road runner" when I was four. If she needed some small thing from Mr. Howard's grocery store, she would cross the road and ask my mom to let me go to the store. While they stood watching, one on either side, I did the errand for her. She always gave me an egg. With that, I could buy a piece of penny candy. It was always a hard choice. I would stand in front of the glass encased treats while Miz Lessie, the store owner, stood patiently waiting for me to decide.

One other incident which happened before I was five would have been the end of me had my brother Jack not sent me running back home. I overheard Jack and some friends making plans to cross the "waste way," a very dangerous thing to try.

On one side of the waste way was the canal. On the other side was a very depressed holding area, like a big pond. A cement walkway about a foot wide with big upright wheels spaced along it separated the canal from the pool of water several feet down below. Should the canal overflow, the wheels could be used to open the gates and control the Canal water to prevent flooding. In my mind's eye, I can still see some of that water cascading down from the canal into a lower section, but I was too young to recognize the danger.

I had seen that walkway before when we were taken to see the locks. It was the "steering wheels" which fascinated me. I decided to follow these adventuresome, older boys. I think I had a nature that said, "anything you can do, I can do" and I may have tried to do it on my own at a later time had not my brother told on me. It could have been the end of me and any of them had we fallen into that swirling chasm. Jack saw me, scolded me harshly, told me he was going to tell Mama what I had done which had me running back home!

"Mr. Howard" and "Miz Lessie" owned one of the stores from which we got our groceries. It bore little resemblance to to-day's "supermarket," but had both food and some tools and other necessities. When Daddy worked in the Navy Yard he got paid on Fridays. It was his night to make his weekly trek to the store where he could catch up with the neighbors and hear or debate any "world news" with the men who gathered there. For Dad's trip to the store on Friday nights, Mom would tell him what was needed, and he would order the next week's supplies, which always included a 25 lb. bag of flour, milk, coffee, and some nice cut of fresh beef. Daddy was very particular about the meat, wanted only the best, so we did not often have it. He ordered the groceries, which Mr. Howard would deliver on Saturday morning. We children looked forward to the bag of penny candy Mr. Howard always had tucked in the grocery box.

The owners lived atop the store and if Mr. Howard was upstairs and Miz Lessie needed him, she would take the broom handle and knock on the ceiling to alert him or to wake him if he was trying to take a nap. Daddy and Mr. Howard were good friends, and he would sometimes invite Daddy to ride into town when he and some other men went to see the local baseball team play. For that, Mom always had to have Daddy's white linen suit starched and ironed. She did it by heating the iron over the cookstove without even a fan to send some cool air on hot summer days. We didn't have a hook-up to the electric lines along Route 17 until I was eight years of age. We could, however, safely leave the doors open at night and usually, the cool breezes would blow through on hot nights.

One of the other stores was called Deep Creek Mercantile, a general store where my mom went to buy things like our shoes and material for our dresses and other clothes. She made most of what we wore. The store was divided between the groceries and what was called "the dry goods." Mr. Seymour took care of the one side, while his wife, a lovely older lady we called "Miz Jeanie" took care of the other side. She had dress material and sewing notions. There was a tiny room about eight-foot square with shoes at the back of that section. The only shoes I recall trying on there were a size 3, so I don't know how old I was at that time, maybe 9 or 10? Miz Jeanie and my mom would visit while Mom made her decision about what to buy, based mainly on what she could afford. I can still see Miz Jeanie; I thought she was so pretty. She was tall, a stately, gentle woman with slightly graying, blonde hair, always friendly, always kind and helpful.

On summer's warm Saturday nights, Mom would take my sister, brother and me and we would walk to the center of the village where we got to know almost everything about almost everybody. We kids played "kick the can" or "hide and seek" while the women sat around and talked. And talked. And talked until we kids were worn out and it was time to make our way down a dark road and head home. One night I was running up ahead and missed the driveway, fell into the ditch, and they all laughed at me. In those days, it seemed quite deep to me. I said, "Mama, I fell in the ditch!" Mom said, "Did you get hurt?" I said "No, but I fell in the ditch." She said, "Well, just crawl out!" Maybe that is a good lesson to learn. When you fall into a ditch, if you are not badly hurt, just "crawl out!"

There were other places of business in our village, including a barber shop, a gas station, a small store run by "Mr. Georgie" and his wife, where she sold some of her cooked food at mealtime, and a small store run by Mr. Brabble, an African American man. When there was a need for any specialty thing, we had to catch the bus and go into "town." The bus ran from Deep Creek to Portsmouth every half hour.

This was the world into which I was born on a cold day at the end of February 1928, in a small house, owned and rented out by the Richmond Cedar Works which handled the logging business centered in the Dismal Swamp. Daddy worked for them.

Shortly after I was born, Daddy and another man went into the construction business and Daddy built a "nice" home with indoor plumbing. As the depression began to hit, his partner absconded with the money and my parents lost the house.

That is when they found the five-acre plot on the Dismal Swamp Canal bank with a very old farmhouse they planned to renovate. The bank agreed to a five dollar a month loan payment. Daddy began putting up a four-room house, designed to have a washroom for Mom, a shop for him and two rooms for Mom's elderly parents. It was not to be. We were all safe, but the old farmhouse burned to the ground just five days after we moved.

Mom had gotten up to prepare Daddy's breakfast. She lit the oven of the kitchen kerosene stove in the farmhouse and had gone back outside. The stove must have malfunctioned, the fire took only minutes to burn the whole house. There was no insurance. They lost almost everything, Mom's treasures which my older brother had sent her from his Navy travels and even the basket of dirty clothes she was planning to wash that day. I was four, but in a month, I would be five, and the sight of a burning house as we sat on a blanket that January night is still one of the pictures in my mind.

The new construction became home until Daddy could build on to the rooms. We were crowded into it, but we had a place to eat and sleep. Neighbors donated furnishings and we survived the depression. Daddy hired a contractor when I was about fourteen years of age, and the house received a new look. It was never a large house, not a fine home, but it was a place they could call their own.

I feel sure the loss almost destroyed them. First, the loss of their beloved daughter in a tragic school accident, then the loss of their nice home because of a greedy business partner, then the fire. Somehow, my parents made it through, but I hear the echo of the legacy left behind for me and my children's lives: we can endure.

Even with the loss from the fire, living on the canal bank proved to be a gift from God. By that time, the road in front of our house was paved; cars and trucks which had earlier made use of the canal for transporting vegetables and people could be seen on the highway. It seemed God honored my parents' hard work and their lack of complaining.

We had our own pork meat, grew most of our vegetables and some fruits on part of the five-acre property. Both Dad and Mom had a "green thumb", so we had all kinds of good fresh food in the summer and vegetables in the winter—turnips, kale and of course, the Southern delicacy, collards. On the north side of our house was a small hole dug into the ground, filled with straw, and covered over from the top, in which my parents stored the end of the season vegetables, including both white and sweet potatoes and green tomatoes. As they were needed, I was often sent out to bring in something. This meant putting my hand into the straw and feeling around, searching for the right ones. I think today that might frighten me a little, because I don't have a good relationship with some of the spider kingdom.

Those veggies did not last all winter, so when they were used up, Mom would open the ones she had canned, or we would have to wait for the summer crop. We always had an abundance of jams, jellies, tomatoes, pickles and vegetables which Mom had "put up" in quart and pint jars during the season. Freezers were unknown; I was older when we got our first electric refrigerator. We lived a "use it up, wear it out, make it do, or do without" kind of lifestyle and likely would not have been able to survive the difficult years of the 1930s had my parents not been frugal, unable to spend because there was so little money coming in. We passed through those post-depression years without being hungry, even though many people were not so fortunate.

Other staples as needed might be corn meal, dried beans, sugar, salt, baking powder and a few canned goods items. During the week, Mom would occasionally walk to the store and get canned pineapple to make an upside-down pineapple cake, lemons for meringue pie, some jello or some spice for making gingerbread. She made a dessert every weekend. Mom's biscuits were the best, but an occasional loaf of bread in the summer with some peanut butter was a wonderful treat. I am still a bread lover, most any kind, any time.

One job my sister and I had was to clean and fill the oil lamps we used before we got electricity. The black soot had to be removed each day. We pumped our water by hand, bringing in buckets for use in the kitchen. It was clear, very cold, and had no chemicals, so the taste was refreshing. It was the duty of my sister and me each Monday night to fill the two big round washtubs outside in preparation for Tuesday's washday. Our answer to today's plastic pools was being able to play in those washtubs when it was not washday. We pumped and filled the tubs early in the morning. By afternoon, the water was warm from the sun, and we played in it.

Before we got electricity, Mom boiled the clothes on washday, using a big black pot under a fire out in the back yard. Those were fun days. When the weather was cold, we came home to a hot baked sweet potato she had put in the coals. A neighbor James always stopped by and would not leave until he got his potato. Mom fed lots of neighbor kids, along with her own.

With four young children to care for, my parents had to find a path out of the maze. We were not the only people who lived through hard times, but today, I honor my parents for the survivors they were. They did not give up, did not expect a handout. Instead, they picked up the pieces and began to put back together the puzzle of their lives. Perhaps unconsciously, they looked for ways to earn money for the family.

My brothers hunted and trapped in the Swamp, adding to our family livelihood. Jack was the better trapper. He would use a little rowboat and paddles they had made, cross the canal and set the traps on the edge of the Swamp. One fortunate experience he had was trapping a mink. In those days, buyers from New York would travel around the area and purchase the pelts. My brothers tanned them, using a rack to hold them tight. It seems impossible now to realize it was Christmas Eve, 1936, when the New Yorker arrived, offered ten dollars for the mink skin. Mom used the money and went into town to have the electricity turned on and we were able to listen to Christmas carols on the radio for the first time. The lines had been installed along the paved road, but each family had to pay to have electricity turned on at their homes.

Daddy also started a small flower nursery on our five-acre property to help with income for our large family. That was when I learned the names of flowers, trees, plants, and got my first love of gardening. My brothers and my father paddled a rowboat down the canal to find special saplings people wanted for their properties. I am not sure where Daddy got the plants, but small bushes, perennials and annuals filled the rows of the field. Daddy walked between them almost every night, picking out grass and checking to see they were growing properly. I was usually right behind him, leaving my somewhat annoyed sister to clear the table and do the dishes. As soon as she missed me, she would be calling me in to dry them. From that time came my love of flowers. I have planted them around the world.

Our busy time was usually Spring and Fall. The best planting time for bushes and trees was when they had spent all their energy in summer and before they fully woke up in the Spring.

That was the dormant season for them. The best buying time for almost everything was in the Spring, when the earth warmed up but before the actual growing season began.

We were all expected to help, especially with keeping the weeds out of the garden. It was repeated so often that I can still hear my father tell my mother as he left for work when he got a job in the Navy Yard, "Get the "younguns" out there to get out the weeds before they take over the place." My life was being molded into what I would become. Today, I can see the need to keep the weeds out of my spiritual life.

In the Spring when the jonquils were blooming, Mom earned money packing the large boxes for Mr. Waldemar Weiss' Flower Farm. They were shipped overnight to New York. We kids earned money cutting the jonquils, one cent for twelve of the big bloom ones and one cent for 25 of the narcissus. It was a way for many "Creekers" to earn money and provided fun time as well. Mom would take a break and go sit with elderly Mrs. Weiss, Waldemar's mother. She was a tiny lady, dressed in long black or dark gray clothes and wore a black bonnet. I remember the beautiful cut glass pieces she had in her house. I think she was German, and I wonder if it was a part of what she brought with her when she came to this country. I wish I had asked Mom about her.

To get to the farm from our house, we had to walk about a mile. After Mom finished a busy day in the field, it was sometimes near dark when we trotted home along that dirt road. Times have brought changes. Those roads are now paved and the fields where the jonquils grew have houses. Only memories of good times remain.

The Navy Yard began to hire just prior to World War II, and Daddy submitted his application. He got the job and became a molder. I never knew exactly what he did. Sometime during those years, he made Evelyn and me metal bracelets out of a metal he called *monel.* It looked like stainless steel, but I have not been able to find any reference to it nor how the Navy Yard used it. When I saw Daddy had put EW initials on my sister's, I asked him to put VW on mine, and he did. Many years later, my sister still had hers, but mine was lost along the way, maybe in college days. I guess I wasn't as good a "keeper."

During the war years, large farms were sending food to be used by the military, so there were some shortages in cities. Most of the people in our area had gardens and the women canned a lot of the family foods, some even canned meats. We had home-made clothes. Mom found many remnants were perfect for our needs. In wartime, large bags of flour, the 25-pound ones we used for our large family were sewn and filled in printed cotton cloth about the size of a pillowcase, cloth which could be used for other things like dish cloths and curtains or even in some cases, prints used for some item of clothing. I recall thinking how pretty some of them were.

Mom always had supper ready when Daddy got home from work, and we all sat down together. When the hot peppers were fresh and green, Mom laid out five or six in front of his plate and he would choose from them, taking a bite with whatever else he was eating. Evelyn and I were told not to touch them, but I knew I just had to taste one. One night when no one was around, I took my first and last bite! It was a personal lesson in obedience. Mom never again had to tell me not to touch them. After supper, my sister and I would clean up the table and wash the dishes. Mom would sit down and work the crossword puzzle.

When the heat of summers without fans or air condition-ing became oppressive, when we were older, we were allowed to go swimming in the Deep Creek Canal across the road from our house. The canal was fed from the Dismal Swamp. It was rich in tannic acid making it safe for swimming but turning it into a brown color. It was our neighborhood "spa." There were a few sandy spots along the banks, opened up when the canal had been dredged. They provided entrances among the wild plum bushes that grew along the roadside. The softly flowing water always re-freshed us. If a snake was taking his swim, someone would yell, and we would all run up on the bank while it swam by. Some were poisonous, but I don't recall anyone ever being bitten.

My mom kept one secret from Daddy. I don't think he ever found out that my brother Willie had $10.00 a month sent to her from his Navy pay. She watched the mail like a hawk. It seemed to arrive on the same day each month. Mama was a penny pincher. We teased about her "pinching a penny until it hollered" but I am sure that is what got us some of the things we had. Daddy would have enjoyed being a rich man, but he did not believe in what he would regard as "foolishness." When we went to the summer resort area called Ocean View for the church picnics, he thought fifty cents was "a'plenty to waste on that foolishness." Mama knew better. She made sure we got a ride on everything, reminded us how to spend our money, using the Fun House and swimming as the last things to do. Those were very happy times for us, probably because of Mama having saved from that $10.00.

Daddy actually had a very soft heart. I once saw him put a package of crackers and cheese on our grocery bill when "Uncle Mike", a black man who often helped us, was standing in front of the store. Daddy asked him if he had had anything to eat that day. He said "Nah suh, I ain't." If I have ever learned anything about generosity, I learned it from my parents.

"Uncle Mike" and Queenie, his wife, were elderly, so tiny and "dried up" but a sweet old couple. They lived on our end of the bridge. Mama and Daddy called on them when they needed help. Mike helped in the garden, and Queenie stayed with us when we were still young and Mama had to go to town for some reason. When Mike helped Daddy, Daddy always gave him vegetables or part of anything we had that he could use.

Once when we had not seen him for a while, he came to the house, probably wanting to have some work if Daddy needed him. I must have heard the expression about sick people being "white and pale." When I saw him that day, I said, "Mike, you look so white and pale." He laughed; told me he had been sick. Mama, standing nearby, told me later it would be hard for Mike to look "white and pale." They were a loving, helpful old couple.

My parents' ability to see beyond the crises which had confronted them brought them through. The veil of immaturity obscured my physical vision when I was young. Today, I see my parents as heroes. I know two upright people who loved their children and saw to it they had their needs provided. They did not depend on government or anything else. We were never rich but now I know we were never poor and hungry, even if the meals were simple and the clothes and house furnishings homemade. Such were the early days of my life. Little did I or anyone else know at the time it would take me from that village into many countries around the world where I would experience similar things.

My parents, Lafayette Williams and Mary Della Doughtie Williams.

Early School Years

When I attended Deep Creek School it only had eleven grades, no kindergarten and no 12th grade (a twelfth year was added a few years later). It was a country school, sons and daughters of farming and dairy families. There were about 250 students when I attended. A few went to college; others pursued vocational careers.

We had good teachers to whom we owe a debt of gratitude. People knew their neighbors and much more about each other's lives. There was a freedom which does not exist today. We

Deep Creek School, Portsmouth, VA, ~1938.

walked the roads at night without fear. I was carefree, loved the out of doors, had a lot of imagination and was an average student for whom school was a necessary part of my life, something to be endured.

In first grade, from day one, we began to learn to write our names in cursive. I knew Myrtle had two tall letters, but not which one, so I added a third. I did learn the alphabet, and to read as well as write. I never learned to print and still find it difficult to do it neatly and have all the letters equal.

One day when I got hungry before lunch, I sneaked my ham biscuit and took a bite of it. I think that was the day Miss Cleaves made me go into the dark cloak closet and stay for a while as punishment. I don't recall being afraid, but neither do I recall sneaking my lunch after that! I think I learned my lesson with this teacher. Today, some parents would object to that, perhaps calling it "cruel and unusual punishment." Mom's idea was if we were doing something wrong in school and were punished for it, we deserved another punishment when we got home. We were expected to obey teachers and elders, a sort of "class action" of the community. I probably never told her about this incident.

If Miss Cleaves remembered, I wonder if she thought my missing a meeting in which I had promised to speak in her church years later was my revenge? I hope not. It was when we were on furlough, a Sunday morning, and my attention was on getting all the kids ready. Richard was going to take them to a different church.

Our second-grade teacher, "Miss Sally," had been at the school for many years. She had taught all of my parents' seven children before me, and we all owed to her the ability to spell. We raised our hands if we could pronounce the words she wrote on the blackboard. I was a good speller, but one day I was stumped when she wrote **t-i-o-n** and asked us how to pronounce it. None of us could do it. I will never forget that she illustrated it with the word transportation. I am grateful to her for my ability to be able to pronounce and spell almost any word.

My third-grade teacher, Miss Deal, was a nature lover. I was a dawdler. Time did not have much significance for me if there was something to do that interested me. My sister gave up on waiting for me to walk to school. I knew that if I was late for school, all I had to do was find something along the way to show Miss Deal and the lateness was excused. It could be a wildflower, a gum tree ball, or an unusual curly piece of wood, just about anything we both concurred had to do with nature. Often, she would tell the class about what I had brought. I learned so many things. Miss Deal also taught us how to have a good handwriting.

Those were also the days when companies sent out small free samples. Along with science and good health habits, she was able to write for samples of so many things. Toothpaste and pictures of birds are two I remember. Miss Deal must have had some hope for me. She was a member of Deep Creek Baptist Church and followed Richard and me in our ministry. Although we had little contact in those adult years, when she passed away, she left me a small amount of money.

Grade four had two special memories for me. I was asked to open a drawer in the teacher's desk to get something for her and saw her secret pack of cigarettes! A teacher's smoking was not very acceptable in those days. Miss Johnson was a good teacher. I think it was at this time that she had us learn to memorize.

There is another memory of something I did which back-fired on me while in Miss Johnson's class. In the afternoon, if all our work was done, we went outside for a little exercise. At the end, we had to line up in straight lines. The reward for those who rode the bus was being able to board the moment the bell rang and get their chosen seats. For those who walked to school, as I did, there was nothing special. One day I was annoyed with some-one who rode the bus and I decided when we lined up, I would stick out my foot. I knew the teacher would not let us go if I did that, but she turned the tables on me, and let everyone but me go! I was beginning to learn school life had boundaries. Another "hard" but very important lesson to learn.

I think this was also the first time I remember taking some-thing which did not belong to me. My "age of innocence" was over. I can't recall just what it was, and I don't recall that anyone knew who had taken it.

In grade five, I can still hear the teacher telling me, "It is not that you talk more than the others, but your voice carries!" It turned out to be a good thing. People don't have a problem hear-ing me when I speak, and I don't usually need a microphone! Miss Chappell, the teacher, would sometimes have "singing competi-tions" where we sang in class. One day, Frank Pierce and I were each vying for best singer. I don't know what he sang, but I sang, "He was just a lonesome cowboy..." She wanted to know where I learned it. I said, "from the radio!" The class voted, and I won the competition! Miss Chappell often had hall duty at our lunch re-cess time. I remember her standing there, eating a chocolate cov-ered popsicle. They cost 10 cents in those days, and I could hardly wait until I had ten extra cents to get one. This was also the year I had something taken from me. I understood stealing.

My sixth-grade teacher, Vivian, was not only beautiful but kind and loving. We all thought she was wonderful. I won a spelling bee in this class and got a tiny crystal pitcher, filled with some small suckers. Many, many years later, I found she was in the Sunday School class my daughter taught. She was ill and, in the hospital, when I visited her. I still had the pitcher and showed it to her, then passed it on to my daughter for a keepsake. We enjoyed those few minutes as adults because I had become a teacher by then.

In seventh grade, I felt like crying when my teacher took off points in my handwriting subject. Miss Deal had taught us so well. This teacher, Miss Waller, also had lovely handwriting. I knew I had nice handwriting. The problem had to do with the way I made my *W* for my last name, Williams. I swirled the final point downward, so it almost looked like the letter *h*. It was just as I had seen Miss Waller sign something before I got in her class. She told me I could not do that. I said, "Well you always do!" I guess handwriting was very important in those days. She had taken a summer course, and found we had to follow the Locker system. The *W* had to have the points at the same height. I didn't swirl any more, and the so-called pretty handwriting no longer seems important to today's students. My husband's writing was never very legible, and my sons seem to think a few up and down strokes constitute handwriting!

I seem to remember it was Mrs. Moore, an older lady, but a very good teacher for our eighth grade. I am indebted to her for my love of literature and poetry. We had to do some group assignments and I was in charge of a group using Tennyson's poems. I made the mistake of using too much time on the poem "Crossing the Bar" which my mom had told me she had also learned in school. Mrs. Moore finally interrupted me, told me I needed to include more of Tennyson's work. I said I had some more, but I think the rest got only a passing mention. I can still quote some of that old poetry if I have just a few seconds to review.

I started high school the same year the Second World War started, 1941. We went through war time, the blackouts, the shortages, rationing and a determined effort to do whatever it took to survive and win the war. Young men age 18 and over were conscripted, sent away from home for training.

The Norfolk Navy Yard, located in Portsmouth, went into high gear and the naval bases around us brought in many young men. We had military all around us, soldiers, sailors, marines. The

Norfolk Navy Yard was a hub of activity, shipbuilding and other trades had opened up jobs for young people and the Navy Yard was hiring. More if not most young people graduating from high school took jobs to learn a trade as soon as they graduated.

High school seemed to bring out more forcibly my competitive side. Mr. Booker was our principal and a member of our church. I liked him, but my smart aleck attitude did bring about some conflict. In my junior year, I was in charge of the Fellowship Club, a group of mostly Christians who had a daily prayer meeting which met in the auditorium and was attended by a good group of students. I think he wanted to get rid of that. He first changed our daily prayer meeting place, said some students had no place to go when it was raining outside, and wanted to dance in the auditorium. It was the age of the jitterbugs. One sister/brother duo had perfected the art and I guess the rest of the kids except for our prayer meeting wanted to learn how to do it. We found a room and continued to meet. After making my commitment to Christ, I attended one dance in the Community Hall. I felt God speaking to me that it was not the place for me. I left. Today 's dances with the bumping and grinding are not for me.

I did not want to attend the junior/senior prom in my junior year. Mr. Booker called me in and in a soft but strong voice, tried to make me see I was making a mistake. Mr. Booker and his wife were highly esteemed in our community. He told me his wife's father had been a pastor. I believe he was sincerely trying to help me, but intimating I was becoming too "religious." Today, I know that Christians young and old always take a risk when they stand for what they believe. I kept to my conviction, and even today, would do the same.

However, after I got home from my first year in college, I visited the school which was still in session. Mr. Booker asked me to speak to the student body about college life. I remember I used the newspaper ads about work opportunities to explain why we need a good education! As I was leaving, he took out five dollars from his wallet and gave it to me. I guess that meant my brashness was forgiven and hopefully, forgotten.

I think Miss Lawson was our chemistry teacher in High School. I did not like chemistry and feigned a wimpy nausea when we had to do one experiment, the one which smells like rotten eggs. I did not like history and Miss Murden tried her best to show me its value. Today, I love studying any of that old stuff and our daughter has excelled in it. She is a history teacher in High School and in the Community College.

Miss Rice was our math teacher. Some of us may have thought she was a heretic when she said it was not a whale which swallowed Jonah, but she also left a legacy for me. It was a time when having an autograph book was the trendy thing to do. We would have our friends write a note in it, probably a bit of a comparison to Face book and social media today. Miss Rice wrote, "Know thyself." I have learned a little about myself, but I think Eternity will be here before I ever achieve that!

Miss West was our English teacher and may have been our Latin teacher, a subject about which we wrote in our books, "Latin is a murderous language, it came from 'cross the seas. It killed out all the Romans, and now it is killing me!"

How little we know of the important things when we are impudent "know it all" teenagers like I was. After I became a teacher, I was thankful for all the Latin I did remember, along with a tiny bit of French and 2 years of Spanish I had in college. They are called "Romance" languages and made it possible for me to understand more of the background of how language developed and operates. We can sometimes break down the meaning of a word when we see how it is put together. I thank language teachers for that.

I graduated from high school in war time in June of 1945, but the war was winding down except for that one final punch. President Truman announced the end of the Second World War, "V-J Day"—Victory over Japan—in September 1945. We were a small group, only about 25 graduates and only a few went to college. I don't recall much about counseling students for careers. Some in my country area followed in their fathers' footsteps and farmed. To their credit, I think everyone in my graduating class had done very well without college by the time they were married and had a family. I was one of those who needed college because I believed God had called me to be a missionary.

My school days before college came and went by so quickly. If I could make a request from God for those teachers who tolerated me, it would be that they got a gold star for all I learned because of them. I am not a "real student," have been very selective in what I want to study, but I have enjoyed all the education I have had.

Faith's Seeds Planted

Ours was not a particularly religious, mission minded home, but my parents were good and loving people who attended church. I was strong willed with a desire to do what I wanted to do with my life, not immoral things, just not having to answer to anyone.

There were two mainline churches in Deep Creek, the Methodist and the Baptist. They stood side by side. The Methodist Church was a painted white wooden building, the Baptist Church was brick. Both were built on the banks of the Deep Creek Canal. I don't think either church felt competitive, and we did engage in some activities together. Revivals and the summer church picnic were two of the special times.

I was eleven when a new pastor, Rev. John Taylor, was called to Deep Creek Baptist Church. We called him "Preacher" and we called his wife, "Clara Mary." They had three children, a daughter in college, training to become a teacher and two sons ready to go to college. The older son, John, was serious minded. The younger one, Verne, was a lot of fun, musical, played the marimba or the xylophone. We were all fascinated as we watched him play in church.

As is the case of every new preacher, the church people talk among themselves and size up the man. We were at church one Sunday when the pastor preached about how we could know we were going to Heaven. I suppose I was trying to "size him up" at my early age. As we came out, I said to my mom, "Nobody knows if you are going to heaven or hell until you die." Then, "if your good deeds outweigh your bad deeds," I

Deep Creek Baptist Church, ~1946.

said, "you will go to Heaven, won't you?" She grunted an "uh huh" and nothing more was said. The Holy Spirit would work in both our lives, and we would each realize we were wrong and make a commitment to Christ.

When I was twelve, some of my friends had "joined the church" but I had said I wasn't interested. I wanted to grow up and do what I wanted to do, drink, smoke, and live like I wanted to live. I wasn't a bad person, had not done any bad things. I was self-willed, adventurous, and curious. I wanted to rule my own life and do whatever I wanted to do. I had to discover those who make the choice for Christ must live as He wants them to live. Even at that young age, I knew becoming a Christian meant having a change in my life, becoming committed to God and His will for me.

The pastor continued his ministry, preaching messages about how we could have a personal relationship with God and about a world that needs to hear of Jesus. I was young, not yet a Christian, not even interested in becoming a Christian, but that seed was implanted in my heart.

Sometime during those "tween-age" years, some older relatives came from Philadelphia for a visit. They drank beer and smoked, and I thought when I was grown up, I would do that, too. It seemed such a "grown up thing" to do, and I wanted to be grown up. It was not that I was a rebel or felt unloved or mistreated. I just didn't want to be told what I could and could not do.

After they left the table one day, my sister and I tasted the beer left in the cans. We thought it tasted terrible! I was cured. Neither of my parents drank and my dad did not approve of drinking. I had once heard him tell my older brothers that the day they started to drink was the day they would have to move out of our house.

About that same time, I began to have some undefined fears. I don't know what they were, but one night I was so fearful, I asked my mom to lie down beside me. She did; I went to sleep but had a fitful dream. It was as if God was showing me what an eternity would be like without Christ. God was already at work in my life.

At age thirteen, I had heard enough Bible teaching to know I was not ready for Heaven. This short period of fear made me decide I needed what we teased was "eternal fire insurance" and helped me make the decision to join the church. I thought being baptized would be enough to get me into Heaven, but foolish enough to say it would not make a difference in my life, and it did not. "The Hound of Heaven" was on my trail. Jesus said, "the seed is the Word of God" (Luke 8:11-15). I had tried to plant that seed in a weed patch, but it had survived.

During World War II, young sailors made the seven-mile bus trip to our church. "Preacher" had a love for people, a vibrant testimony, and a strong appeal to make our lives count for Christ. Many sailors, raised in the church back home, found a spiritual retreat at our church. Looking back, I realize having the military around us was a kind of cultural experience, an opportunity to hear how other parts of the US lived. Soon we had a large group of young people, some of whom later went into the ministry or, like I, became missionaries.

The church had a weekly radio program with the young people. Our theme song was "I Would Love to Tell You What I Think of Jesus." It is by faith that we hear God speaking to us. The Spirit of God, like the wind, was blowing that seed and it was taking root in my life and heart.

"The wind blows where it wishes and you hear the sound of it, but do not know where it comes from and where it is going; so is everyone who is born of the Spirit." (John 3:8)

But what is faith? I doubt that as a teenager I could have answered that question. I am not sure I can, even today. It was more of an inner compulsion which said, "Just follow me." I was fifteen; I knew I was a sinner, not a big sinner, just a sinner, separated from God because of mankind's lost condition. I did hear that voice; I understood I needed God's forgiveness.

It was a small thing that convicted me enough to understand the need for repentance. I had sneaked away and gone alone to the movies. My parents did not mind the movie-going but did not want us attending on Sunday. It was that disobedience and deceitfulness which caused me to understand wrongdoing when I was fifteen years of age and to finally understand why I needed God's forgiveness. I went to church that night and when the pastor gave the invitation, I went forward, saying I wanted to rededicate my life to Christ. My life was changed as that seed of salvation was planted in my heart. Jesus said to Nicodemus, "You must be born again" (John 3:3). I had a new DNA. I made a full commitment to Christ.

The change that came to me was a light shining in darkness. 1 John 2:15 became my mantra, my sacred counsel: "Do not love the world nor the things in the world. If anyone loves the world, the love of the Father is not in him." There were many things I would not do, but the one thing I wanted was that everyone should know about Christ, so I talked about Him a lot.

I had gotten to be somewhat of a leader in high school, on the student council, a cheerleader, involved in many activities of the church, but somewhat obnoxious by wanting everyone to know I was a Christian. I had a prayer list of twenty-five people for whom I prayed regularly. It was post war time and we had a lot of Christian activities which had been started in the area. Youth for Christ, the Fellowship Club, after church "Singspiration," and prayer times all added to my Christian growth.

By the next year, that tiny mustard-sized seed had taken root and was beginning to grow in my heart. It was time for the annual revival in the church. We went to these special meetings every summer. For three weeks that year we heard wonderful music, both singing and instrumental, by Herb Hoover, and a great message by a man named Bill Piper.

After the first couple of meetings, I was on my knees by my bedside one night when I understood a "silent" voice and knew God was calling me to be a missionary. (Little did I know that had been God's plan for me from my birth. I heard that story the night before my future husband and I sailed for Pakistan as missionaries—the story about my mother's pregnancy and promise to God.) A missionary from China had spoken in our church about the orphanage he and his wife had started. They needed young people to begin to prepare as workers. I assumed that was God's call to me. I believed I was headed for China; only after China closed its doors to outsiders, did I know God had other plans for me.

I did not know how this missionary would influence my life, but I did know one thing about China. When we went to the ocean for our annual church picnic, there were lots of tourist items for sale, most of them made in China, referred to as "cheap." It was a different China than that orient land of today. One of those cheap tourist items was a celluloid doll, somewhat like a more modern kewpie doll. Her "dress" was pasted on feathers, a little risqué, but I didn't realize that at my young age. I begged each year, and finally, Mom got one for me. The celluloid was pliable, so I had to be sure it did not get squeezed. Celluloid was a forerunner of plastic. I treasured it for a long time.

I did not know it at that time, but Isaiah spoke about hearing God speaking. Isaiah 30:21 says, "Your ears will hear a word behind you, 'This is the way, walk in it,' whenever you turn to the right or to the left." How did I know it was the voice of God and not just a thought I might have gotten while listening to the preacher? I knew because I had no desire at that time to prepare for missionary service.

Therefore, I struggled with the call for most of the revival. WHAT? ME, LORD? A village girl from a lowly background? How could that possibly be? But I felt that call so strongly, I promised that "if I still feel this way in the morning, I will tell everyone." I could not. The meetings went on. I guess God had to keep me going to them until I had the courage to tell the story. I was answering a call inaudible to everyone but myself. The last night of the meetings, I went forward to tell the church. It was one of my father's rare appearances, but he was there. It was a very tender moment when he came up to hug me.

I had a part-time job in high school and each Friday, I would leave work, cross the river by the ferry, walk through what was then called "the red-light district" and go to the YMCA, not acknowledging any fear. I could have been in danger! There, a group of young people met to study the book of Romans with a college professor, Mr. George Kissinger, from Hampden Sydney College. The Romans Road study was a wonderful introduction to the Bible teaching I would use all my life. I think everyone in the class was older than I, mostly married couples, John and Lolly Dunlap who were just starting Tabernacle Church and some of their friends, Evelyn and Carlton Long from Highland Baptist, some sailors stationed in Portsmouth. We walked back to the ferry and crossed to Portsmouth where we caught our busses. Mom, bless her, was waiting for the bus and me when I got back to Deep Creek.

When the study was over, there was always a group walking back and taking the ferry from Norfolk to Portsmouth. I was fortunate not to have to return by myself. I would catch the last bus to Deep Creek where Mom would come and wait at Mr. Sawyer's gas station. We walked that dark road down an unlighted Route 17 to our house. We were thankful for the occasional car passing. It lit up just enough of the highway to keep us from getting off the road. Light is one of God's special blessings.

I knew I would need schooling to be a missionary. How would I get that? I was going to be a senior in High School. What plans should I make? It was not faith that moved me to believe I could get an education; more likely it was something akin to presumption, a faith substitute—just presuming on God for whatever we want to happen. I certainly did not know how it could come about, but in the end, it did.

"For the vision is yet for the appointed time;
It hastens toward the goal and it will not fail.
Though it tarries, wait for it;
For it will certainly come, it will not delay." (Habakkuk 2:3)

I was not like Habakkuk or Abraham or Moses or any of those great heroes of the faith. I was probably more like the disciple who asked Jesus where they could get bread to feed the five thousand (see Matthew 14:13-21).

When I announced to everyone I was going to college and going to be a missionary, I had not really thought of how it would happen. My Dad had retired from work because of a heart condition. My Mom wanted to know where I thought I would get the money. Never giving "faith" a thought, I said I believed my brothers would help me. I would come to realize how much we underestimate God when we fail to see how He can provide, just as He did in the wilderness for His people.

Waiting to see the fulfillment of a vision that would last a lifetime would be a life-long process. What I wanted was to go wherever, whenever, and do whatever God wanted from my life.

****

I have often wondered why God called me. I was not a candidate of quality and even I know it. I was brought up in what could only be termed "humble" circumstances. We did not use the word "poverty", but I think it would have been applicable by today's standards. I had no particular skills or talent, had been only an average student, was both naïve and somewhat gullible. What could I offer to God? I had chosen Him because I believed He had chosen me. Whatever His purpose for me was to be, that was my desire. He would have to perform it and perfect my way.

Years later, I would discover that I was not the only one who questioned my calling. When I became a Christian, I found myself wanting to tell everyone about my faith. It was the most important thing in my life, so much so, I even wrote a letter to the editor, and it was published in the newspaper.

Not everyone appreciated the stand I was taking. After my mom passed away, my sister and I were going through her "box of memories," all little memorabilia bits housed in an old cigar box. We found a letter, addressed in the handwriting of a kindergartner, but obviously written by an adult. It was addressed to me at school, but since the mail carrier knew our family, he had delivered it to our home. Mom had opened and read it, decided I did not need to have it. "Who do you think you are?" it said, "We know what you are!" It was impossible to know who had written it. Mom had kept it, may have forgotten about it or she may have wanted me to find it someday.

By that time, I was an older Christian, recently retired from the Mission. Sadly, I could not get it out of my mind. Who was that person? What did she mean? I was sure it was a woman. Men don't write letters like that. Was there any way I could find out who the person was and why she wrote as she did? I was sure the person would have changed her mind. Our ministry had been written up several times in the local paper. The church and all the community had been gracious and welcoming.

My sister and I decided it would be a futile search, but there was still a nagging root of bitterness. I had to come to the place where I sought God's forgiveness for myself and for that person. Around the same time, I got an email from a British friend whose husband was a writer. She is publishing some of his material. He knew nothing of this, nor did she, but the reflection he wrote sounded like something I needed to hear decades ago. "Single handed we cannot fight off the assaults from directions all round us that might destroy us..." If reading that note after decades bothered me, it might have destroyed a part of me when I was a teenager.

Jesus said, "But if you do not forgive others, then your Father will not forgive your transgressions." (Matthew 6:15). Forgiveness is the heart of God. I had earlier written an article on forgiveness after our son was attacked and so badly hurt. It was as if I had to renew my promise to be forgiving.

Where God Guides, He Provides

"And the Lord said, "If you had faith like a mustard seed, you would say to this mulberry tree, 'Be uprooted and be planted in the sea'; and it would obey you." (Luke 17:6)

"And without faith it is impossible to please Him, for he who comes to God must believe that He is and that He is a rewarder of those who seek Him." (Hebrews 11:6)

If faith is like a mustard seed, it needs to be planted in ground that will nourish it and cause it to grow. It needs the nutrients we find in the Word of God. But the writer says, "without faith it is impossible to please God…" so I need faith and I need the Word and I need to be planted and I need to grow if I am a Christian.

It is by faith that we hear the voice of God. But how do we describe faith? It is elusive. If asked to explain or prove my faith, I guess my answer would be having faith is something like putting my hand into a bucket of water and taking it back out. The hand looks wet, but others do not know the experience until it happens to them. The water on my hand is not much affected by that action. Only I am. When I speak of my Christian faith, I mean I am putting my whole dependence on God, trusting Him to do what the Scriptures say He can and will do.

Stepping Out in Faith

I had boldly announced my plan to go to college and become a missionary. However, as high school graduation neared, I was still undecided where, or how, to get the training I would need. My parents had no money and I had none, except the small amount I made each week working at a five and dime store.

College was not easy for me; I dare say that in those days, village schools did not prepare students as did large city schools. Only a few from our small country school planned to attend college. Educationally, my Bible knowledge by that time was about on the same par as my secular studies. To attend college meant I would need funds, I would need books, I would need travel expenses, shoes, and clothes.

"Now faith is the assurance of things hoped for, the conviction of things not seen. For by it the men of old gained approval. By faith we understand ..." (Hebrews 11:1-3)

What was it I could understand if I had faith? What I now know is that faith secures the substance and substance is the evidence that God has heard the prayers we have asked of Him. I still doubt that I had faith. As I look back, I can only credit God's faithfulness. Perhaps my tiny grain of faith was strong enough to keep my focus on what I believed God was calling me to do. Here were some of His promises I thought I could claim:

"And my God will supply all your needs according to His riches in glory in Christ Jesus." (Philippians 4:19)

"The world and everything in it is mine ... the cattle on a thousand hills... (Psalm 50)

"The fear of the Lord is pure ... more desirable than gold ..." (Psalm 19)

"He brought Israel out with silver and gold ..." (Psalm 105)

My brother Jack and his wife offered to help if I would go to secretarial school. I thanked them but said I couldn't do that. The state senator's wife, a member of our church, talked to me about going to a Baptist college. She did not know that I had no money to go to any college!

I had an application for a Bible college and had filled in all but one detail, "Why do you wish to come to Bible College?" I wanted to write it was because I felt God was leading me there. I had friends there, but somehow, I did not have enough peace to put the words on the paper, and the application was still lying on my dresser when Preacher Taylor took me home from church one night.

He asked about my plans. His third child was graduating from Bob Jones College, at that time located in Cleveland, Tennessee (the school would move to Greenville, South Carolina and be renamed Bob Jones University in 1947). He and his wife would be willing to give me fifty dollars of the sixty needed for monthly tuition and room and board if I would go there. The Taylors understood what I did

Preacher John Taylor. He and his wife were such a wonderful blessing to me!

not, that I needed the spiritual guidance, the culture it would provide for me, and the love of the people in a school like that. I could work on campus to meet the remainder needed to pay my bill.

For my graduation gift, my parents had given me a suitcase. My mom sewed my clothes. My brother paid for my trip, and I had enough money to arrive and pay for my books. God had met the needs. When school opened in September 1945, I was enrolled, trusting God to supply the rest of my needs. There were so many times when I saw God provide, using the limited income of family members, as well as church people, and new college friends.

Because of the housing shortage on campus, Nell Sunday Hall, the teacher's house had been turned into a residence for students. I roomed there with two others on one side and three on the other, a bathroom in between. Coming from the country, for me that was a real luxury! One of my roommates had been given her own bank account; two of my roommates were sisters, children of a millionaire father and mother. Now, there is another bit of God's humor—putting me with girls who had never known financial need! The sisters each received $50.00 a month spending money. But when their parents, the Barges, came to visit, they always brought a gift for each of us.

After completing my first year of college, I went back to visit my high school friends. We had had a prayer meeting and time of fellowship, which I had led in those years. The principal, also a member of our church, had not been happy about our doing this, but when I went back to visit, he opened his wallet and gave me a five-dollar bill. Afterwards, he and his wife always had a kind word for me. I guess they decided I would somehow make it!

To help with my tuition and room and board, I had a job waiting tables in the college dining room. The Administration had strict rules but prided itself on students getting to know each other. We were given table assignments in the dining common for a period of time, maybe a month. Food was served to each table. The table settings had to be properly done, even to spreading a tablecloth for Sunday dinner. Table manners were also stressed. I would forever be thankful for that training. I grew up in a large family. My Mom did all the cooking, but my sister and I had the chore of setting the table and washing the dishes by hand. If forks were the only cutlery needed, that is all we put on the table. No sense putting out knives and spoons if we did not need them!

The war was over, but some rationing still went on. There was a substitute for butter. I will call it a forerunner for margarine. It was a white oil-based substitute, but we had a packet to mix in and color it yellow, making it look more appealing. The taste was acceptable. The stores sold a substitute for coffee, but surprisingly, we had the real thing and real cream. It was my first experience with learning we could "float" cream on the top of the coffee. The school had students from all over the US. I think it was those Midwesterners who taught us how to do that. Much of the meat in my area was pork; the "Middies" probably had more beef and rich milk.

Sugar was rationed, but we had syrup. One of the staples in the college diet was grits. I think it was the Yankees who thought the grits tasted better being bathed in syrup. That "Suth'n" delicacy turnip greens and cornbread was a frequent lunch meal. They did the same thing with the cornbread; they defiled it with syrup. Soon it caught on and many of us became copycats. It may have been a desire for something sweet in a time when sugar was hard to get.

During those college years, on one occasion I was desperately in need of the stockings we were required to wear. I had cried out to God, weeping, asking Him to send the money so I could buy them. A friend found out about it and offered me $5.00 and when I said I did not know how I could repay it, she said I wouldn't need to do that. I bought the needed hose, silk ones, so easily run, but just a couple days later, a package came; it held two pairs of nylon hose, the only ones ever sent me. Mrs. W.H.C. Deal from my home church apparently had been able to procure them; they were not easy to find in those early post-war days. The same day, $5.00 came from someone else. I have been left wondering how much better it would have been had I not taken my friend's five dollars and just waited a little longer on the Lord, but I had been so embarrassed to wear stockings full of runs. In His graciousness, I was able to repay the "fiver" given me but also never to forget that lesson of waiting on the Lord.

I did not want anyone to know of my needs, but at one point when I faced a serious financial problem, these roommates thought I should ask their father for a loan to help me out. He sent $100.00, which I promised to pay back. I never forgot that promise, but I had no idea how I could repay the loan, but I knew I would someday keep my promise. After we became missionaries, my husband got some extra money from his military service and said I could use it to repay the loan. I sent it to my lender, Mr. Barge, who returned the money, saying he would have accepted it only if I had not gone into the Lord's service. Since we had done that, he did not want repayment.

On another occasion, the pastor and his wife, who had been my source, were in an accident, totaling their car and putting them in the hospital. Thus, I got behind on school payments and was told I could not take my exams until the bills were paid. At the same time, I had an emergency appendectomy with no insurance to pay for it. My brother Woodie came from Virginia and paid some of the medical expenses. A girlfriend from Florida told her church, and they sent money to help me. I took my exams and returned home to Virginia. The next day, I got two extra medical bills for tests the hospital had done, one for $15.00 and one for $10.00. I had the promise of a job but had not yet started. Then, one of the greatest surprises of all, the next letters held money. That's right! There were two checks for just those amounts, sent from the church in Florida. Apparently, some people had planned to send earlier and had not. Was I living by faith? Not sure I even knew the meaning of the word. It was GOD's faithfulness! My prayer is that God will reward those who had faith in me. Learning those lessons would be a life-long process.

"For the vision is yet for the appointed time … Though it delays, wait for it …" (Habakkuk 2:3)

The key words were **WAIT for HIS time,** and that is often when faith breaks down. Waiting is one of the hardest things we learn to do. We think God has forgotten. Sometimes, we also have forgotten the prayers when we get the answers. On occasion, we do not immediately get the answers because a spiritual battle is always going on around us. That is what was told Daniel in his day; his experience was like this:

"Don't be afraid, Daniel; from the first day … your prayers were heard … But the prince of the kingdom of Persia opposed me for twenty-one days … I have come to help you." (Daniel 10:10-13)

My mom said she always knew I would be a teacher because I got children around me and took the lead in playing games. In one of my education classes or in the books I had to study I recall a statement like this: "Put any group of children or people together and one will always emerge as a leader." I guess I must confess that was often me!

Without some guidance, few young people know how to look at the future, decide what their talent or talents are and pursue the right courses. This may have been truer in the 1940s than it is today with counselors. I started out in college as a Christian Education major. That meant subjects like Bible, Sunday School ministries, dealing with problems in the classroom. All of this was helpful for the life God had planned for me. In the middle of my third year, I decided some secular education classes would be helpful for teaching and to my advantage. I added those classes to my degree. I was not much of a student, but I made it through and got my BA degree in 1949.

My mom and me at my college graduation, 1949.

Meeting Richard

I grew up liking boys. I didn't want to be a boy, just wanted to do all the things they could do. I always seemed to have a boyfriend but when I got to know the man who would become my husband, G. Richard Thompson, I knew this kind of love was the real thing and I never wanted anyone else. My mom was a "young" 78 when Daddy died. There were some widowers in the church, and I asked Mom if she would ever consider getting

51

married again. I still remember her very firm, "No sirree! Once around is enough!" I feel the same way. Richard was my "one and only," far from perfect as was so much else about both of us but I can happily say there was never anyone else who ever interested me. When God gave us to each other we knew we were the right match. I don't think I consulted with anybody about him, no marriage counselors in that day.

I met Richard in college. We each believed God had called us into His service. Richard was headed to India, where he had been born and lived to his early teen years. His parents were Methodist missionaries who had met, married, and served in the villages for almost 40 years. His father's latest assignment was as pastor of the Methodist Church in the port city of Karachi. Their home became a "home away from home" for young British soldiers who served on the frontier of Afghanistan. These young men were at the coast for their "R and R." As Richard heard them talk of the need for a Christian

A photo of Richard's family, (from L to R), Dad Thompson, Jim, Wayne, Richard, and mom Vivian.

witness in that tribal land, he felt God's call and believed it was where God wanted him to go.

His family had returned to the US when World War II was eminent. The Methodist Mission asked his dad to return to India where they felt he could minister to the people left there including the British troops. He reminded them he had three young sons. The Mission said others were making sacrifices and missionaries should also be doing that. It was true and although he did not want to go, he felt pressured and consented to make the long and dangerous journey.

In April 1942, his mom, Vivian, who had suffered from headaches, went for tests. It was discovered she had a brain tumor and was sent to Columbia University Hospital in New York for surgery. I think the family was taken by surprise when she died in April 1943 without fully recovering from the surgery. The letter to tell his dad took three months to reach him. Therefore, it fell to Richard's Aunt Zelma to decide what to do about the boys. The oldest, Olin Wayne, went off to college, Richard stayed with his Aunt Zelma in New York to finish high school and the youngest, Jim, was placed in boarding school. His father eventually remarried in India.

By this time, the war had heated up and almost everyone and all of life was influenced. Richard graduated high school and with his gown on his arm left immediately to go to the nearest recruiting office to join the Navy. He served for three years, half of that time overseas, where he met other young Christian men, all being nurtured in their faith by becoming a part of the Christian group called The Navigators. After the war ended, he returned to the US and looked for a Christian college to prepare for his future.

With thousands of young men returning from the war and wanting to make use of the GI Bill, it was not easy to find a spot. The college enrollment was full, but God... It was another of the ways of God, those happenings that take place "behind the veil" where God is in charge. Richard wanted an education that would prepare him for Christian ministry. The "No Room Here" sign was out when he applied to the first college. His next choice was Bob Jones College. It was there we first met in 1946.

A friend from Richard's hometown was the fiancée of a friend of mine. Both of them wanted us to meet. We couldn't have been more different! I was a country child who had rarely been out of my small village setting, but now at age seventeen, was away from home, in my second year of college, further down south, studying to be a missionary. I was hoping my faith would sustain me to get the needed education; I had no money. He had been born in India where his parents were missionaries. His grandparents had also served and founded a seminary there. My world view was limited to a sprawling community of farms, country stores and a place where everyone knew everyone else, where in true Southern style we addressed adults with Ma'am and Sir, and Miz and Mr. He had lived and traveled around the world, now was considered a "Yankee" and understood little of those formalities. My family was blue collar class, farming background, little formal education. He was from a polished, educated family, several generations that included missionaries and ministers.

Our first date was different; we went to church. I was a Southerner and proud of it, outgoing, no doubt with a "Suth'n drawl", usually the originator of easy conversation and curious about who he was. Richard was a very quiet, private person, a Yankee by adoption, from New York. Not knowing just how to approach this, I began by asking if he had been in the service. He said yes, to which I asked how long. He said, "Three years." I then asked if he had been overseas. He said he had, for 18 months. The church service was beginning. Not being able to get conversation out of him, I was quiet. Sometime later, I recalled that first date and asked why he did not talk. He said, "We are not supposed to talk in church." He was a Methodist; I was a Baptist. People in my Baptist church visited with each other to catch up on all the news.

That was not our last date. He then invited me to go to a soccer game. In India, soccer was the sportsman's game. I had been a high school cheerleader for football, knew nothing about soccer. He attempted to explain a few things, finally gave up. He then began to talk about some studying he had to do; nine weeks exams were coming up. I asked if he wanted to go study. He did not answer, so I turned my attention back to the game. Finally, he said "No," but I didn't know why he was saying it. I said, "No what?" He said he did not want to go and study.

It seems after getting out of the Navy, he had visited his grandmother in a retirement facility in Florida. She had said, "Richard, you will have to watch those Southern girls. They are fast!" He thought I had said, "Do you want to go steady!" I wasn't sure what to make of him, was he really okay, the kind of guy I wanted to spend time with? When the names for high grades were posted after the nine weeks exams, he was on the list. I was not. I was the one who should have gone to "study!"

Despite this rocky start, we continued dating. In high school, I had worked in the library, so to pay off my $10.00 a month scholarship, I had asked to do the same job. On one of our dates, Richard and I met in the library because we had to do some research. Richard had two special loves from the time I got to know him. He loved maps and visiting new places. Had he stayed in the military he would have made a great "reconnaissance" man, one to scout out new territories.

At the library there was a very large world map, likely the first world map I had ever seen. He very proudly pointed out the country of India where he planned to go, showing me places with which he was familiar from childhood. It seems immature to say I planned to go to China when I didn't even know where China was, except that it was in the Far East. Seeing this map of the world displayed was my first introduction to how much he wanted to be "back home" to the place of his birth. We then saw China where I was expecting to go, and I was introduced to Asia.

I would find there was more to Richard's prominent family and their professionalism than anything in my country back-ground. It left me a little insecure about the relationship when he had me pull a book from the stacks, *Who's Who In America*. We found the write-up about his grandfather, a scholar who had five different titles with the entry of his name. This gentleman was obviously a godly giant, a statesman, archaeologist, and educator. What he had accomplished was beyond anything I had ever known. I teased about this being Richard's "pedigree." Was this the right relationship for me?

Our relationship had been like a math study. Up to this point, it had been "adding" but very soon we would understand "dividing." As we continued to discuss our future in missions, we discovered we were both committed to missions, but he to India and I to China. That caused us a little problem; neither was willing to change course. We have joked about how God had to intervene. When we quit dating because of the plans we had made, things changed. We like to say God had to make a whole new country just to get two stubborn young people together!

In 1946, the British released control of India and India's religious persuasions brought about the country's division into two parts, one for the Hindus and one for Muslims. By 1947, the agreement was sealed. Muslims were in the majority in two areas, each on a different side of India. One became East Pakistan, on the Bengal side (which eventually became the country of Bangladesh). The other, West Pakistan, on that same northwestern Muslim frontier where he wanted to go. I would later learn the word Pakistan meant "land of the pure," from two Persian words, *pak* (pure, holy), *i* (of) and *stan* (land).

At the same time, it was a period of upheaval in China. The country was closing its doors to missionaries. They were being put out, told to return to their home countries. China wanted to be free of foreign domination of any sort. I would not be able to go to China.

About six weeks after our "break-up", we were back together, and the future was settled. Shortly after we started dating again, he told me he loved me and wanted to marry me. We were in the dating parlor at Bob Jones University, no kisses, not even a hug. He came home to visit one time, met Mom and Dad, and stayed with my sister Evelyn. She told me he was a nice guest and that he always took off his socks and hung them over the chair! There was not much further talk about him, just acceptance even though the family knew nothing about who I was marrying.

Becoming Mrs. Myrtle Virginia Thompson

By the Spring of 1948, we were engaged with plans to go to Pakistan. The night I got my engagement ring I went in to show it to my mom. That was after Richard left to catch the last bus into town where he was staying with my sister in Portsmouth. Mom was in bed. She had one bit of advice: "Yes, now you love him so much you wish you could eat him and five years from now you will wish you had!" (But I never wished that.)

We graduated in June 1949. Mom came for the graduation, and we went back home to Deep Creek. Richard went off to sell Bibles as a summer job. We stayed in touch by letters, no cell phones, not even landlines in my home. I worked at a furniture store in Norfolk.

Richard's college graduation, 1949.

I spent the summer, busy thinking about plans and having my sister Evelyn and sister-in-law Ellie help me. I sent out 100 invitations, not enough for all I would like to invite but all I could afford. The cost for printing was $18.00 and I still have the bill and some of those details somewhere.

I did not see Richard all summer until he came for the wedding. His dad and stepmom, Emma, were already in town, as was his Aunt Zelma and another friend with her. There had been very little money for this wedding, it was God's great gift, provided by others. Daddy wanted one of the ladies from Mr. Howard's grocery store (one of those more "society knowledgeable") to be the mistress of ceremonies. She wasn't interested (I am thankful!) but Mrs. Cuthriell was willing and a dear Christian in the church. She also had a little rehearsal party for us.

Ellie made my gown from a beautiful sari Aunt Zelma had gotten during a trip to India. I wore Richard's mother's handmade lace veil from India as well as her silk petticoat. Mom made the bridesmaids and flower girl's dresses, colors were orchid, yellow, pale green and white organdy (flower girl), all in the same style as my dress. My sister-in-law Ellie's friend, May Lee Boulds, who taught music for a living, was the organist, would not accept payment, and wrote me the sweetest note. We had "Because" and I think the other was "O Love that will not let me go..." a favorite of Richard's mom. There was a third song, a Christian

57

commitment song we both liked. Dad Thompson and Preacher Taylor did the ceremony, so we were twice blessed!

I had ordered two palms from the florist and two baskets of flowers. It was all I could afford. The florist arrived the night of the rehearsal, saw the church and said it would never do to have only those things. Daddy said we would have more, I said it was all we could afford. It was the only time in my life I ever talked back to him. I moved away from where they were standing. The florist came back to me and said "I am going to give you this wedding. I remember it was your father who went into the Dismal Swamp and got some trees I wanted and planted them for me." I couldn't believe what she did for me, her most expensive wedding. The altar was banked with palms with lilting candelabra and flowers, just beautiful! I was told it was one of the most beautiful the church had ever had; another special story which reminds me God has always seemed to spoil me with blessings!

Our wedding day.

(Olin) Wayne, Richard's older brother was the singer—he was singing in a night club in NY at that time—and his younger brother Jim was best man. The other male attendants were boys from my church. We got a telegram from Jim the day before the wedding—"very sorry cannot arrive until Wed." (the day after the wedding). Richard's stepmom, Emma, got that changed in a hurry! I had four attendants, my sister Evelyn as maid of honor, two friends and Teenie, my niece, a junior bridesmaid. I had chosen 6:30 as the time because in those days 5-6 was when most people ate supper (no way to provide for that) and 7:00 was a "society" event, meant a dinner reception after the wedding.

It had rained all day but stopped later in the afternoon before the wedding. I had spent part of the day riding a bicycle to collect flowers from Mrs. Sawyer's chicken yard where her white rose of sharon was plentiful and in bloom. She had said I could have them. We used them to decorate the Community Hall for the reception where my sister-in-law Ellie had done a beautifully decorated three-layer wedding cake (traditional) and punch, nuts, and mints, that's all, folks!

While everyone was going over to the community hall my brother Jack had taken us from the church back to the house to get my engagement ring which I had forgotten to put on! All the way there he was tooting the horn to celebrate.

Richard's Aunt Zelma had sold Richard her car, and he was planning the honeymoon—it had to be Niagara Falls with a stop in New York on the way to have my first curry dinner in a very nice Indian restaurant. We were away two weeks, ended up going about 100 miles into Canada, stayed in places where they had a room for rent (not uncommon in those post war days) and had a wonderful time.

We arrived back, said goodbye to family and left immediately for Bob Jones University to complete Richard's studies. He had one more year on the GI Bill and planned to use it for completing his master's degree. I like to say half of that degree belongs to me for doing the typing! The papers were not allowed to have any corrections and I was not a great typist, but I guess they were all okay, he got the MA!

Richard's Aunt Zelma did so much for both of us. We could never adequately express how grateful we were to both of families!

We bought a very small and old 18-foot travel trailer, already set up in a trailer camp owned by one of the students from the university. The plans for "tiny houses" on wheels young couples are opting for today bear no resemblance to what we had. Ours was old, gray on the outside. We painted the inside a neutral color, put up a small cover for the entrance way and planted a tree I dug out of the woods. It was our first home. It was adequate, since we would be spending a lot of time on campus, and I planned to work part time.

One big difference in these new models and our old one was the scant sufficiency of anything modern. Our double bed mattress tucked in the three corners of one end, would not become the picture perfect the showrooms advertised. Fitted sheets were likely not yet a part of the American entrepreneurism. Next were two very small closets, one for hanging clothes with a place for the heater next to it, on the entry side of the trailer. On the other side was another closet which may have been intended as a place for a shower. We used it for storage. There was no stove, but a small counter space where we could place our broiler oven and a double hot plate, next to the sink. We needed a table. My brother-in-law, back in Portsmouth, Virginia, designed, built, and shipped one for us. It was about ten inches wide when folded up, with two drop down leaves making it 36 inches wide when it was opened. A pull-out couch filled the other end. We had a couple of chairs and maybe some other small pieces. It was small, inexpensive, but we felt it would be adequate. I look back and see how God was already shaping my life to fit into the life of Pakistan, the "do without many luxuries" where we cooked on a two-burner oil stove with a tin oven that sat on top if I wanted to bake.

We lived there that year (1949) on the GI Bill, $105.00 each month. Richard had a small savings account from his Navy days, but we did not want to use that, so we counted our pennies. I found a part time job in a nice department store. The twenty-five cents we had left over each month was enough for an ice cream treat to enjoy with our neighbors who had even less because of their baby's needs. We went out once a month and paid five cents for each of the four of us. It was a delicious small treat. The experience of doing without was a great teacher!

In May 1950, a group of graduates were planning a trip to meet with the Evangelical Mission Alliance (TEAM) in Chicago during their Annual Conference. They invited us to join them. Six of us crowded into the station wagon which one student owned and drove all night to avoid having a motel bill. It was a tiring, long trip which ended up with all of us making plans to serve with the mission. Some did not make it for health or other reasons, but we did. Memories of how God had us in His planning calendar still wash over me like a flood. Is it not true He is able to do exceedingly above all we can ask or think?

We learned that TEAM was an interdenominational, faith mission with missionaries in about seventeen different countries. It had been started by Fredrik Franson, a great man of God who had served in China. It had originally been the Scandinavian Alliance Mission with mostly Scandinavian people serving; it was renamed in 1950 because of the influx of non-Scandinavian missionaries.

* * * * * * * * * * * *

Some years later, feeling like a powerless Christian, helpless to see the remedy for the needed changes in my own life, let alone for those to whom I felt called to minister, I began to reexamine my thinking. Was it irrational to believe God had really spoken to me to do something for which I was ill-equipped? I remembered Moses had a similar experience when He cried out to God:

"Please, Lord, I have never been eloquent ..." (Exodus 4:10)

Because it was the way I felt, I think he might have added, "Neither have I had the experience for all this; send someone else!"

When Gideon was trying to hide his wheat from the Midianites who were stalking the land, God met him on the threshing floor.

If it was God's voice I had heard, I needed once again to make a full surrender of my life to Christ. In later years, I would see how God would accept my gift placed on His altar, but He would take me at my word and remind me that everything I thought I was as a person must be surrendered to Him. We don't hear much about that kind of "total submission" contract today. It is relegated to "super spiritualism" or mysticism. There was not a lot of good, healthy spiritual reading material available, but writings of C. S. Lewis were being spread around, and I read some of them. It may have been Lewis's comments which had spoken to me. In *A Grief Observed*, Lewis makes this comment:

> Your bid for God or no God...will not be serious if nothing much is staked on it. And you will never discover how serious it was until the stakes are raised horribly high; until you find that you are playing not for counters or for sixpences, but for every penny you have in the world. Nothing else will shake a man—or at any rate a man like me—out of his merely verbal thinking and ...if my house was a house of cards, the sooner it was knocked down, the better.[1]

I was certainly no match mentally or spiritually for understanding the writings of C. S. Lewis, but I thought I knew what he meant when he said we had to be "shaken out of our merely verbal thinking." Just to say I was a Christian was not enough. There was more. But what was that elusive "more"? I read what Paul wrote in Philippians, and began to quote it as my "life verse":

---

[1] C. S. Lewis, *A Grief Observed,* (New York, NY: HarperCollins Publishing, 1961), 37-8.

"That I may know Him and the power of His resurrection and the fellowship of His sufferings, being conformed to His death; in order that I may attain to the resurrection from the dead." (Philippians 3:10-11)

It was a little frightening, but I knew that was my heart cry, too, and I began to put some thought into what it meant for me, personally, something other than words or a message to give to others. Of what use is a "dishrag Christian"? In order to be used of God, the dishrag must be wrung out.

Later, I would hear someone say the verse in Philippians must be understood in reverse order. In other words, to have the power which transforms lives, one must be "made conformable to His death," and we must enter into the "fellowship of His sufferings." That was the part I did not like. I had joined with the congregation on so many occasions, singing

"Have Thine own Way, Lord, Have thine own way,
Thou art the Potter, I am the clay,
mold me and make me, after Thy will,
while I am waiting, yielded and still,"[2]

But the question was, did I really mean it?

In the Old Testament, the potter's house, the potter and the clay he used to form the vessels on the wheel are used as illustrations of how God dealt with His people. Here is what two of God's servants said:

Shall the potter be considered as equal with the clay,
That what is made would say to its maker,
"He did not make me";
Or what is formed say to him who formed it,
"He has no understanding?" (Isaiah 29:16)

---

[2] Adelaide A. Pollard, "Have Thine Own Way Lord," 1906. Public Domain.

"But now, O Lord, You are our Father,
We are the clay, and You our potter;
And all of us are the work of Your hand" (Isaiah 64:8)

"Behold, like the clay in the potter's hand, so are you in
My hand ..." (Jeremiah 18:6)

In the New Testament, Paul reminds us that the potter has power over the clay:

"Or does not the potter have a right over the clay, to
make from the same lump one vessel for honorable use and an-
other for common use?" (Romans 9:21)

If I believed that, what difference did it make that I, an insignificant person from an insignificant village and at an insignificant age had felt God calling me to be a missionary? The words of a chorus, "Every Moment of Every Day" by Norman Clayton, sung in our youth group came whirling back to remind me. In that hymn, Mr. Clayton wrote about yielding to Jesus to be what He wants us to be.

Not every Christian hears this inaudible voice and responds in the same way that I did. God has "different strokes for different folks." Robert Frost understood this and said it best:

"Two roads diverged in the woods and I—I took the road less traveled by."[3]

I took that road "less traveled by. That is what has made me different.

---

[3] Robert Frost, "The Road Not Taken," In *Mountain Interval*, (New York, NY: Henry Holt and Company, 1920). Public Domain.

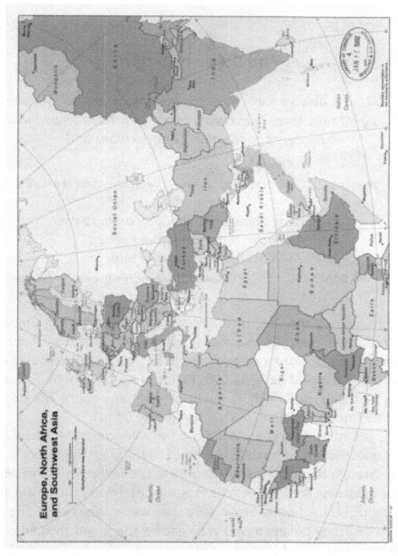

Richard and I would end up serving as missionaries with TEAM in three different countries in the Middle East and Southwest Asia: Pakistan, Iran and the United Arab Emirates.

The Sojourn Begins

"And God is able to make all grace abound to you, so that always having all sufficiency in everything, you may have an abundance for every good deed" (2 Corinthians 9:8)

"Then they spoke against God;
They said, "Can God prepare a table in the wilderness? ...

"He rained down manna upon them to eat
And gave them food from heaven.
Man did eat the bread of angels;
He sent them food in abundance" (Psalm 78:19, 24-5)

During the visit to the mission headquarters in Chicago, Richard and I learned the meaning of "faith missions." It meant raising funds for support, equipment, and travel. When our Director said we would need $2,000, I blurted out I did not know anyone who had that much money! Not great and noble, but honest words from one who expected to "live by faith."

Can God "prepare a table in the wilderness?" It was a cynical question asked by the children of Israel when they were walking through the wilderness. Asaph was the writer. In Psalm 78 he was recording some of Israel's experiences. I don't think I am cynical, but I think I understand why they were. What were they to do when they believed God was leading them and they knew of no resources on which they could depend?

This would not be the only time I would ask the same question. Could God do for me what seemed the impossible? Yes! He did for the children of Israel. We saw Him do it for us. God, who owns the cattle on a thousand hills, the wealth of every mine, the Creator and Sustainer of the Universe, has untold means to meet our every need!

My lack of faith had not bothered God. Money, equipment, and support came in. In just three months and a series of amazing ways, we discovered God's storehouse was stocked full and a "mere" two thousand dollars was no problem for Him. He had an ample supply for us.

A Whirlwind of Events

In June, while working as a "missionary speaker" at a children's camp in Georgia, I lost my appetite and began to feel nauseated. The older members working there diagnosed the problem. We would be welcoming a little one in about nine months! It was something we had not counted on, and I found it hard to believe. The confirmation of my pregnancy came as a surprise, just prior to our college graduation. Richard immediately decided we needed to be in Pakistan when the baby was born, just as he had been born in India. It was a long shot to believe it could happen, "but God..."

In September, we received the news from TEAM that all the paperwork was in order, but before we could leave, we had to raise the needed funds for our support, travel, and outfit. God again smiled on the adventure. Our first meeting was in Elgin Bible Church in Illinois where a college friend's father was pastor. After that, other churches and individuals promised support when they got the news. Our largest gift was from a college couple we barely knew, four hundred dollars.

From gifts of five and ten dollars to gifts of baby clothing and personal needs, filling nine pieces in all, trunks, boxes and suitcases, everything and more came in. Preacher John Taylor had become pastor of Grace Baptist Church in Norfolk, Virginia. He was our Joshua, leading us into "the land of promise." They became our "sending church."

This church was born in a small store front which had been vacated and sold. Preacher Taylor began the ministry with a small group which had been growing and now was interested in missionary outreach. The church group had provided so much of what we needed and expected to use in Pakistan. "Preacher" and some men from the church had packed our nine pieces of baggage for shipping. A two-burner kerosene stove, a few pots and pans, tableware, linens, adult clothes, and necessities for the baby were packed in boxes, suitcases, even an old humpback trunk someone had offered. Traveling halfway around the world from the US to Pakistan would mean we needed warm clothes when we started out, but clothes for the hot weather when we reached the Mediterranean area were packed in suitcases to travel with us.

Preacher Taylor at the ground-breaking for Grace Baptist Church, Norfolk, VA, 1956. We were home on our first home leave from Pakistan and were fortunate to be able to attend. This church was such a huge blessing for us and were our "sending church."

Our life became like a whirlwind. In less than six months, we had finished up college work, Richard's MA, my BA, visited the mission headquarters, applied to become missionaries, been accepted by the mission, taught in two children's Bible Mission camps, raised our support and travel funds, gathered an outfit including baby needs, and were on our way. Much of this while I suffered from morning sickness during the last three months of that time.

A Mother's Secret

Of Mary in the Bible, it was said she, "treasured all these things, pondering them in her heart" (Luke 2:19). Mothers are like that; they lock some secrets in their hearts, perhaps forever unknown, but this one of my mom's escaped. It was one she had never told until the night before we left home to go to New York in preparation for going to Pakistan.

Our tickets were in hand; our trunks and suitcases were packed. We had been able to get most of our required immunization shots. We were novices, but everything had gone like clockwork. We had tentatively planned for an early "family" Christmas on December 21. It would lessen my sadness at having to be away from home at a special family time. We could leave Portsmouth with our luggage and make the four-hour trip to New York on the 22nd to board the ship on the 23rd.

Then came the news: some shots were not available locally, including Yellow Fever. We would have to get that and any other shots we needed in New York. We should plan on leaving immediately for New York so as to be there for two weeks because the dosage for some shots required they be given a week apart. The die was cast; in order to get the shots and make our ship connections, we would have to leave early on December 9. There could be no delay if we wanted to board that ship! TEAM had an apartment in New York, so housing would not be a problem. The host and hostess would meet us and help us get everything done.

We hastily made our final preparations before leaving Portsmouth, Virginia. We went that night to give my parents the news. We would not see them again for five years. We wanted to tell them as much as we could about what lay up ahead for us but in fact, we knew very little. We ourselves had been acting in faith, taking each step as we went along.

I can still see them as they were that night: Daddy sitting in his gooseneck rocker by the big oil heater in the living room, Mom, in the little hallway next to the living room, sitting at the sewing machine, working on Christmas gifts for the family. They seemed so old at the time, but Mom was just sixty, Daddy was nearing seventy. The first words out of my mouth were about our having to leave the next day. Moms were, "Oh, no!" Daddy did not say anything.

I was not close to my mom like my sister was; I was a "daddy's girl" who followed him every step I could. I always felt different, but it was not something as a child I could put into words. One day I asked my mom if I was adopted. She answered, "With all these young'uns, would I adopt another?" As my own children were born and began to grow up, I saw how different they were. I understood how each child is unique in some special way.

My loving parents had weathered storms of uncertainty for over four decades, times full of good memories and bad, struggles with life and the sudden death of their ten-year-old daughter from a school related accident, the depression, loss of the house they had worked so hard to build, loss of another house because of a fire, wartime concerns, sons who had gone off in battle zones but thankfully, had returned safely, then the loss of a son just after wartime. She had not said it, but I was sure she was thinking, "And now, another child is going far away. Will she return?"

Mom was an incredibly strong woman. She had to be in order to endure some of the trials she and Daddy faced. However, that night when we visited the last time for what we both expected would be at least five years, she was different. It was only the second time I had ever seen her tears, not a big crying episode, just tear-filled eyes that told me she was deeply feeling our leaving. It was then she related the story of her pregnancy with me and promise to God (as told in the Preface to this book). At the time she made that promise, she must have had no idea that God would hold her to it! When she finished, with tears in her eyes, she added, "but I never thought He would take you so far away from me!"

****

As odd as it seems, what Mom told me that night was never again discussed. Now I wish we had. Some sacred secrets when revealed need to be kept in the treasure box of the heart. I guess this is where that one had its final lodging.

Mom has been gone from us for decades, gently carried in the arms of her Heavenly Father, laid to rest beside my dad and the daughter they lost 16 months before I was born. Several decades have passed since that night when we sat together by the oil heater in the tiny living room, and she shared her secret. Memories, like directions on a map, leave their imprint on our minds. I have relived them over and over.

Preparing for the Mission Field

We left our home in Virginia on December 9, 1950, had a two weeks' stay in New York so that we could get the required yellow fever and other shots not obtainable in our area, and take care of the final travel plans with the travel agent.

We knew little about the field to which we would be going, and not much more about New York, but God has HIS people everywhere. TEAM had a Norwegian couple in New York who kept an apartment for people just like us; they had room. Across the street was a Norwegian church with "*Velcomen*" carved in stone. The welcome with these new friends could not have been warmer.

When we got to the clinic where the needed shots were given, I was told if I had any adverse effects from the shots, we would not be able to travel. No one was worried about Richard, who had been immunized many times as a "missionary kid" and in the military. Therefore, I went first, then stood nearby as Richard got his shots. He did not do as well. I had to help him find the

71

door as he tottered around feeling the wall! Luckily, there were no other ill effects.

The travel agent from Menno Travel in New York was a great help. He was shocked that I was venturing out in the late stage of my pregnancy and said, "Well, you don't look it, so don't tell anybody!" It was the travel agent who suggested we purchase some grocery items to take to the China Inland Mission in London where we would be staying. It was so soon after the war that Britain was still feeling the effects of rationing and food shortages. He told us the ship would keep them in cold storage, so we bought several dozen eggs, some pounds of bacon, some jars of peanut butter and maybe other things.

Fellow TEAM missionaries Dick and Marjorie Winchell were due to sail on a different ship the same day, headed for Africa. They took us to the port for boarding the *Queen Elizabeth* before they gave their car over to someone. It was another hurdle overcome for us. God's love sees to it that every need is met. His provision is boundless. He tells of His riches in the Psalms and in the book of Job. The amazing thing is that He is willing to share them with us!

We set sail in December 1950, after having made somewhat hurried plans in order to be at our mission station before our baby's birth. Both the travel agent in New York, and after we got aboard, the ship's doctor had wondered at the wisdom of our leaving the US this late into my pregnancy, but earlier, all had been approved. Since Richard had been born in India, also of missionary parents, it was his desire that our child be born in what he thought of as "my country."

Setting Sail

We boarded the ship on Friday afternoon, the 23rd, got settled, and too excited to sleep, stayed up to watch as we passed by the Statue of Liberty about 2:00 A.M. on the 24th, Christmas Eve day. Our few days crossing the Atlantic were uneventful. We had a little Christmas Day celebration in our room with the little tree we had taken along and the gifts from our family. It was my first Christmas away from them and both my parents and I, as well as other family members, felt a little sad. As children, my sister and I pored over the Sears catalog, the "wish book" as we called it, noting what we wanted for Christmas. Christmas at our house was never a big affair, with large gifts. Rather, as a rule there was usually only one gift from "Santa Claus." How could he carry so many around the world? One was enough. Richard was fine; he was "going back!"

The 25th was Sunday. In those days, the ship regularly held Christian services. Richard was ordained and although a novice, was invited to lead it. Richard was surprised when the Chief Steward asked him to do the upcoming Sunday worship service; there may not have been another ordained minister or vicar aboard the ship. His early years in India provided him a slightly familiar advantage with the Anglican traditional services. After hesitating a moment, he accepted, feeling it was an honor. He handled it very nicely. Richard had a beautiful voice and knew the tunes of the songs we sang.

The trip on the beautiful *Queen Elizabeth I* was an introduction to formal living. The dining room table was laid with all kinds of cutlery for meals. At my country home where my sister and I were the ones to set the table and wash the dishes, if only a fork was needed, that is all we placed at the table, except for my dad's place. He always had to have a knife to cut up the green peppers he ate with his supper each night, and a spoon for his coffee.

On our honeymoon, we had visited Richard's aunt, who took us to a very fancy restaurant. I felt embarrassed that I was not sure how to eat the meal. Back at school, we were living in a tiny trailer. We had been given a Betty Crocker cookbook. When I found it contained more than recipes, I used it to teach myself table etiquette. Each Sunday, I prepared a meal and used our wedding silver and other wedding gift table finery. I used as many pieces of my new wedding silver as I could. Aboard the ship, I felt at ease until I saw a small fork and spoon placed at the top of my plate which had not been mentioned in my Betty Crocker cookbook! I just watched the people at the table next to ours and saw it was a British way, used for dessert.

During this trip we met another missionary, Ruby Severtsen, who was going out to work with the World Mission Prayer League (WMPL), a Lutheran group which worked on the frontier in Peshawar. From the moment we saw her in the eleva-

tor, there was a common bond. She was engaged to Leonard Patzold who was finishing up some degree work and would be coming later. When she learned I was expecting a baby, she made me her charge. We compared notes

Richard, me and Ruby Severtsen onboard the *Queen Elizabeth*, 1950.

and found we would be together on the next ship when we sailed through the Mediterranean Sea. Her mission station was located further north in Pakistan, on the border of Afghanistan. We became friends, and by the time we landed in Southampton, it seemed we had known each other for years. When she married, I let her wear my wedding dress. We remained good friends during all the years we were in the country.

Learning Experiences, the British Culture

After passing through customs, we boarded the boat train to London. Ruby's arrangements were with the family of a friend, "A man carrying a book under his arm would meet her." We helped her search the crowd and saw no one with a book, but Americans traveling in those days were easily recognized, and the man found her. He was not carrying a book. We parted but would meet again about nine days later on the Scottish ship *Cilicia* to begin the next part of our trip.

TEAM had arranged for us to stay at the China Inland Mission (CIM), a faith mission group founded by Hudson Taylor in the 1800s. They had a lovely large home in London where retired and other missionaries could stay. China had closed its doors to missions and the CIM was receiving some of their missionaries, but they had room for us, and the building was heated, a very important part of that blessing. Since neither my clothes nor shoes were considered heavy enough for the cold weather in England, the ladies expressed a lot of concern and wanted me to go out and buy some "woolies." I did not want to spend the money, so I was careful of how long we were out in the cold.

All of England was still experiencing rationing five years after the war ended, but probably because of concern for this organization, the CIM could get some special rations of food and except for one morning, we enjoyed the meals. One morning I could smell the breakfast cooking, maybe kippers on toast? I knew what would happen if I tried to eat it. I decided not to get out of bed. It didn't work; the hostess came knocking at the door and I had to explain.

We had a travelogue about tourist places, but in 1950, England was still suffering the post war experiences of being bombed. Many places were not yet rebuilt and may never be. We saw Westminster Abbey with its treasure trove of history and Buckingham Palace, the royal residence.

What was more exciting about seeing the King's residence was that we got to see close up King George the Sixth, the Queen and Princess Margaret. Just after we arrived at the front gate, we stepped up to one of the guards who walk back and forth in front of the entrance and asked if the King and Queen were by any chance coming. He replied without moving a facial muscle, "In about 15 minutes." It was only later that we learned that approaching the guards in front of the palace is a positive "no, no."

We stood by the gates, waiting. Sure enough, the car came in sight. Since it was an unexpected arrival, we were in the front line with only a few people around. Our brand-new camera was turned on; alas, Richard had not known it had to be cocked. We got a close-up view, saw the famous royal wave and in a nano-second, it was over, no picture. All we got was a quick glance and that famous royal wave.

Today, we await the coming of the King of Kings Who will invite us to enter His palace in the beyond, where Jesus said, "In my Father's house are many dwelling places" (John 14). We will attend the royal reception and spend our days there forever after. What will it be like? We can only imagine it by using the Scripture as it declares it.

Since we were going to an area of the world very much influenced by the British culture, it was probably to our advantage that we had several very interesting moments—learning experiences—while we were at the Mission House that week in London. First was that "not everyone in London was equal" (not so blessed?). This mission house, the China Inland Mission, was heated, whereas many places in England were not. Ruby stayed with a family who had no heat and said she was sure her thermometer registered 32 degrees one morning!

Staying in the CIM home was my "101 course" on how to behave with people in a different cultural background than I had in my growing up years—what to do and the discipline of doing things a different way. Whereas I had been used to a "three hearty meals a day" culture, the missionary mealtime routine was lighter meals in this home, breakfast, then "elevensees" (just a cup of something to drink to refresh us,) lunch, then tea at 4:00, and dinner, all served on time.

The China I had thought of serving was now closing its doors to missionaries, and the CIM home was welcoming return-ees every day. The first ones from this large group of people were arriving. What a privilege it was to hear about China. I wondered if I would have been able to learn the language. Knowing I would not have to learn it brought a sigh of relief. Little did I know what I was in for with learning the language of Pakistan, in characters, and written from right to left.

The repatriation had started just as we were leaving England; otherwise, there would have been no room for us. We met some of them. They told of hardships they had endured before they left. About those jars of peanut butter, that almost essential delicacy for Americans? As we packed up, the hostess brought out those jars. I did not want to take them, wanted these new friends to enjoy them. She then confessed the missionaries returning to England from China had existed on peanut butter during those war days and never wanted to see it again! After we arrived on our station, I admit to being very happy we had that peanut butter!

As we prepared for this next lap of our journey, we got the idea to buy some chocolates to take to our Pakistani co-workers. We went to a shop, looked at all that delicious and beautiful assortment, and made our selection, then were asked for our "ration tickets." It seems we could have gotten those because we were tourists, but we did not know it, so we had to leave empty-handed. There was no time to go to the ration office. Americans had abandoned rationing years before. To this day, we feel no one makes chocolates like the British. Well, maybe a few other countries do!

We had one final laugh on ourselves before we left. Richard called a taxi to take us from the home to board the boat train which ran from London to Liverpool. We would embark on the *Cilicia* from Liverpool. Maybe it was the Cockney accent, but when Richard tried to explain the location of the Mission, the driver called out, "Wat kin' o' commission?" or something that sounded like that. They finally got it straight. The taxis all had a list of payment charges posted inside the cab. When we wanted to pay, we thought we were giving a generous tip with the payment but were asked if we were wasting our money. We got that sorted out when he let us know we were cheating him; that listed charge was out of date. We gave him the extra, then wound our way to the pier for the Scottish ship *Cilicia* for the next lap of our trip. But what a wonderful experience and introduction to mission life we had during that first trip to London.

Besides Ruby, still traveling with us, there were several British missionaries aboard the *Cilicia*, returning for service in Pakistan. We became instant friends and were blessed by many ways in which they helped us adjust before we got to our destination. An interesting footnote in Richard's Mom's diary when she went out to India in the early 1900s, a three-month trip via China, was that they had to study language aboard the ship! We would have to wait for that.

The Next Leg of Our Sojourn

Shortly after we boarded the Scottish ship, I had to visit the ship's doctor for some reason, and Ruby told him how far along I was in my pregnancy. He wondered who had allowed me to come that late in my pregnancy. I told him if it was a baby girl, born aboard the ship, and he had to deliver her, I would name her Cilicia Ann. I doubt it brought him any comfort and it did not happen.

When we went through the Suez Canal, passengers were allowed to get off at one end, travel up to see the Sphinx and the Pyramids, even go through the tunnel inside one, and also see the Cairo Museum with its artifacts about "ancient Egypt." At the opposite end, passengers would be delivered to the ship and reboard. Richard took advantage of that on this first lap, and on our return, 5 ½ years later, he kept the children, and I made the trip, also visiting Alexandria.

For those who did not take that tour, we could watch as the ship slowly moved through the Canal. At times, we could view both sides of the white shore sand. Going through the canal took a whole day. It is only wide enough for one of the big ships. I seem to recall at some points it seemed we could reach out and touch the desert sands on each side of the ship. Most of the time, it was deserted areas. Only occasionally could we see that life, perhaps Bedouin tents, were pitched further out in the sand. Except for what we saw on each end of the canal, we saw very little vegetation during most of that day. Along the way, I noticed some areas cut out. I will call them "way by" places, so if the ship had to pass another, smaller boat, there was a "way by" for the smaller boat to dock.

Also, the ship brought aboard some entertainment. Especially fascinating was the Gali Gali man who did magic tricks unimaginable, like throwing a ring overboard and then having it reappear in someone's pocket. It was a fun thing, and it was no longer a problem believing the stories of those ten plagues in Moses' day being replicated.

At each end of the canal, we were allowed to go aboard and shop, while the vendors haunted every move we made. One of our old suitcases had broken open, and we needed to get one. The ship's strong suggestion was that we take a guide if we left the ship. We took their advice but apparently, he had his own friends. That guide walked us over village paths for a good ten minutes! We had no idea where we were going, and I was beginning to feel a little panicky. Our final destination was in a little leather-making shop. Before we could purchase anything, we had to have coffee. Ahh, the friendliness of the Middle East! A small cup was poured for each of us. All I could think of was that it might be poisoned and no one aboard the ship knew where we were. They would never find us if anything went wrong. I said I did not want any. Richard thought that would be insulting and told me since we were now in the Middle East, we needed to partake of their hospitality. I still refused. He took one sip but noticed a lump in it. He rolled the lump around in his mouth, thought it might be a spice, but remembering my warning to him, spit it out. It was a dead fly! The plague of Egypt was still in abundance. The quick apology of the shop keeper could not convince him he should have another cup. We bought out suitcase and returned safely to the ship.

We had some Bible-time get-togethers aboard the ship. At the end of the trip, a British lady whose name I can't recall, and don't recall ever meeting again, gave me these verses, which are still with me, and which gave me insight into knowing a little better the promises of God and how I could trust Him, even in the difficult times. One was Zephaniah 3:17 and one Habakkuk 3:17-19. Just to keep in mind that God Himself can rejoice over us, that He will joy over us with singing is enough to set me singing! And I did, often, sing of His great Love.

"The Lord thy God in the midst of thee is mighty;
He will save, he will rejoice over thee with joy;
He will rest in his love, he will joy over thee with singing." (Zeph-
aniah 3:17, KJV)

And ...

"Although the fig tree shall not blossom,
Neither shall fruit be in the vines;
The labour of the olive shall fail,
And the fields shall yield no meat;
The flock shall be cut off from the fold,
And there shall be no herd in the stalls:
Yet I will rejoice in the Lord,
I will joy in the God of my salvation.
The Lord God is my strength,
And he will make my feet like hinds' feet,
And he will make me to walk upon mine high places." (Habakkuk
3:17-19, KJV)

We had gone out as "faith missionaries." What if...? Could there ever be a need God would not supply? The verse said we could trust Him. We would have to believe that. Today we know He is indeed trustworthy.

****

The God Factor That Became a Sojourn

"Abraham went out, not knowing where he was going...(he) journeyed on, going on still..." The word used for

Abraham's journeyings is "sojourned." That means he would be moving around, not staying in one place. He was acting in faith, just doing what God was leading him to do. The New Testament says of him, "... faith was reckoned to Abraham for righteousness..."

Those whom God called in the past are really no different from those He has called throughout the ages. All of these and many more are experiences or emotions which prove how really human most of us Christians are in our daily walk. We have fears, we feel incompetent, we shrink back, but then, we may decide to step forward and say we will obey.

Psalm 78 begins with "I will open my mouth in a parable." A parable is an earthly story with a heavenly meaning. I like to think parables like this one draw us into the arena where we learn to "play the game of faith." As we win, we are given the opportunity to find God is big enough for every need we have. God has His reasons for His high calling of people like me. One of those is to "show to the generations to come the praises of the Lord and His strength and His wonderful works that He has done."

God's servants have always had to act in faith. It would be no different for Richard and me. Moses said, "Oh, Lord, I am not eloquent..." Make that, "I need help!" God said to Gideon, "Go in this thy might..." The Lord promised to be with him. Isaiah lived in the King's palace. He heard God ask, "Whom shall I send and who will go for me?" He answered, "Here am I, send me." It was the call we believed we were answering.

A missionary living in a foreign country and with people of a different culture wants to be victorious in the battles being waged. Because we believe God has called us, we want to see answers when we pray, to be "result oriented" in our prayer life. It is not always like that. Praying in faith is different from praying to "get results."

When we pray to get results, God becomes a "puppet god" for us. When answers are not quickly forthcoming, we may be like those who serve a foreign god and try to do more to make Him answer. Our God is not like that. Sometimes, there are roadblocks when we think we should be moving ahead. It is then the "faith tank" becomes empty.

Faith is not like a seed which continues to grow after it has first sprouted, although when we look back, we know what it has done for us. What we might regard as "faith" might be known by another name, such as hope or belief, or even supposition. What is regarded as "faith" is sometimes a desire to "entice God" into doing what we want, thereby making Him less than God. Faith does not "draw interest" like a bank account where something is deposited and left on hold to be used later, and yet, it is that very "bank account" on which we rely when we are in need. God "has done it in the past" and will He not do it again just because we prayed?

Jeremiah wrote, "Shall the thing formed say to Him that formed it, 'Why hast thou made me thus'?" This was my personal problem. Who was I to take on this ministry? Jesus told His disciples to "go into all the world and preach the Gospel." A disciple is one who sits at the feet of another for the purpose of learning. I had been sitting at Jesus' feet, wanting to get to know him better. Paul wrote, "Faith comes by hearing and hearing by the Word of God." I wanted to hear what God had to say and obey it, but to take on a missionary ministry?

Our Arrival in Pakistan

"'For I know the plans that I have for you,' declares the Lord,
'plans for welfare and not for calamity to give you a future and a
hope.'" (Jeremiah 29:11)

"It's just beautiful," were my first words as I looked around at new surroundings in a small cantonment area, set in a bowl with a ring of the snow-clad Himalayan Mountain foothills, in the northwest frontier area of Pakistan. The district of Hazara, located in a bowl like setting in this northwest corner of Pakistan, is 3500-4000 feet high. The area is heavily wooded, a welcome sight after the barrenness of the desert areas we had witnessed a few hours earlier. Wherever the sun could peek through the trees that frosty morning, we saw glistening patches of snow, silvery streaks adorning the white of the newly fallen snow signaling winter. In the far distance, the high mountains with reputations like K2

The snowy mountains surrounding Abbottabad, ~1951.

and Nanga Parbat gleamed with the brightness of fresh white snow. The mountains looked stacked, one on another, shown like a picture on a postcard, or a deck of cards laid out by number, the lowest to the highest, with valleys in between. We would experience something like that one day when we thought we were

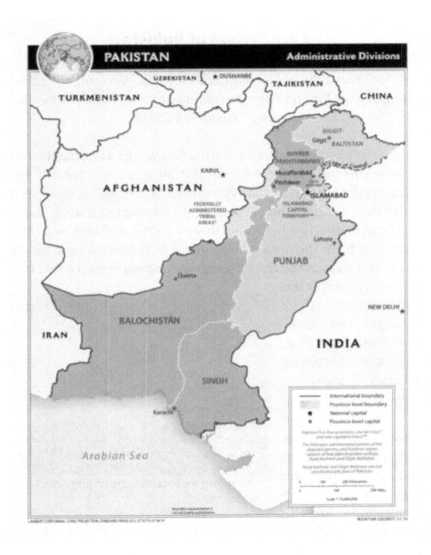

84

nearing our goal on a mountain trek, only to find we had to cross another valley before reaching the higher hills.

The date was January 26, 1951. From a small village in America to village life in a country thousands of miles from home, I was probably one of the most unlikely persons to have answered God's call to travel across the world, but here we were, my husband Richard and I, meeting people we had not known before, senior missionaries who would help us monitor our activities and equip us for the ministry to which we had come. We were entering into a brand-new lifestyle, everything about our life new, our baby still in my "baby carrier" from which she would emerge a month later. The very way in which we had become acquainted with the Scandinavian Alliance Mission, as it was then called, and been accepted by them, had been seemingly coincidental happenings which had come together and created a space for us in God's harvest field.

Now, we believed we were where God wanted us to be, in Pakistan, just five years earlier, a part of the sub-continent of India. Everything new, our experiences and theirs. We would grow together, some experiences would be difficult, others delightful, all compressed tightly in the Hand of the God we had come to serve, all known to Him, unknown to us. We would ask Him to lead us. Some additional promises on which we were resting, written over two millennia ago, from Jeremiah and Isaiah were the following:

"Stand...and see...and ask...Where the good way is and walk in it." (Jeremiah 6:16)

"You shall be My people and I will be your God." (Jeremiah 30:22)

The steadfast of mind You will keep in perfect peace,
Because he trusts in You.
Trust in the Lord forever,
For in God the Lord, we have an everlasting Rock. (Isaiah 26:3,4)

We knew God would be sufficient for anything we faced.

The Arrival!

Dad Thompson came over from India to meet us at the ship when it landed in Karachi. A Methodist missionary, he had already served for about 35 years when we arrived. He and Emma had worked with the refugees when India was divided in 1946. Once again, we two pilgrims experienced the help we needed to get us further on the way. He had arranged for us to stay the night with an Anglo-Indian family from the Methodist Church at 74 Garden Road, a church and house well known to Richard, now being pastored by an Anglo-Indian minister. Richard's family had lived there in the 1930s when his dad had been the pastor.

Our arrival in Karachi, 1951. From L to R, the Anglo-Indian minister, Dad Thompson, me, and Richard in front of the *Cilicia*.

More new experiences, the first of which was a tour of the local open-air market. There were rows and rows of tables with large containers of fruits, vegetables, and dry fried lentils ("*chana*"), which both men sampled, expressing how tasty they were. My first bite reminded me of the hot peppers my own father grew and enjoyed back in America, but they were too hot for me! I also watched Dad Thompson shop for a leather purse for his dear Emma. I would not understand until later why he wanted to buy the purse in Pakistan; leather hides were not abundant in India where the cow is sacred.

Richard and his dad enjoyed those few hours, just reminiscing. Then, it was back to the parsonage for dinner. It was "old home week" for Dad Thompson and the large dinner table had been set for several other guests besides the three of us. Plates were stacked at the end, and the hostess served each one with the food set in front of her place. Each plate was passed around. What was probably intended to be something which everyone else would regard as a delicacy was something of a shock to me. The meat entree was "hump." To one who knew of a hump as something only a camel had, I didn't even want to try it! Just after all the plates were served and everyone was enjoying the meal, I tried to slip my meat onto Richard's plate, but I got caught! "Oh, you don't like hump?" said our hostess. I think Richard spoke his kindest words, explaining that this pregnancy had changed a lot of my tastes! However, no one bothered to tell me what "hump" was. I would find out later that it was actually the hump of the Brahmin bull, which was treated with spices and became much like our corned beef.

Dinner over, it was time to retire to our rooms where we found fresh warm water in a large pitcher, a wash basin, and a towel. Our six-week journey crossing land and ocean, then boarding a train to climb into the foothills of the Himalayan mountains, would soon be coming to an end, but our life as career missionaries was just beginning. It had been a long day. A cool breeze was blowing through the lattice work covering the open windows. Sleep came very quickly.

After a good night's rest and some more visiting, we said our final goodbyes to the people at the Mission House and prepared to board the train in the late afternoon. Dad Thompson had helped us arrange our trip up country. We had water, some sandwiches, and some thick quilts for our bedding. No sleeper service for missionary travel! Richard's Mom was reportedly once asked by a British soldier friend, "Why do you travel second class?" to which she replied, "There was no room in the third class!" The thousand-mile trip would take two nights and one full day. We would arrive on the second morning.

There was room in the compartment for several people who were traveling short distances but at night, we could reserve the compartment for sleeping. These little box compartments had wide boards strung from near the top of the train and held by a chain which could be pulled tight against the wall for the daytime but let down at night. In later years when we visited Granpa and Granma Thompson in India, we had special thick quilts (*rezais*) sewn like sleeping bags. We were able to attach the strings to the chains to keep the quilts and the kids from falling off as the train rumbled and bounced along.

Our Journey Ends at 24 Pine View Road

The British left behind many good things, one of which was the British rail line which went from Karachi to Peshawar on the Afghan border. We had brief stops in the large and historic cities of Lahore and Rawalpindi. I think what must impress westerners more than anything else is the mass of people who always seem to be standing around. At the train station, there were those who were waiting for the train, the "coolies" who carried luggage, railway workers and those just trying to find some odd job. No doubt others were just "observers" wanting to see who was coming and going; they did not have anything else to do. The poverty was obvious.

Our thousand-mile trip by train started in Karachi and ran through the dusty Sindh Desert. As we departed Karachi, Richard saw some familiar sights. It was as if his heart had never left his boyhood home. He was happy to be a part of India again, even though it was now Pakistan.

We got supper on the train. Soon it was night and the only thing to be seen along the way was the small light of an occasional village. The train made several stops. The next morning, we were again able to get breakfast from the dining room on the train, fried eggs, bread, and tea. The all-day ride through the desert was hot. Opening the windows meant more sand blowing in our faces and on our sweaty clothes. I seem to remember the dining car was no longer available. For lunch, we ate the sandwiches in our tiffin basket and drank from our bottle of water. Most of the stations at which we stopped had huge pots of boiling tea, which Richard enjoyed.

One of the stops the train made was at Taxila, a village about 55 miles from Abbottabad. The first TEAM missionaries, Dr. Andrew and Olive Karsgaard, along with nurses Karen Pedersen and Marian Temple, worked at the United Presbyterian Hospital in Taxila, and came to the train to welcome us. The village of Taxila dates back to the days of Alexander the Great. Vestiges of the Greek influence have been uncovered by the archaeologists and preserved in museums. Alexander and his army had traveled this area up to the Indus Valley where Richard would later encounter people who orally recounted the history of Alexander's army being stopped there.

Bill Pietsch, a young single missionary, met the train in Haripur, one station before the last stop in Havelian. From there, the train took a westward turn on flatter land and headed to Peshawar, near the Khyber Pass into Afghanistan. The train track was not laid to climb the hills. We still had a nine-mile trip, into the foothills to our station.

Bill had been in Pakistan only a short time but had already learned his way around. We would have to rent a taxi for this part of our travel. Without his help it would have meant negotiating the cost. We would not have known about charges or other passengers, since as a rule, as many as would fit in could ride together. We got acquainted as we rode around curves, up and down hills, passing other vehicles on what seemed not much more than a one lane road, watching for oxcarts and sheep herds moving on the same road. We were thankful to find the roads paved and on occasion, a "lay by", a wider margin to help in case of needing to pass. The British had built the roads for the Government Transport System. They were adequate, but narrow, extending up to 3500 feet of the steep mountain ranges and beyond. All the while I was looking out from the not too clean windows of the ancient station wagon, wondering, "Are we there yet?"

The old taxi slowly made its way up the winding road in the ups and downs of the hills that morning, passing loaded carts and rich farmland. The twists and turns as we climbed the hills made our bodies sway against each other, but nine miles later, we finally entered a populated area, a gathering of buildings and what we knew must be our destination, Abbottabad, the Mission Headquarters of TEAM, 24 Wilde Road, later changed to Pine View Road. The paved road led up an incline to mountain villages we could view above our house.

We arrived to see the members of our new missionary family, five adults and three children, all dressed in wool coats, hats, and mittens, holding a sign, "Welcome Thompsons!"

Me with our welcoming committee for our arrival in Pakistan, 1951. Back row, L to R, Carl Davis, me, Agnes Davis, Mabel and Don Fredlund, Bill Pietsch. In front are the Davis children.

Bill was from California, Don and Mabel Fredlund from Canada and Carl and Agnes Davis, the senior missionaries on site, from Illinois. None of them were accustomed to a Southerner's accent. For the next several months I would be teased by everyone I met about my "Suth'n drawl."

The first view of the Mission Headquarters was of a very old, large but attractive house, likely built in the 1800s or at the latest, at the turn of the 20th century, for the British officers stationed in the cantonment. It was later purchased and given over to the work of the United Presbyterian Mission. The house was set on a compound, a word the British used to describe a plot of land with a group of buildings. There was a high mud brick wall along one side of the compound. To this day, I have no idea what was on the other side of that wall! Nor do I know why I was never curious enough to go and see.

The mission house and our mission headquarters. 24 Pine View Road, Abbottabad.

The main property entrance wound through and around the side of the house, with an exit at the back. While waiting for the men to unload our belongings, I surveyed my surroundings. Remnants of the last snow glistened in the sun that morning. Its clay covered outside walls were set on stone underpinnings, the trim on the house and the posts holding the wide front verandah were painted green. There was a very large double bay window across the front with the main door entrance on the verandah side. About a quarter mile away was a little cottage on the property belonging to St. Luke's Anglican Church.

These old houses, the Mission House and St. Luke's Cottage beside the church, surely would have had a tale to tell had

91

they been able to talk. They had known many a get-together, and there would likely have been many stories they could have told.

As we entered the Mission House from the verandah, there was a very large reception room, possibly used for entertaining. At any rate, it would serve as a gathering place for our missionary meetings in years to come. There were various rooms on either side, probably bedrooms, a study and a dressing room. Behind the reception room was a nice sized dining room, and another small room like a mud room, with storage cabinets and a huge sink with running water. The mud room was connected by a short-covered walkway to the outside kitchen, but there was no running water in the kitchen. I imagined this house had what were considered some "modern amenities" at the time of its building.

There were two bathrooms, which also had running water, and "WCs," located above the commode. Flushing was done by pulling the long chain which hung down beside the tank. Each bathroom had a large solid cement form about 30 inches high and two feet square, with a rim that formed a basin. At the bottom was a drain area, an exit for the wastewater and a nice access for mice and rats.

This plot of land had earlier been purchased and given over to the United Presbyterian Mission which worked in those northern reaches. Those missionaries were elderly, ready for retirement, and TEAM, new to the area, had been invited by their mission to take over the work and the property was acceded to our mission.

Connected to that wall and along a main road at the back of the house, was a tall thick hedge, making a barrier to separate and hide from visibility some smaller mud brick quarters. In the front of the house was a big flower bed, extending along the front, then some steps which led down into a packed clay area, possibly designed as a play area, since there was no grass. Further out, a deep ravine separated the compound from a side road. The trees were enormous, sycamores was my first impression. A year later, after we moved into that house, the gardener found what looked like a clump of orchids and brought the flowers into the house for me. But orchids in a land of winter cold and snow? Maybe just iris.

At the time of our arrival, the small buildings behind the main house were being used as rooms for the Pakistani teachers who ran the mission school for national children, where I would assist and teach after a year of language study. There was no building for the school; the children met outside on the compound unless there was inclement weather. In that case, the teachers would clear out a room in the Mission House and they would meet there. They were not meeting on the day of our arrival.

We washed the sand and dirt off our faces and hands and went in the dining room to meet the *khansama*. In the true language of Urdu, the meaning of *khansama* or *khansaman*, was the person who cared for the household "*saman*," or belongings. In this case, he was the cook and bearer, or server who brought in the food from the outside kitchen. He had laid a special table and a welcome breakfast was ready.

The Mission property was located on the main paved road, which wound down from the hills above to the bazaar below the Mission House. Just a short distance from the house, and nearer the bazaar, was a covered shed housing the *"tonga wala"* stalls where one could hire, for a few cents, a ride in a horse-drawn "carriage" (really just an open cart with a back seat for passengers and not much of a place to hold on) to move around the city. Most of our local travel would be by *tonga* or walking; we would only use a bus or taxi if going long distances. We would early on welcome the closeness of the *tonga* stand and the availability of a ride to get where we needed or wanted to go, since at that time, no one in the mission had a car. But it was the warmth of that first meeting which made us feel secure, already appreciated, and welcomed by a new "family" of people.

We Learn Some History of this New Area

The British had ruled India for two hundred years before the country was divided in 1947. They were gone, but vestiges of their leadership were left behind. During their rule they had designated certain areas as cantonments, districts or areas of a town where troops were stationed.

The cantonment where our mission was located, Abbottabad, had been a district headquarters. The first District Commissioner, Mr. Abbott was the honoree when it was named. *Abad* is the word for abode or city of, and thus, Abbottabad, the "abode of Abbott," a beautiful area 3500 feet in the mountains located in the Hazara district of Pakistan. It would be home to us for the next seventeen and a half years, with several breaks when we returned to the US to reunite with family, our supporting churches, and our Mission Board.

Missionaries with TEAM of Wheaton, Illinois, were among the new groups which had first entered the country just prior to partition. TEAM's ministry focus was three-fold: educational, evangelistic, and medical. The educational and medical work, while meeting real physical needs, also provided a path for meeting spiritual needs and opened doors for evangelism.

A medical team led by Dr. Andrew Karsgaard from Canada and some nurses were the first to go out in 1946. They were working under the umbrella of the United Presbyterian Hospital in Taxila. In fact, TEAM would remain under the umbrella of the United Presbyterians for about five years before having their own status in the country. TEAM's vision was to establish, in time, our own hospital in the far north areas.

That vision came to fruition in late 1955 when the mission broke ground on Bach Christian Hospital at Qalandarabad in the Mansehra area. All of the missionaries had voted to contribute funds each month for the effort and the land was purchased from a local wealthy landowner. Prior to this, Dr. Karsgaard and the nurses working with him were completing their medical work, including up to 20 or 30 cataract surgeries a

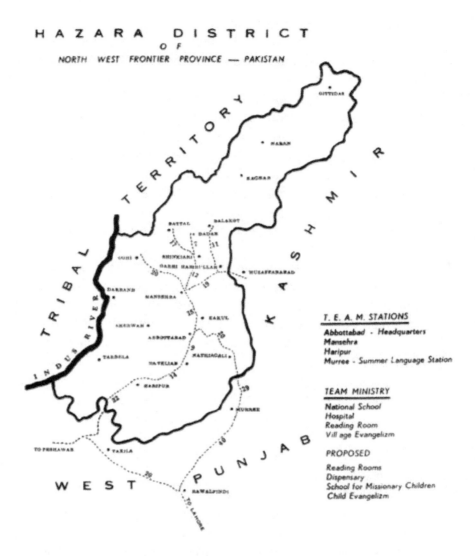

The Hazara district of North West Pakistan where our TEAM ministries and stations were located, 1954.

day, in mud houses or rented garages in the area in addition to running a small clinic and dispensary.

The Carl Davis family arrived in 1947. They would head up the work in Abbottabad. The work consisted of managing the school located on the mission compound and the reading room located in the Abbottabad bazaar. The reading room, with various Christian reading materials, was also a place for entertaining questions from locals and anyone wanting to discuss Christianity.

Carl and Agnes were our senior missionaries, only a little older, but far more mature, and much like parents for us. Carl and Richard made a good evangelistic team. They used Carl's motorcycle and sidecar to visit villages around Abbottabad. Agnes had a wonderful spirit and laugh. It was hard to be discouraged when she was around.

The Fredlunds and Bill Pietsch had arrived soon after and were already working in the villages of Mansehra and Haripur doing evangelism. Karen Pedersen, a single nurse from Canada, arrived just before us and went to live with the Fredlunds in Mansehra and to assist Dr. Karsgaard. Karen and Bill eventually married in Pakistan.

The number was growing. God was calling His workmen from many places. For faith to grow, it needs the climate of "faith-full" people. We found those in our missionary family.

Living in Villages

Pakistan is a vast land of villages. There, among a strong and resilient people, many of whom were and are tribal people, living without many of the modern amenities and some things Americans take for granted, was where we would spend the next seventeen plus years of our lives, happily welcoming three of our five children who know that country as the land of their birth.

During these years, we would learn a new culture, a new language, a new way of life, a new kind of dress, a new diet, but mostly, everything that was foreign and new would become natural and routine.

The greatest privilege for me would be learning that it was *a sojourn into faith,* not totally unlike the sojourn experienced by God's people in the Old Testament, and even, I sometimes later thought, in a very slight way, like the Bedouins of Arabia who traverse the desert and set up their tents, or the *khane ba dosh* who annually passed through our area in Pakistan in camel caravans, traversing long routes which led to and from the high hills of Pakistan and Afghanistan, all without complaint, to graze their cattle. We

A caravan of *khane ba dosh* in Pakistan, ~1951.

would see them with their camels and animals, and their young and old people. Those who could walk did, and others were perched high on a camel, holding onto a child or maybe a baby lamb or a few chickens. *Khane ba dosh* means *"the people who carry their house on their back,"* a very apt description of their lifestyle.

The reason I can relate to them in a small way is that I cannot count how many times we moved in those days, but it was many. During the children's boarding school years, housing for the children was not available during the summer. Parents rented houses and mothers, happy to escape the heat of the "plains", moved up to the 7,000-foot mountains to care for them, then moved back down around September, when boarding reopened. Abbottabad, located at 3500 feet, was not that hot, but when there is no refrigeration or fan, one can feel the intensity of the summer sun, even after it goes down. On a few occasions in the early years, we moved our beds outside the home and slept under mosquito nets.

Maybe it is not fair to say I almost felt like the Bedouins *or khane ba dosh*. I must admit, our life was much more pleasant, but I have moved around a lot. At last count, I have crossed the two big oceans 20 times and lived in four countries, including the US, while visiting extensively in two others.

Village life meant living amongst, and visiting with, the very poor. Villagers live simple lives, often using only one room for sleeping, with a small verandah outside for cooking. Some have a *baithak,* comparable to a "sitting room" where they can entertain guests.

During our time there, the country was made up of East Pakistan and West Pakistan, two parts separated by a thousand miles. With a population of about 75 million people, it was, at the time, the largest Muslim nation and the least developed of major countries. What a formidable wall it presented for Christian missions!

Further complicating the picture was a very low literacy rate and a confusion of six main languages and many dialects. Though the new constitution guaranteed religious liberty, the whole outlook for the new field was uncertain. Two factions in national government were struggling, one for absolute Islamic monopoly, the other for national progress.

Pakistan was a mainly Muslim country with a small percentage of Christians and other religious groups. One aspect of the Muslim faith which presented a challenge to witnessing to them was their strong sense of community. Unlike our Christian faith which demands making a choice to be a Christian, a child born into Islam is from the first understood to be a Muslim.

Muslims in Pakistan lived in Muslim communities or neighborhoods. Mosques, the places of worship, abounded. The call to prayer was made from the mosque by using a loudspeaker or electronic devices. The first call is just before daybreak, the next at noon, a third in the afternoon, a fourth at sunset and the last, just before bedtime. The Muslim does ablutions before prayer and washes face, arms, feet, etc. If he cannot get to the mosque, he will lay out a small mat or find a clean place on which he can prostrate himself. This practice was followed even when traveling—if on a bus, the bus would stop near a source of water so the passengers could properly pray.

Most Christians in Pakistan lived separately, in *bastees*, or neighborhoods and were economically challenged. These "Christian communities" were not formed of converts in the usual sense. In that area of Pakistan, during the turn of the century in the 1900s, great numbers of low caste or outcaste Hindus embraced Christianity in a mass movement, probably more motivated by social and economic benefits than by faith in Christ. However, through later missionary evangelistic efforts, such as the efforts of "praying" John Hyde, many became true believers.

At the time of partitioning in 1947, more Hindus declared themselves Christians. For some, at least, this may have been a way to escape the massacres by Muslim extremists, since Christians were considered separate and thus escaped. This lack of a clear-cut idea of what a believer is, had weakened the Gospel impact. Pakistanis spoke of four kinds of Christians: *nasli*, one born in a Christian home; *magli*, one who imitates; *asli*, one who has truly accepted Christ, and *fasli*, one who bears fruit.

Christian churches were few in number, but there were some vibrant, witnessing Christians. TEAM operated a small school in Abbottabad. One of our first assignments was to help with the running of the school and to have morning devotions, in Urdu, with the Christian teachers.

Songs from the Past that Still Have a Message
There were two churches for Christians in Abbottabad. One was a Presbyterian church, born out of the missionary efforts during the days of John Hyde, whose congregation consisted primarily of Hindu converts. The other was St. Luke's Anglican church.

We usually worshipped at St. Luke's church while we were in Abbottabad. St. Luke's church was a beautiful stone building, built in 1864 as a place of worship for the British when they ruled India, with beautiful grounds kept by an excellent gardener. The Padre was Pakistani; his wife was always kind and helpful to us.

The congregation was small, but faithful. It consisted of the Christian teachers who taught at the little mission school, some local Pakistani businesspeople and TEAM missionaries. Services were in English and followed the Anglican tradition of worship which were quite different from the evangelistic tradition that Richard and I had previously observed.

We were often invited to sing duets during the "Evensong" service at the church, a little worship service, mostly Anglican passages of Scriptures and prayers, about five or six o'clock on Sunday evenings. I well remember one of the songs we sang, probably the

A gathering outside of St. Luke's church in Abbottabad after a wedding, ~1950s.

first time we sang in the church. The song we chose to sing would not have been a familiar one to those coming from the Anglican tradition. Messages like this are not heard today, I am sad to say, but they should be. Our Love and thanks to God for such a wonderful provision for our salvation.

"There's a line that is drawn by rejecting our Lord,
Where the call of His Spirit is lost,
As you hurry along with the pleasure-mad throng.
Have you counted, have you counted the cost?"

Chorus: "Have you counted the cost,
if your soul should be lost
Though you gain the whole world for your own
Even now, it may be, that the line you have crossed
Have you counted, have you counted the cost?"

"You may barter your hope of eternity's morn
For a moment of joy at the most;
For the glitter of sin, and the things it will win,
Have you counted, have you counted the cost?"

"While the door of His mercy is open to you,
Ere the depth of His love you exhaust,
Won't you come and be healed,
won't you whisper, 'I yield?'
Have you counted, have you counted the cost?"[4]

I had to look this up to be sure I remembered the words. Elizabeth and our boys used to tell me when I forgot words, I just inserted my own. I still do and she still does!

****

This would be the start of my earthly pilgrimage, a lifetime learning experience about my faith and the faith of others, and to a large measure, a discovery of what is, and what is not, important in life. The seed of biblical faith, planted in my heart at an earlier age, had taken root and the experiences would aid in my walk as a Christina mother. I would come to know the joy of the Lord as

---

[4] Arthur J. Hodge, "Have You Counted the Cost?" 1923. Public Domain.

my strength, and happiness as its byproduct. It was grace, God's wonderful undeserved grace, which had brought us to this place. All would not be a journey of ease nor of delight. During those years, there would be battles and discouragement, even lapses in faith as we wondered if and how God would work out the situation facing us. Through it all, we would come to know the promises of God are for real and now, so many years later, I look back in amazement at how very real our God is!

Of Abraham, it was said "he journeyed onward, not knowing..." where he would stop. He "looked for a city whose architect and builder was God..." This was our journey, too. The years following would take us to places near where his entourage had traveled several millennia before. Neither the travel adventures nor the lessons were exactly the same, but like the early men and women of faith whose records of wandering are found in the Scriptures, we would become students in the same school.

"Faith is the substance of things hoped for, the evidence of things not seen" said the biblical writer about the Hebrew people. It—faith—is the plan for all who follow God's plan. Unlike Abraham and Sarah who may have walked and traveled by camel caravan, we had the privilege of modern transportation as we traveled halfway around the world by means of a ferry, cars, ships, trains, and the "elderly" taxi, thankful for each conveyance.

Our Life as Missionaries Begin

"Your ears will hear a word behind you, "This is the way, walk in it," whenever you turn to the right or to the left." (Isaiah 30:21)

The story of our arrival in Pakistan with a baby in my *bacche dana* ("baby holder" in the language of Urdu) left a few we met along the way in a bit of a shock. Not many adults would think it wise for a young person expecting a baby in a few weeks to be traveling halfway around the world. Interestingly, my own obstetrician had not advised against it. However, Dr. Karsgaard, already in Pakistan, had said we should arrive at the latest by the end of six months. That had not been possible, given delays of shots needed and ship connections. We decided to go anyway. My husband wanted his baby to be born in Pakistan.

Apart from God, there is no explanation how we happened to be there. We were so inexperienced, so young, needing to be trained like one trains a child. We were literally moving by faith into the unknown. We mostly did what we were told by our elders. There is a wonderful promise in Isaiah 30:21: "when you go in the way, you will hear a voice behind you saying, 'This is the way; walk you in it'." We did try to listen to that voice.

Our First Homes in Pakistan

Our first home after arriving in Pakistan was St. Luke's Cottage, which was next door to St. Luke's Anglican Church. Our cottage was separated from the church by a well-kept hedge. It was set on a long plot of land, with mostly weeds growing on it. I don't recall now who kept them cut down, but someone must have, possibly to use for fodder. Across the back of the land was a street that led to the movie house in Abbottabad, and in its opposite direction, led out of town.

It would be a while before we could move in; our luggage and outfit cases were not yet upcountry from Karachi. Thus, for the first two weeks, we would be living with the Davises, our senior missionaries, in the Mission House. About two weeks after our arrival, we went 55 miles south to Taxila, to the Presbyterian Hospital where our Mission would be holding its Annual Conference. The Frontier Fellowship Conference was also meeting during this time. It was an annual event, a time when missionaries from all the different organizations working on the frontier met for fellowship and prayer. The Hospital hosted the conference, which lasted several days. It was a great time of refreshing and a time for us to get to know who was working in the area.

Since by this time, it was so close to my expected delivery date in mid-March, Dr. Karsgaard would not allow me to return to Abbottabad with the Davises. Baby Elizabeth was in the same hurry she is today. She decided not to wait around; she emerged somewhat unexpectedly from my "baby carrier" on February 26, 1951, the day after my 23rd birthday. As a child, I had said I did not want children until I was "at least 23 years old!" When we returned to Abbottabad, she had her first *tonga* ride when we went from the hospital to the bus. A few days later, we moved into St. Luke's Cottage.

Elizabeth's first tonga ride going home from the hospital, Abbottabad, Feb. 1951.

St. Luke's Cottage was a four-room house with a half wrap porch. A vine planted on its outside edge kept out the sun and provided some privacy from the street. Inside were two rooms on either side at the front, and two at the back. A small kitchen area was behind one back room and a small "bathroom" behind the other back room.

Our first home in Pakistan, St. Luke's Cottage.

We used the right side for a living room and dining room and the left side for bedrooms. An electric wire with a bulb at the end was strung from the ceiling in each room. The floors were cement, some were covered with old *chatai*, made from hemp, and much like some of the new rope floor coverings we see today. It was winter, and COLD in the cottage. For heating, we purchased a small, but very good, portable oil heater which we kept in the front room where we had a couch and a chair. At night, we slept under heavy cotton quilts, purchased from the bazaar, and used hot water bottles, which we had been told to bring with us from the US. I am not sure they can even be found in the stores today. Some missionaries who did not have them sometimes filled regular bottles with hot water or heated a brick and wrapped it for the warmth, great innovations in the third world countries where heat is needed!

A year later, when the Davises went on furlough, we moved into 24 Wilde Rd, later changed to Pine View Road (to make it more respectable sounding when missionaries were living there? Nah!). Wilde was likely the name of some British official. This road led up into the hills where the pine and other trees were in abundance.

Learning the Language

About four months after we arrived in Pakistan, we packed up our things and our baby daughter Elizabeth, loaded them in a taxi and left for "the hills" of Murree and language school.

The "hill station" of Murree is seven thousand feet above sea level in the Himalayan Mountains of West Pakistan. When India was partitioned, Murree became the "gathering place" for both missionaries and Pakistanis. India had many places in the cool hills of their country, but Murree was the one left by the British to Pakistan. From the days of the British, it was referred to as "the hills" or "the hill station." Property owners had built homes there to escape the heat of summer. During the time of the partition of India, Hindus who fled left behind beautiful homes, some of which had been destroyed, while others were left standing. Some repayment was made or claimed and those became rental properties in later years.

A generation or two earlier, Presbyterian missionaries had put together a program and a book to teach us how to learn to read, write and speak the language. Children from those days were now back as missionaries. They and trained nationals were our teachers. Now there were some missionaries who were second or third generation people serving there. Those children had grown up with the people. TEAM people were newcomers.

The United Presbyterians, under which our mission initially operated, were extremely insistent on missionaries learning the language; they had set up a wonderful language learning guide and program which we had to follow, since we were under their umbrella.

Richard had the accent, knew much of the Urdu language, but he spoke it like the Indian children with whom he grew up, i.e., sometimes grammatically incorrect. The language is written in character, from right to left and has aspirates which can change the meaning of the word if pronounced without aspirating. I had to learn it through the proverbial "sweat and tears"—lots of those! Adding to my challenge was that I had to walk back and

106

forth each day from the language school to where we were staying to feed Elizabeth.

Things would be different for us. The culture does not adjust to missionaries or those who visit. We would have to adjust, specifically I would have to adjust. Richard was "at home." While trying to teach me, our first language teacher spent time each day praising him for his language progress.

A year later, when I took my first-year exam, Richard was taking his second-year exam. I have a streak of competitiveness in me, I never gave up. When he finished his fifth-year exam, I was still struggling, raising three children, taking care of the Mission House hospitality and by that time, in charge of the school. It was a proud, proud day when I passed the fifth-year exam, something few missionary women attempted. It was not a requirement for women, but I was in education and thought I should do it. The only part of that exam with which I had a problem was translating JFK's State of the Union speech! The Voice of America had sent it out in a Bulletin, the Missionary Language Committee had pounced on it and decided we should take the challenge. Ugh!

And if learning Urdu wasn't challenge enough, during our second term, primarily because of Richard's ministry to the tribal areas in the north, we decided we should also learn Pushtu, which was the primary language of that area. In 1961, Richard, after taking and passing his first Pushtu examination, preached a sermon in that language! Around that time, a burden was laid on my heart to interrupt my Pushtu study (which I rarely heard spoken) and study Hendko which was the language spoken all around me. I began to study informally. While I spoke Urdu, in order to reach the heart and proclaim the message of salvation to the people I met, I felt I needed to know Hendko.

But I often said the reason I did try to learn it was because I couldn't shut up when others were speaking, and I did not know what they were saying. In Genesis 11 the Bible tells us how all these languages began. Some of the people wanted to build a tower to reach to heaven to worship their god, not the Creator God. To thwart their plans, the true God brought about the inability to speak to each other. Imagine a man asking for a log or a piece of equipment when he was working on that tower, only to find the other person had no idea what he was talking about!

I had a similar experience during my first days in Pakistan. A man came by with a large stack of letters. I assumed he was looking for work and we needed some help. It was the custom for anyone wanting work to bring their "resume" in that form. The person hiring knew to look for what was **not** said, not what was said. If no mention was made of honesty, there was question about whether or not he would steal. This man was trying to communicate with me, but I had not yet begun to study the language and I could not understand. I read through some of his letters. He kept speaking in Urdu, and I kept answering in English to come back the next day, that I would tell "Sahib." When Richard, who understood the language, returned home, he said the man was not looking for work, he wanted me to rewrite all that stack of letters!

I personally thank God for the insistence on language study; I learned in the years following that no one really understands a culture without knowing the language, and to minister to people, we must understand both, as well as the customs of the people.

I would also come to understand that learning the language also means learning to distinguish between different sounds and accents. One false move of the voice or tongue can cause confusion! Although I had intensively studied the language, enabling me to communicate quite well, there were similar words which I could confuse when speaking.

We had a mountain man helping us in our home; his dialect was slightly different, but we got along just fine—until the day I called him in and asked him to go and, or so I thought, buy me a long bamboo pole. He looked very puzzled, so I tried again. His puzzled look was as confusing to me as my request was to him, so I took him into the room where I planned to use the pole as a curtain rod.

When he understood what I wanted, he covered his mouth to hide the smile, and said, "Yes, Madam." But the smile alerted me to a wrong word. I thought for a moment, and then, with "Is it … or …" spoke two different words. In his very gracious manner, he corrected me. Instead of asking for a long bamboo pole, which would fit across two windows, and on which I could hang my curtains, I was asking for a very long buffalo, which I could place at the top of the windows and on which I could hang my curtains!

That was not the only time I confused words. Another occasion I recall is somewhat more embarrassing! One morning, I got up early to catch the 5:30 A.M. bus to go shopping for school supplies in a bigger city, 75 miles away. The trip took two to three hours, depending on what stops were made and how long it took for most of the men travelers to drink a cup of tea.

A *kacha* bus, typical mode of transportation in Pakistan. The other was the government bus, which did not include room on top for riders.

I was the only woman on the bus that morning. Just 25 miles on the way, I knew I had to have a rest stop, but where, how? There were no public restrooms anywhere around—at least, not as far as I knew. I think most villagers used the wheat fields. When the men got off to drink tea, I set out to find some place where I could be hidden. There was nothing but the emerging wheat. Seeing some small huts about 25 yards away, I hurried toward them, only to find a group of men—no women. I bolstered up my courage and asked what I thought I wanted. Laughter! The moment the words came out, I knew I had made a mistake.

Instead of asking where I could "make water", I was asking where I could "make whiskey"!

Our Ministry Work

I had expected Richard and I would work together in our ministry projects. I thought it was right for couples to be seen working together. I would take up his slack and he would take up mine. What naivete! We were going to a land and country where custom and culture would never allow that. Islam has some very great differences for both of those lifestyles. The husband is expected to make the living, the wife to keep the house and bear children, very preferably, a son. Culture demands the married woman be kept behind the veil, no man except her brothers be allowed to see her face or be in contact with her. Thus, I would not participate in most of Richard's ministry activities, such as his "treks" and evangelism among the men of the villages.

My ministry would primarily be with the school children and hospitality and visiting with women. Since my college training was in education, it was natural that after completing my language studies, I would be involved with the small school that met on the mission compound. Classes were normally held under the trees, with the students seated on low wooden stools and using slates and chalk. After each lesson was done, the slate would be rinsed in a pot of

Some of the children who attended the small school on the mission compound, Abbottabad, 1950s.

water set aside for that purpose. Only one small copy book was needed; it was used for writing. The Mission charged a small fee for each student, many of whom were from the poor Christian families, but Muslim children were also in attendance. Still fixed in my memory is the sight of children in flip flops, even during cold weather! Two boys from a Muslim better class family had leather shoes, made by the local cobbler.

Our ministry during our years in Pakistan was with Pakistani Christians and with Muslims. There was a small group of Christians in Abbottabad, but otherwise, few or none in the other areas in which we lived or visited. It might be surprising to think we would need to minister to Christians in a primarily Muslim nation, but it was needed. There was just as much a need for revival amongst that group, as there was (and still is) in the US. We prayed for these Christians and were depending on them to help with the ministry in the Hazara District. We longed for the day when the work would be indigenous, but first these Christians needed further teaching!

The Pakistan Military Academy at Kakul, the equivalent of our West Point, was about three miles from Abbottabad. It trained some of the finest men from Pakistan as well as from other parts of the Middle East and Africa. Among them were Christians, and the British Brigadier in charge was a Christian, as was his wife. We first got to know Brigadier and Mrs. Tarver when Carl and Agnes Davis invited us for dinner in the TEAM mission bungalow. They were a very lovely couple, easy to be with and very outgoing. After Carl and Agnes left for home leave, the lot fell to Richard to head up the weekly services at the academy. It was a rare privilege to have invitations to some of their special functions.

It seems strange to call hospitality and helping someone a "missionary's ministry," but I would learn hospitality was a wonderful, effective and godly way of sharing our faith. Hospitality may involve helping someone. The Mission Headquarters station was where I got my start.

These were wonderful times and there were always funny incidents. If it was not a wrong language word choice, it was some other *faux pas*, like my spilling the soup at the Davis' table when Brigadier and Mrs. Tarver were having dinner with all of us. Ohhh!

It was said that "the first year or two, the people laughed with you; after that, they laughed at you."

Learning the culture, as well as the language, along with being at ease with all kinds of people, is an important part of being a missionary. It was very important, but admittedly, we felt more at ease when we were "with our own." We were so young and there was so much to learn. Our lives would touch many others, the very poor and the very rich, and we would have to learn how to adapt to each.

So many things come to mind, like a blocked septic system when a guest arrived at the Mission Headquarters station while we were living there. Our guest of honor, a Scottish businessman, David Thomson, knew more about fixing the system than we did! Boy! what embarrassment and also what a blessing! It was a whole new lesson. We were able to get someone from the town who took car of this septic system business and David supervised the whole thing! David later joined TEAM as a missionary, married Ann Morris, a single lady missionary, and became a wonderful help to all of us.

Another incident had to do with Dewey, an attaché in the US military, stationed in Karachi. He came to visit us in Abbottabad and was there on a day when Richard would go to the PMA for Friday service. Dewey was a precious fellow Christian, very unwilling to cause trouble for anyone. In those days, there was no clothing one could pack which did not wrinkle. He had brought his good suit, tie and shirt. I thought I had better check on whether or not they needed pressing, and of course, they did. The Military Academy young men were always immaculate; we needed to be that way, too. Dewey was ready before Richard, and sat outside, reading his Bible, when I saw he had on one black sock and one white! It was very obvious! Should we tell him? We decided we had to tell him. We called him in, and his reply was that the man who did his wash had paired them up that way! He had not wanted to bother us again. Well, we found him a matching pair, and all was well. Missionary life is like a mystery novel, you never know what is next and how you will need to deal with a problem!

People came and went during the times we lived at the Mission Headquarters, stopping in for a break or for a cup of tea. At one point it was a place where we could have guests for an overnight. During one of our early hostings at the headquarters station, we had a number of new arrivals. Dr. Karsgaard and his family, along with five nurses, arrived. We had them crowded in every room.

The Karsgaard family were soon on their way to Mansehra where they would establish a clinic and begin the plans for the TEAM hospital. The nurses stayed for a short period. Feeding people in a new land where food choices were very limited was something of a challenge. One of the nurses did not like onions in her food. They are a very important part of the diet in Pakistan. The British left behind a tradition about mealtimes. Breakfast was early in the morning, meaning the need for a mid-morning break, "elevensees" a cup of tea and a "biscuit," in our language, a cookie. Lunch was about 12:30, then at 4:00 we had tea, a slightly more "formal" time for some people. For us, it was tea and sometimes something special, along with it, but usually, just more cookies. Dinner was between six and seven, depending on schedules. Beef (water buffalo) and lamb (goat) were the meat choices, chicken and fish were rare.

Our missionary team continued to grow our first year in Pakistan as evidenced by this photo from the early 1950s.

In addition to his varied duties at the mission stations, Richard's ministry took him far afield. He trekked to a lot of mountain villages in a kind of "reconnaissance ministry" or "frontier evangelism" speaking to the tribal people about God. His ministry was primarily to the tribal people in the Northwest region of Pakistan between Kashmir and Afghanistan.

Richard would say that one of the hardest parts of the ministry was gaining the people's confidence. He would have to convince them that he was not part of the US Government sent there to spy on them! The people needed to see the missionaries living their religion. The medical and educational work of the mission were practical methods for revealing the love of Christ and gradually convincing the people you were there to help.

Picture of a typical tribal villiage in Pakistan, 1950s.

He wrote home of one particular visit to one of the thirteen villages in the mountains west of Abbottabad he and another missionary, Vern Rock, made in the spring of 1953. Vern and his wife, Wanda, arrived in Pakistan the year after we did. Entering the village, after the customary tea and eggs, the way opened to present the Gospel. Soon a typical argument was thrust upon them—How can Jesus be God's Son? Vern and Richard told the man (a religious leader) that they would like to hear how the Quran could show the men gathered God's plan of salvation, particularly how to be freed from the power of sin. Then they would appreciate the opportunity to do the same from the *Injeel* (New Testament). The villagers agreed, but the man left in a huff saying, "This hut is no place to bring a Holy Book!"

Vern and Richard were then taken to the village mosque. After the noonday prayers some fifty men squatted around them with three *maulvis* (priests) directly in front. In an unusual way the Lord undertook giving real liberty in spirit and language as the message of freedom from both the penalty and power of sin was presented. From the faces of those listening it was evident they realized this was God's way. We prayed for the work of the Spirit in the hearts of these and other villagers reached on this and all of Richard's other treks.

Picture of Richard on trek to a tribal village and some of the men of the village. Guns were prevalent in this part of Pakistan.

Planting Seeds

The Scripture has much to say about gardening; it seems to carry over into the spiritual part of our lives in both the Old and New Testaments. One of the things gardeners do is to look and see if what they have planted has grown. As I reminisce about our time in Pakistan, I think about what had been or what we wish had been. Like gardeners, missionaries also pray for growth and fruit.

James was one of those I have thought about. He was from a mountain village and came to us shortly after we arrived in Pakistan. His story was that he had come across a Bible and with his family, had read it nightly by candlelight, not wanting to be found out. The family had come to believe but wanted to know more. He came several times, then we never saw him again.

Another was a young man Richard met while trekking in the mountains. He had professed Christ while living in India, then, later, crossed into Pakistan. After meeting Richard, he made a recommitment of his life to Christ and began to witness boldly. A short time later, his body was found at the bottom of a bridge, in a dry riverbed. The police called it "suicide."

Still another was Zara—a young, wealthy, "progressive" Muslim who early in life was orphaned but was educated and teaching in a nearby Catholic school. We got to know her through another missionary family. When that family went on home leave, she began visiting us. One late night I decided to confront her with her need to know Christ. It was a very strong spiritual battle. She wept but did not pray to do that. However, she came again the next day to tell me she had become a Christian. She studied the Bible with me, then with one of the missionary men who was better able to answer her questions, was baptized. Then, suddenly, she stopped coming to see the missionaries. A few months later, someone saw her fully robed in Muslim dress, uncharacteristic of her. She crossed the street to avoid facing that missionary. Jesus told a story that might apply—Luke 11:24-26. We did not see nor hear from her again.

Tribal people came to the higher mountains each summer to help with the harvest. One woman was a regular as she came to our door to sell wild blackberries she had picked in the woods. We always looked for her; we used the berries for making jam. The last summer I saw her, she looked ill and told me she was. We sat down on the cement floor of our verandah, and I tried in Urdu to explain the Gospel to her. I prayed she would be able to understand, even though she spoke a tribal language. She tried several times to pray with me this simple prayer: "Oh God, save me through the blood of the Lord Jesus Christ," but she could not get out all the words. I recall thinking "Oh, God, loose her and let her go!" I then asked her to try it one more time. She did and was able to say that prayer; she left me with a smile on her face. The next morning, she trudged back up the hill, still with a smile on her face, but she had no berries. She looked weak and said again she was not well, but "still praying it" (the prayer—"*Ae Khuda, Yesu Masih ke khun se mujhe bacha!*"). Will we see her in Heaven? That is the basis of my faith and I expect to see Jesus someday.

And who can forget the tribal rulers and people with whom Richard had contact? One special one asked, "Can't I be a Muslim and a Christian at the same time?" Richard had to tell him he had to make a choice. Interestingly, our Mission hospital workers continued to meet with that man's family when they came to the hospital and would sit and talk. Some seeds are planted but take longer to germinate and grow.

A Pakistani Sister

In addition to insisting on language training, the United Presbyterian missionaries had done one other thing. They had training schools for young people. The boys had a technical school in which they learned trades, and the girls were trained for other things. Some were trained as "Bible women" or Bible teachers. Miss Nazir was one of those. She and Miss Rehmat, another Bible teacher, came to work with and for our mission. They provided a bridge of opportunity in ministry to women and children and were a tremendous help as we learned the language and culture. We were so thankful for them and their ministry. They were both girls of fine character with cheerful dispositions, and good workers. While Nazir worked as a faithful Bible woman, she really wanted to be a nurse. After some years, she was able to go for training.

We met Nazir again some years later when we went to the United Arab Emirates (UAE). Nazir had also had a change; she was working in the TEAM hospital in Al Ain. Once more, we found a young lady mature in her ways who also loved ministering in the Pakistani church of expatriates while also serving as a nurse. She was faithful in all she did and was a light for Christ. In order to prepare for the day when she would have to retire, she sent most of her money home to her brother, who was to save it for her.

Instead, he spent the money, and when she returned from the UAE, there was only a little of it left. A Pakistani pastor and his wife, Kathy and Arif Khan took her in. She remained with them for a while.

We lost touch with her for a while, so I am not sure of the circumstances during the next period of her life. Letters she sent indicated she somehow lost her (few) belongings and moved out into a Muslim village where she started a small clinic, caring for the women and children. Another missionary helped her to obtain Bibles and other literature, which she had been able to give away. She also found a way to take some local Muslim children to a Sunday School class. In her letter, she was not complaining, only glad that she could do what she was doing.

Nazir was an honest, faithful, and loving servant of the Lord as long as she lived. Her work in Pakistan was a very worthy cause; many women and children were not able to make the trip to a larger clinic or hospital when they need medical attention. Village life in Pakistan is not easy; medical facilities are not that accessible for many people, especially for those in the villages. Nazir was an answer to that need, in addition to being a witness for Christ.

Feelings of Discouragement and Loneliness

Have you had the experience of feeling discouraged or lonely? You may have if you remember that Christians are the objects of Satan's fiery darts. Missionaries working in his territory are more so than ever his target. There was a time when Richard and I both were very discouraged and one point at which I felt lonely because I was alone, humanly speaking.

The times of discouragement came during our first term, when we were actually the busiest, with about 17 different responsibilities. There was a lot of ministry to be done, but it seemed like nothing much was happening.

We were living in a rich, fruit bearing area with many fruits available in season, but we did not feel God was working with us to do what we thought He had called us to do, that is, bear spiritual fruit. Our senior missionaries, the Carl Davises, left for furlough just one year after we arrived in Pakistan. We moved into the headquarters house where we would each have responsibilities, everything from studying language to entertaining people who dropped in, running a small Christian day school for Pakistani children, taking care of the reading room in the little town, conducting Bible studies and worship services, and raising our family. After only a couple of years, we both began to feel drained, like nothing was happening and maybe we were in the wrong place.

Then a charismatic mission with several young people and an older couple moved into the other side of our town. We welcomed them, happy for the friendship of those who not only spoke our language but knew our Lord. Soon they were conducting nightly services and things were happening that seemed like the kind of fruits for which we had been yearning. Some of the small group of national Christians were being awakened and revived. The group had healing meetings, and some spoke in tongues. It was contagious for these national Christians. Although we did not agree with these parts of their ministry, we did yearn for some of their fruit! We wanted to see national "Christians" know and understand the reality of their commitment. We wanted to see new life in them.

But it wasn't happening to us. We seemed to be in a dry and barren land. Sometime during our third year, we both wondered if God really wanted us in Pakistan. We were not disillusioned with missions, just with ourselves and what we were doing. If the charismatics were seeing results, why weren't we? Maybe we should return to the US and get jobs. We would gladly support others whom God would send out. I think we were both ready to question whether or not we were really in God's will.

At this point, some new missionaries arrived on the field. Our big house was divided into two apartments, and we had two young women living in the other apartment. Rosie and Marge Stewart had come out to work with children. While doing language study, they were also busy translating children's songs into the Urdu language. I think this made me, especially, feel even more insecure. One day while chatting with them in their apartment, I noticed a tract their parents had sent them. It was published by the American Sunday School Union, and its title was "The Life that Wins." They let me take it home to read it. When I first began, I thought "This is too deep for me right now; I will do it when I have my devotions in the morning."

A few days later, on my knees beside my bed, I did read that tract, and God used it to teach me a lesson I needed to learn. It was a lesson I should have remembered from my early days of being a Christian; I had been taught it before, both by my pastor and by a Bible teacher when I was a teenager, but it had not taken hold of my life. Its message was simple: God Himself indwells the believer and will work through the "yieldedness" of His children to accomplish what HE wants. I rose from my knees with the wonderful assurance that God had placed us where we were to do what HE wanted with us. Later, when Richard read the tract, he was so moved by it that he went to share it with Vern, another missionary.

The tongues and healing movement was not necessary to do the work to which God had called us; what WAS necessary was to remember that Christ needed to be preeminent in our lives, a living reality within us. And as for tongues, what I wanted was to speak the Urdu language correctly. I knew it would be labor intensive to study several hours a day, but I did it. God answered my prayers and even with family responsibilities, I managed to pass the full five-year course during our second term.

Now that our focus had changed, we no longer had to be concerned with what God was doing in the lives of our charismatic friends. We knew He had called us to be "fruit-bearers" but we are only branches; it is the VINE that produces the fruit. Those days of discouragement passed. Now we were willing to wait and see what God would do in answer to our renewed "yieldedness." We have no idea today what was accomplished, but we had a small vision of what could be done. I report with sadness that our charismatic friends did not stay too many years. Still, I thank God for any eternal work they accomplished.

Almost as soon as we arrived in Pakistan, Richard was "on duty" and often away. However, usually he was within reach if I should need him—in the reading room, or someplace nearby. During our second term we hoped to get into village work. We had a good measure of the language and were supposed to "know the ropes" and be mature in the ministry to which God had called us, but there were other lessons to be learned.

I think this next "big and valuable lesson" for me came from having to be alone. From his missionary childhood in India and hearing from British soldiers of the need in what was then northwest India, Richard had had a burden for the tribal people in the frontier area. He and Vern wanted to try to work in a village bordering tribal territory, many miles away, where westerners were unknown, and no one had taken the Gospel. Their plans were to rent a room and go each weekend, but they would also spend one week out of the month up in those hills. They wanted to be available and establish contacts—to meet with any of the men who wanted to discuss the Gospel. I helped them get ready and pack up for that first trip. As soon as they left, the loneliness set in. What if something happened to me? or to him? What would I do? How could I get word to anyone? I did not even know the exact location where they would be. The children were small, and I was absolutely alone in a village where I had already felt some hostility, nothing serious, but I feared it could be potentially difficult.

I got on my knees to pray for them and myself. Strangely, God became more real to me during those days and weeks. I spent more time learning of Him as I studied the Scriptures. It never occurred to me to check on Wanda, Vern's wife, who was also alone! They lived about 40 miles from us, but there was a way to travel by bus and we could have gotten together had either of us thought about it. I don't suppose either of us did. Maybe we were both trying to be "courageous"!

The Scriptures are as good in times of loneliness as they were when I had been discouraged. The Bible has such wonderful words of comfort. The verse which spoke to me that first day was Isaiah 54:5, "Thy Maker is thy husband; the Lord of Hosts is His Name." I was not alone. He would be there if I had an earthly need. It drew me into a closer fellowship with the Lord.

Our Growing Family

Elizabeth was one year old and there were no other missionary kids around for her to play with. All her little friends were older, already school children in the Abbottabad Christian School for Pakistani children, where she was loved by both the teachers and the children as she trailed along when I conducted the daily routine. We decided we had to get a playmate for her. It didn't take long, just over nine months!

While we waited, we searched through a book of boys' names; we knew it had to be a boy. George was rejected; Richard didn't like that for his son, even though it was his own and his dad's name. There was no question about the middle name; it would be Richard. As we looked down the list, one or the other of us rejected every name except Douglas. We kept coming back to that. Thus, before he was born, he was Dougie.

His brother was not planned, but God must have decided Doug would need a playmate, too, and 15 months later, Jimmy joined our family. Now there were two babies to care for, but we had Bilobai, a wonderful Christian *ayah*. She was in charge of Doug, and I can never thank God enough for having had a wonderful Christian for our little boy.

Doug always seemed older than his young years. He seemed born with a plan in mind, and he always worked to carry it out, from taking apart toys to wanting to take Mary Beth, another missionary child, on a three-mile hike each way and go with another couple to the movies when they were all about 15! We were up in Murree; fortunately, none of the moms liked that idea! Another plan was to make Christmas gifts for his siblings and pocket the rupees he was given for them. Mom said "no" to that one, too, but today I know his ability to have a plan is what has put him where he is. He has excelled in his field.

"Dougie"—now Doug—was no more than three when "Jimmy"—now Jim—would come crying to me, telling me Doug had taken apart some toy that was Jim's. The problem was that while Doug could take it apart, I was not able to put it back together again and I think he took apart every toy he ever had. I recall thinking God surely must have a special place for Doug's ability, but I did not think it would be as a star student in school. He hated kindergarten!

Because Doug was sandwiched between big sister Elizabeth, who seemed never to have a problem with any schoolwork, and Jim, very much like her, I came to realize "all children are not created equal." For that, we can thank a gracious, loving Heavenly Father, the Creator God, since if we were all just alike, most of us could not do some of the necessary things we need to do to survive.

I saw early that no two children are alike, even if born of the same parents. Although I probably started out trying to treat them all alike, I soon learned I needed to treat them as individuals. (Oh, yes, I am pretty sure they will differ with me on that! When I could not figure out which boy was the culprit, they were all treated equally—they all got the paddle!)

Doug had a strong will, but strong-willed children also have leadership ability. Doug and Jim were mostly inseparable, but while Jim was able to "squiggle" out of things, Doug was very transparent, unable to present a false front. He is still like that: "what you see or hear from Doug is the real Doug." The downside of that was, it meant often he was the one who got caught. The "Christian teaching" of the day was to "spank a child until he cried and then spank until he shut up." How do you do that with a child who was not a "cry baby"? He took his punishment without a lot of tears. I think he now says he deserved what he got.

Speaking of getting caught, he was only about three years old when he slipped away from the *ayah*, Bilobai, and me when we were doing the wash out behind our house. Suddenly, I heard the gardener, who was working in the front yard, calling out to tell me Doug was standing in water up to his little waist. We had a *hauz* in which we kept water for the garden. It was a six-foot-wide cemented square. He had climbed down into it but could not climb out. He was not hurt, and only wet up to his waist. Thanks, Lord, for preserving our Doug from drowning!

Moving to Brarkot

TEAM policy during our time in Pakistan was that missionaries would serve five to five and a half years in the field and then return home for leave. As the time for our first home leave neared, Richard and I had determined that we wanted to serve in the villages during our next term. During that same time frame, TEAM was asked if they would be interested in continuing a ministry which included running a small dispensary started by a British missionary organization in the Azad Kashmir area of Pakistan. TEAM agreed and two nurses, Ruth Arvidson and Dawn Bursma, were assigned but they first needed to complete language training. Thus, Richard and I were asked if we would be interested in moving there in the interim just a six-month period. We decided it would be a good introduction to all that village life implies.

We moved to Brarkot in Azad Kashmir in the fall of 1955. Brarkot was in a hilly area, what was then a long winding uphill road from our headquarters station in Abbottabad. The courtyard of this village house we lived in had a wall around it, and the area seemed quite safe. By that time, we had three small children who survived there beautifully. If we had had an emergency, I don't know what we would have done. I think transportation was at a premium, I don't recall anyone having a car in that area. The local bus traveled between Mansehra (fifteen miles from Abbottabad) and Brarkot, going one way in the morning and returning in the afternoon.

The village houses in general and the one in Brarkot was very different from the old British bungalows. For beginners, most had a wall around them, which the British bungalows did not have. This house had two sections, what we might think of as a "Pakistani or Indian duplex". The side we lived in had two stories, with one room on top for sleeping, and one down for eating or relaxing. There were several small rooms on either side, one used for a kitchen, one for bathroom commodes (which had to be emptied at least once or twice a day), a room with a cement vat in which to store water, and a room we used for storage.

Water was brought from the spring a short distance away, by a "*mashkee*" (water boy) who hauled the water in a sewn-up goat skin. He brought two in the morning and two in the evening. It is hard to remember how far from our house was the spring, but it was near a river where we often took the children for a walk.

The ceiling between the up and down stairs was made with supporting beams and branches, overlaid with smooth mud plaster and whitewashed, as were the walls. I can still see that occasional chunk of mud falling down onto our dining room table, especially if someone happened to walk upstairs. We were told the whitewash was good for keeping out bugs and I don't recall having a problem with them.

During our time in Brarkot, I handled the small clinic that had been started by the British missionary ladies. Although untrained, I soon learned how to pass out simple medications for eyes, sores, malaria, vitamins and worm treatments. Each Wednesday, Dr. Karsgaard and a medical team travelled the 22 miles into the mountains to care for the more serious problems. After Ruth completed her language training and came to Brarkot, she and I conducted a weekly children's Bible hour.

Richard contacted the men and some men made a confession of faith under his ministry. We were wonderfully received by the people, with their small gifts of corn and eggs, and, on one occasion, a chicken. We rejoiced that we had the privilege of being witnesses and ministering in an area where, at the time and to our knowledge, there was not a single professing Christian.

Another "ministry" in Brarkot was to local women of Sikh background who had married Muslim men. Periodically, the police would round up the women and the men would have to pay to get them back. The women would sometimes ask us to hide them in our storage room. When the police left, the village children would come and tell us, and the women would go back home!

Ruth and I teaching a children's Bible class in Brarkot, ~1955.

Brarkot was a wonderful introduction to village life in Pakistan. Although we were only there a few short months, it reinforced our desire to return to another village during our second term.

****

As I reflect back on those first years in Pakistan, I am amazed to think that a young woman from a small village in the US who had never traveled overseas, would find herself living half-way around the world, far from family, in a foreign country where it was a struggle sometimes to communicate. But then I serve an amazing God! And it was only by His providence and power that I found myself serving Him in Pakistan, with my loving husband and three small children. I recall the psalmist who wrote: "I will instruct you and show you the way you should walk, give you counsel and watch over you" (Psalm 32:8). And although, we were very much looking forward to going back to the US to see our family and friends, our hearts belonged to this land and these people and we were eager to return to continue the work God had called us to.

Going Where God Sends

"Before I formed you in the womb I knew you,
And before you were born I consecrated you;
I have appointed you a prophet to the nations." (Jeremiah 1:5)

It was March 1956 and we had completed the first five years of our missionary career while living in the tiny village of Brarkot. It had been a great experience. The time had quickly passed, and we were getting ready for our first home leave. We wanted to do village work after our planned return a year later. Brarkot had been a good introduction.

We would use the time at home to reconnect with family and churches while broadening our support base, doing lots of speaking, traveling, studying, and upgrading our education, and getting some rest.

There was great excitement at thoughts of seeing family and showing off our three little ones, all born in Pakistan. We had celebrated baby Jimmy's second birthday just days before we were due to leave. His brother Doug was fifteen months older, age three. Elizabeth, the big sister was five. They were so much fun.

Another Surprise Addition

The next addition to our family was unplanned.

It was my job to pack and prepare us for the trip home, while beloved hubby took care of travel details. It was a tiring job, knowing what to take, what to leave behind for others, what to get rid of and what to store. As we prepared to leave the village, I felt exhausted. When the villagers started their fires for cooking, using cow patties (straw and dung) and mustard oil for frying, I began to feel uncomfortable in my stomach. I was sure it was nothing serious, just the over tiredness and the two smells that were getting to me. The days for turning over the work had been busy days. I was stretched to the limit. Yes, of course that was the problem. I was over worked.

Then along comes Paul Lundgren, a fellow missionary, making a last visit to us in Brarkot, wanting to offer his help. Hearing the problem, he pronounced me pregnant. "I couldn't be," I declared. Morning nausea had plagued me with the others, but this was night sickness. He laughed and said, "I will have to teach you the facts of life!" It was annoying. I hated the teasing and his telling the other missionaries. We had not planned on having more children.

After we left the village and headed home by ship to the USA, the night sickness stopped, but there were other reasons which made me think Paul might be right. As soon as we got back home in America, I made an appointment with our

Boarding the train in preparation for our first home leave in 1956. Richard holding baby Jimmy, Doug, Elizabeth and me.

family doctor. He was a huge man who always insisted on a big "fatherly" hug. We had been put in touch with him through his sister, a wonderful Bible teacher, but we knew he was not a Christian. In one of the Bible studies, she had asked prayer for him. He had never charged us for all the things he did for us, one of the many kindnesses people did to make our lives as faith missionaries a little easier. We considered it to be God's providing, even as He has promised.

As I walked into the examining room, I said, "Oh, doctor, I think I am pregnant, and I just don't want to be!" I am sure I was near tears. We had our family. We had already endured a lot of teasing because our children were so close in age. I was pregnant when we went to Pakistan, pregnant twice while there and returning to the US, pregnant again. I wanted to get on with my life, not have to endure those long months again, buying and wearing maternity clothes, not having to spend money we needed for our daily needs and for getting back to Pakistan. I wanted to be free to do some of the things which I thought would make my year in the US a time of enjoyment, and I was pregnant! Pregnant again!

I was utterly forgetful God had always been there from the time I became a Christian and gave my heart to the Lord. He was there when I needed funds to go to college. He had met every need when we had decided to go to Pakistan. I was annoyed, so disappointed at being pregnant.

The doctor confirmed I was pregnant, then said in a very matter of fact way, as if an alternative, "*Do you want to get rid of it?*"

That "**it**" had such an ominous tone it shook me into reality. "Oh, my, no!" I said quickly. I suppose I thought some miracle could be performed that would say I was not pregnant, but it didn't happen. I honestly think this doctor might have terminated my pregnancy without hesitation if I had asked him to do it.

As I left the office that day, I decided I needed to change doctors. Before my next visit, I called and talked to him. I said I had gotten used to a lady doctor while overseas, and while I deeply appreciated all his care for us, there was a lady doctor near where we lived, and I wanted to use her. I did not dare tell him the three other kids had been delivered by men doctors. He was not happy. Within a few days, we got his bill. It was just one more thing to add to the expenses of having another baby.

A bathtub soak is a good place for a mom to reflect. Nighttime, kids in bed, no one to disturb the thinking processes. As I sat there that night, I said aloud in a firm voice, as though ordering the God Who in fact had arranged all this, "Lord, you ordered this baby. You will have to pay for it!" How dare we tiny people on earth to speak in such a manner to the God of all creation! What an unfaithful child I was to think, to say such a thing to God, my Father! He was the One Who had paid my way all my life and from age sixteen had made it possible for me to go to college and for us to go as missionaries. Faith can often seem elusive. Right then, it was in short supply. Such was my case.

But God, my loving Father. He took me at my word. Shortly after I began to see the new lady doctor, I knew this had been the right move. She seemed to take an interest in our family. She told me little about her own life, a story in itself. I doubt I had ever expressed my needs to her, but one day after my check up, she said, "You are going to need a crib. Take this slip of paper and go over to the pharmacy next door and pick out one. Tell the pharmacist to put it on my account." Was God keeping His promise in response to my demands? It was amazing. It seemed everyone who knew me wanted to share in the needs for this baby. Indeed, God was keeping His end of the bargain.

Robert Marshall Thompson was born on September the 26th, 1956. He was named for two men of faith. Robert Kerr from Newcastle on Tyne, England, who had known his dad's family from the days of being in the British Army, stationed on the frontier of then India. He had searched out the family and gotten in contact with us when he sent a letter to the Methodist Mission in India and it was forwarded to us. He wanted to know what had happened to young Richard, who always begged for chocolates. He was a humble man of God, a coal miner, gracious, able to interact with us even though he had not known us nor we him and dear Ella, his wife. We had met this wonderful family when we returned home via England in 1956.

The name Marshall was the name of Dad's best friend from high school, here in the US. Dick Marshall became the head of the rescue mission in Pittsburgh, PA. He loved the Lord, was a go-getter, had a beautiful voice, and became one of our supporters in ministry. Does Bob seem well named? We think so.

130

I believe all his siblings would agree that from his earliest days, Bob was a different child. When he was just a toddler, one day I found him sitting in a corner, berating himself, saying "Bobb-um!" He had done something he knew he should not have done. I don't know what that was but at some point, he must have known sitting in the corner for a behavior problem was the punishment. His older brothers sometimes teased him. Today, they respect what he has become. I think I can say he took on some of the characteristics of the two men for whom he was named, even though he never knew them, and they were unrelated.

From his earliest days, he seemed to have an understanding of what God wanted in his life. Today, Bob is senior pastor of a large and growing church in Hickory, North Carolina where he has celebrated over 25 years in Corinth Reformed Church, a beautiful 150-year-old church which looks like a mini-Gothic cathedral. He and his wife Linda both have a strong faith in God, strong leadership qualities and a ministry with an outreach to the world. God has given them the privilege of growing people in faith, including me, his mom. I am so glad God allowed me to carry him for nine months and then see why God needed him for HIS service.

What would have been the loss if I had chosen an abortion?

I learned to read Jeremiah 1:5 and Psalm 139 with new meaning and a greater wonder, but there was no special revelation about what God had in store for this child who under other circumstances might have been aborted. Thankfully, God is a God of Grace.

****

Our lives have been so blessed. Jesus has led us all the way. Bob was not our last child, but as we have watched God's workings in his life, we know the reality of that story in Moses, "Take this child and raise it for me and I will give thee thy wages." When a fifth child, David, was born on our second home leave in 1963, we immediately gave him to God, just as we had earlier

131

given the first four babies. We have been paid, repaid and OVER-PAID by God, especially paid from the blessing of not "getting rid of" our baby Bob and not losing the privilege of having five precious children who have brought us great blessings in our lives. We can say with the Psalmist, "Children are the heritage of the Lord and the fruit of the womb is HIS reward" (Psalm 127:3).

I still sometimes bow my head in sadness at the foolish and selfish thoughts I had, but I feel sure they are the same as many other women have had. For most of us, pregnancy is not an easy experience. Thankfully, the God we serve protected His "private selection" and allowed Bob to see the light of day.

God Provides Again

We had arrived in the US for our first home leave in April 1956, expecting to stay about a year and return to Pakistan in the spring of 1957.

Whether it was my fault that we had to stay longer—until October—I don't know. We had only been home for about three months when Richard began talking of making our plans to return. At that time, I was beginning to feel the effects of my fourth pregnancy. I recall saying to Richard, "Please let me feel we are home (in America) before you talk of getting back home (to Pakistan)!" I was enjoying my family and the love they and the churches were showering on us. It wasn't that I didn't want and plan to return.

Raising our funds to return was a delayed and slow process. In spite of meetings, we received few honorariums and promises of support. Pastor John Woods of Jackson Memorial Baptist—my brother Woodie and sister-in-law Ellie's church—was a fine man who took a fatherly liking to me. Knowing of the problem, one day he said, "Myrtle, if you will switch and go under the Southern Baptist Board, I can promise you will never have a need." It was an enticing thought, and I had no doubt he would have been able to keep to that promise.

132

It only took a moment for me to answer. I thanked him, said I knew he could and would do that, but "God has led us into TEAM and has not led us out."

It was a period of testing for seventeen months. Had my desire to "let me feel at home for a while" been wrong? Selfish? Unwilling to obey the rules? This mission did not permit us to return without sufficient funds, so in one sense, I was not responsible for the delay, but I do wonder how God would judge it. Son Bob was born, and we began to enjoy our home leave. And in the end, God did provide the necessary funds.

Seeing family was one of the many blessings of home leaves. This is a photo of me with my siblings and parents during our first home leave in 1957. Back, L to R, my brothers Bennie, Jack, Woody and Willie. Front L to R, me, sisters Evelyn and Hettie, and my parents, Della and Lafayette Williams. Two siblings were deceased: Percy (1948) and Mertie (1926).

At the end of that first home leave, we were supposed to board the ship on October 23, 1957, but the freighter had some delay and would not leave until the 24th. We were sailing out of Berkley Piers in Norfolk on the ship *Media*. We had been booked to leave in September, but the shipping company, which was carrying a tobacco shipment, had a change of plans. Since sufficient funds were not raised by September, we were happy for the delay. My sister Evelyn said, "God must want them to go. He not only sends the ship to the door, He delayed it so they could get ready!"

We had a lot of stuff to pack, both for ourselves and for others. I, the planner, had to decide between the necessities and the niceties. Missionaries going abroad in the middle of the 20th century needed to take some items not available in a third world country. Most personal items were not available, along with some outerwear, underwear, and shoes. We had the 50-gallon drums, cleaned and ready, but not much to pack in them. We could hire a tailor to sit on our verandah and using a hand cranked Singer machine, turn out very nice things for all of us, but the kids going into boarding school needed jeans, lots of socks, warm sweaters and coats, some bedding, enough to last about four or five years. It seemed an endless supply of a wide variety needed for both extreme cold and hot weather, stormy days and wear and tear. Besides these things, there were some practical kitchen and household items we wanted to take.

Also, we did not feel we had all our finances. We estimated we needed about $200.00 more and had been praying for it to come in. The reason for this was we had agreed to take a lot of things for families, as well as the school and hospital. We just assumed we would pay duty on some of those large 53 pieces that were going with us as "accompanied baggage" (and those 53 pieces did not include the kids!) It was a lot to care for! In addition, transshipping in England meant watching as baggage was transferred for the next lap of the trip.

Along with family members, I thought I could count people from fifteen different churches as we said our farewells. Our Preacher, John Taylor, had a little dedicatory service for us. As we hugged and shook hands, several gave us money. We thanked them and put it in our pockets. Elizabeth had run on ahead and found our cabin. When we caught up with her, we overheard the answer to a reporter's question: "Would you say you have traveled a lot?" A pause, and then, "Yes, I guess so." At age six, she had crossed the ocean, traveled in England, and seen quite a bit of the U.S.

We started to settle in but were told lunch was being served. We found our way to the dining room. After that, it was no problem for the whole family to take a nap. Our next stop would be New York. When we woke up, it was almost time for us to go to dinner. As we dressed, we remembered the money and counted it. A total of $207.00 had been put in our hands! MORE than what we had thought we might need. We had prayer and thanked our faithful God who had seen fit to answer our prayers at what seemed to us like the last minute.

Boarding the ship for the return to Pakistan, 1957. Me, Richard holding baby Bob, Elizabeth, Doug, and Jim in front. This photo appeared in one of the local VA newspapers who often interviewed us when we were home on leave. Photo: Virginian Pilot.

Norma Culler and Don Stoddard and family got on board in New York. From there we would go to Southampton, England and stay for a visit before continuing, onboard a different ship, to Karachi.

Adventures on the Sea

Even on board the ship, our missionary work continued as God provided wonderful opportunities to share His word and the good news with our fellow passengers! I remember one young lady who one night poured out her longing heart. She said she knew the Lord, but we could sense that she did not know all the Lord wanted for us when our hearts are grieving. She had lost both parents a few months previously and her next closest relative was a cousin in Scotland, where she was going to visit. We told her how Christ alone can satisfy such a longing heart and be

135

a sustenance to her in every hour. We prayed that our words brought her the peace she seemed to need and into a closer relationship with the Lord.

Another opportunity to minister was to four young men, three British and one Scotsman, whose dining table was across from ours. We gave one of them a small booklet of Scripture verses which he said he read many times before leaving the ship. To the Scotsman I gave a little Salvation Bible. Another female passenger, who was French, remarked that although missionaries were all right, but "you are always trying to convert someone!" I remember one occasion in the dining hall, she held up an apple and said it was what Eve had eaten. Her table was next to ours and the remark seemed to be directed to us, so I replied, "The Bible does not say it was an apple." That brought on a long discussion and provided opportunities to bring her thoughts to the real Word of God. She also accepted a Bible and told me, before we left the ship, that she had read it through many times. Then there was the Austrian lady who took a "fancy" to our daughter. In talking to her one night, she told me she was not a Christian, but very interested in becoming one. She did not make the decision to receive Christ into her heart, but we continued to pray that she would! And on and on I could go, telling of the four members of the orchestra and others on board who questioned us about the Scriptures, and what we believed, or became interested in what we were doing. So even before returning to Pakistan and our "mission field," we found ourselves with opportunities to be missionaries and talk to people about God and His plan of salvation! We prayed that all those seeds we sowed, would bear fruit!

Our adventure on the sea came about on our way to England. We had a very bad storm which lasted several days with gale winds and stormy seas. One night, the ship made a terrific lurch, which sent baby Bobby and his crib flying across the room! Estimates were that the ship listed as much as 25-30 degrees! Most folks, like ourselves, wondered what was coming next. One of the British young men was thrown against his wardrobe door and as he tried to stand up, the door broke, and he injured his back. This was one of the things that set him to thinking about his own needs, spiritually thinking. Perhaps it was the same way when some of Jesus' disciples cried out to Jesus to save them on a stormy sea such as this (Luke 8:22-24). We talked with this young man for several hours one night after the storm and he told us no one had ever told him about God's love in Christ and man's need of coming into that relationship though he had always attended church! So, we prayed for these fellow contacts, that they would come to know the Lord and that He alone can "rebuke the wind and the raging waves" and save them (Luke 8:24-25).

Our week in England was indescribable. Although with four small children and rainy cold days, we did not try to "sight-see." During that week, we spoke with a group we had visited before, conducted a service, and visited with friends in their homes. Our English friends were just wonderful to us and we definitely felt a part of that group who upheld us in prayer!

We then boarded the ship *Circassia* and headed for Karachi. On board, we assisted with the services and conducted Sunday School. We made many friends on this part of our trip as well. We were aware that we were already "touching" foreign soil because the majority of people on the ship seemed to be Indian or Pakistani. Richard had wonderful talks with some of the men. I did little else other than take care of our children, for while there was a nursery, the children pleaded with me not to make them go in. Being the only children about the *Media* had left them a bit spoiled. The *Circassia* did not lack for children, however, for there were over sixty children on board. I felt very secure at night, however, to know they were in bed asleep, and could not fall overboard!

Pakistan, at Last!

The lights of Karachi came into view on the night of November 26th, and we could hardly sleep that night. At the customs shed, we decided to wait until the other passengers had cleared out. By then, there was another little miracle—maybe the

Customs man was tired; but he waved us on! The funds we were so concerned about? There was no duty to pay!

We arrived at Haripur, our southernmost station, and were met by a number of our missionaries who had a warm welcome and breakfast ready for us, after which we visited a number of our stations, and saw our new hospital for the first time. It is a thrill to see how the work had progressed! In Abbottabad, the school children from the Mission School greeted us with songs and poems, written especially for this occasion.

It was then time to travel to Mansehra where we would initially be serving this term. Two days after arriving, I came down with the flu. Everyone else soon followed, with Richard being the last to succumb. Even our Pakistani cook, who had been on hand to greet us and welcome us back became ill! A few days later, all were up and over the sickness and readjusting to food, water, and life in general. It was so good to be HOME again! And though we immensely enjoyed our home leave, and the lovely "help" from friends and family, we knew this is where the Lord had called us to serve. We asked our supporters to bow with us at His feet and thank and praise Him for all His wonderful ways and His guidance which made possible our return.

Murree and Boarding School

It was after the return from this first home leave that we had to start preparing Elizabeth to attend the boarding school in Murree, 125 miles away from where we would be living in Mansehra and 7,000 feet in the mountains. The various mission groups serving in Pakistan had realized the need for a school for missionary children about the same time we were leaving for home leave. The United Presbyterian mission had acquired a large facility in Murree, Sandes Home, which had previously been used by the British military for R&R. It was a multiple room building, suitable for large meetings and groups of people. Additionally, the British had built an Anglican church in Murree which was now vacant. The church became the school's classrooms and Sandes

Home was used for boarding. Caleb Cutherell, with TEAM, was appointed as the engineer to build a new hostel in Murree for boarding.

The hostel in Murree. Look at that snow!

Elizabeth turned seven in February of 1958 and started boarding school in March, in the middle of a term. The boarding school operated from September through June with winters off (instead of summer) because of the snowy weather.

Children attending the school were boarded at the school facilities until the middle or end of May when the boarding for the school was unavailable. Then mothers (and fathers who were studying at the language school in Murree) moved some belongings up to Murree to a rented house and the children lived with their parents until September when the next school term started. The rented house, Bexley Cottage, was a huge house with some smaller ones around it. Missionaries (often single people) would serve as "boarding parents" and stay with the children in the boarding facility during the school term. I stayed there one term as one of the "boarding parents."

On Saturdays, the children did special activities. Sometimes they were allowed to walk the three miles to the Murree Bazaar shopping area to spend their allowance, which was anything from five cents to a quarter depending on their ages. As they got older, they had more privileges. Boarding school for most children was a pleasant experience.

****

Unfortunately, tragedy would strike Murree Christian School many years after we left Pakistan. On August 5, 2002, several gunmen stormed the compound, killing two Pakistani guards and four other Pakistani staff and wounding the mother of one of the students. The fact that no students were injured or killed was indeed a miracle! The school subsequently closed its elementary section and transferred the high school division to Thailand. Just a few days after the attack at Murree, three young men threw grenades at the staff of the Christian Hospital in Taxila as they were leaving the morning chapel service, killing four and injuring over twenty.

We received these details in a letter written to us by dear friends who had visited in Pakistan soon after these tragic events. They commented on the remarkable and inspiring absence of bitterness and the spirit of forgiveness that was in the hearts of those who had been witness to these events. They were amazed at the evidence of God's grace and power; this was forgiveness that only comes as the fruit of God's Spirit.

Living in Mansehra

When we returned in 1957, we moved into another village house in Mansehra. We were able to purchase a used '52 pickup truck with funds which had been provided by one of our supporting churches in the US. To reach our Mansehra house, which was up on a hill, I could walk from the bus stop in the shopping area, get a taxi or if our truck was available, walk to the mission house where it was parked and drive to and from the bottom of the hill. Vehicles could not drive up to our house because we had to cross a stream. There was no bridge at that time. One was built later, after a massive storm tore through the stream, causing some flooding. No houses were affected, because all were on higher ground, but crossing was almost impossible for a few days.

The stones in the river had been placed close together. It was easy to get from one stone to the next, a proverbial "hop, skip and a jump." During those first years, we became adept as we jumped or stepped across the stream by hopping on those rocks, just like the locals did. Hopping those rocks was the same way our household goods was brought to us when we moved there. It was amazing the balance these men had as they carried the heavy loads and furniture. A short distance upstream, we could see women washing their clothes and placing them on the bigger rocks to dry.

After crossing, we had a short walk up to our house. On the way was a huge stone marker with an inscription. The inscription had been dulled by time but was obvious enough to be an attention getter. We could not read it but were told it had been there since the days of King Ashoka. He ruled part of the northern area of what was then called Hindustan ("land of the Hindus") in the third century BC, after Alexander the Great's visit. After King Ashoka, there was another interlude of a ruling power in the area. Islam began its thrust in about the ninth century AD, almost twelve hundred years later.

Ashoka inherited and ruled the Punjab region, including what today is part of Afghanistan. He converted from Brahmanism to Buddhism and was said to have a high moral code and a love for animals as well as people. His edicts, carved in stone, may have been a part of this inscription. The stones placed in prominent places was one-way early rulers communicated.

This section of Mansehra was about a mile from the shopping area. It was like a little community or subdivision in itself. There were some larger houses, but several village houses were attached, one to the other, with a walkway or path or sometimes a small drainage indentation in the ground, not big enough to call a ditch, but adequate during the monsoon weather to take the water away from the houses. There was one separating our house from those behind us.

Our house was a long row of four rooms with a verandah stretching all the way across the front of the rooms. Two rooms were connected. The other rooms were separate, like individual rooms with separate doors. At one end was a room attached in an L shape fashion. We used it for our kitchen. On the other side of the courtyard were two small rooms, one for the cement enclosed container where the water was stored, and the other a bathroom, of sorts, no modern facilities, but a box for the seat, with a can under it.

Water was brought in from a spring somewhere in the village, five *mushkis* a day. A *mushki* is the skin of an animal, probably a goat? It is sewn up so it would not leak. The commodes were taken care of by a person who came and kept them clean. I am thankful we knew nothing more about either of these situations. Both may have been at places "down by the river." We boiled the water.

We had a small yard about 35-40 feet in front of the house, up to the six-foot stone wall. There was a large double entry gate. The yard and stone wall were extended around the side of our house, a short few feet to the back. A small path separated our house from the small but nice home next door where the assistant principal of the local college lived.

Behind the back of our house was a small drainage ditch, and across that, a row of rooms, equal to the length of our house, where different families lived. Each had a small porch. They could use the area to make their tea and cook their food. I believe they

Our children and the Karsgaard children by the wall at our house in Manshera.

142

were caretakers for a landowner. There was an open space where the children could play together.

Adjoined to our house on the other side was the high wall separating us from a large nice two-story home, owned by a family whose father owned a taxi business.

While living in Manshera, Richard resumed his treks, often into new, virgin, untouched areas, to establish contact. He mainly trekked north of Mansehra about twenty miles but would cover two to three times that distance on a trek! He would often be gone for up to ten days. In many of these places, Richard and others who accompanied him, were the first non-natives the people had ever seen. They had never heard of the Good News, neither in preaching nor in a tract. Eventually, Richard wanted us to move to one of these villages, but there was no suitable housing available. Richard and others had a "shack" of one room about twenty miles from Mansehra where they would stay and would hold weekend services. We claimed the promise, "Some from every tribe, tongue, kindred and nation" and wondered who it would be from that area!

Blessings Among the Difficulties

Shortly after we moved to the village in Mansehra, there were some serious problems. I was often alone except for our young children while Richard was on his treks. Some of the village children began to taunt our children. If the gate happened to be left open, a child would run in and steal anything he could lay his hands on, even taking things off the clothesline. These boys could stand on a roof above our house and would urinate into our courtyard or throw in feces. The missionary family who had lived there before us had had no such problem. I wondered why it was directed at us. I began to pray and ask God to make me love these people and be friends, or else to remove me from this village. I did not want to be there under those constant, daily pressures. Could I find blessing in some of the difficulties of life? Yes, and I did.

An associate with Billy Graham was speaking in Rawalpindi. Richard and the boys and I went to hear him. When the meetings were over, Richard was asked to stay, but I wanted to come home. We traveled the almost 100 miles by taxi, arriving in the late afternoon, just before dark. It was a hot September night. Our house had one opening for a window in each room, with screen on the outside, and a wooden shutter on the inside, no glass.

The monsoons were over, but the air was still damp. The house was hot and steamy. It had been locked up and we did not have fans. I opened the window shutters, but kept the door closed because of bugs. Our little bichon dog was on the verandah. Suddenly, I heard him barking and a man's voice shout, "*Hutto!*"—get out of the way. I realized the man had climbed the outside wall, gotten into the courtyard, and was coming up to my verandah. I quickly locked the shutters and went to the back of the house and called to the neighbors, "Will you please come and help me? A man is in my courtyard, and I am here alone."

A man's voice answered, "Right away!" By the time the two men got there, the person had escaped, but I had to go out into the courtyard and unlock the gate so they could come in and search the house. I admit to being afraid! The end of that story was that it changed our whole situation. No longer did the young boys do those ugly things, but also, when these men met me outside, they would ask, "Is everything alright?" The problem turned into a blessing.

This same family had five girls. The mother was expecting again. She had another girl. In that culture, boys are more desirable than girls, but this family accepted their lot and seemed happy. When the baby was just a few months old, she became ill. The mother asked me to come and see her. I knew immediately the baby should see the doctor. The hospital was a few miles from us, but I could drive her in the truck and offered. She said no, but the next morning, about 5:30, she sent word she would go. I drove the mom and baby to the hospital. Dr. Phyllis Irwin, a missionary doctor with TEAM, immediately confirmed meningitis. There was nothing to be done at that late date. The baby died. Bodies are buried the same day.

They sent word to me. The people do not eat until after the body is in the grave. A group of men were coming to take the body to the cemetery. By this time, it was late afternoon.

I went over to mourn with the family. I knew the children would be hungry. I filled my pockets with cookies not knowing if I would offend. I did not offer them to the adults, but the mothers understood. Both children and adults seemed genuinely grateful.

A few weeks later, the mother sent for me again. She said, "please come, my heart is hurting me." We were just ready to leave for Abbottabad. I knew if I went, I would not be able to leave quickly, so I asked her to come to my house. What could I offer this grieving mother? I gave her some words from the Psalms, and I think I prayed for her. There would be one more visit with her before we moved away.

Jean Sodeman, a fellow missionary, and I started visiting the people in this village. We had a lot of fun. We could both speak the language and enjoyed being with the people. This was personal contact with women and children, and I couldn't fulfill all the many responses to "friendship" I got. After all, one finds it difficult to win people to Christ unless Christ in the missionary attracts people to the missionary!

On one occasion, we came across an older couple with no children. The man had been to our hospital and been treated for a heart problem. We went to see how he was doing. He was lying on a mat on the floor but seemed to be doing well. His wife was about five feet tall and five feet around. She began telling us her about her aches and pains. We thought she wanted sympathy, so we did not take her seriously.

Richard and I had been out of town, visiting friends. We had gotten back late at night. The next morning, early, there was a loud banging of urgency on my gate. I went to open it and some women and young girls were there, all crying and saying "Masi died! Masi is dead!" She had died and was already buried. It was very sad. They had just observed Eid, a celebration (like our

145

Christmas.) She had cooked a lot of rich food for her family and friends. She may have had some kind of attack. We never knew. I think we both wished we had paid more attention to her when she tried to tell us she was having some physical problems. One of many times I felt I failed someone.

God did answer my prayer and made me love them, but He took me seriously when I was having a problem with the children. I had said I did not want to be in that village. Now I did not want to leave, but we were asked to relocate.

One of our nurses, Norma Culler, passed away with fulminating jaundice. Norma was a very close friend. She had gone out on the ship with us when we left in 1957. Jaundice had struck several missionaries in other areas, but she was the only one in TEAM. She did not live but a few days. She is buried in the cemetery on the hospital grounds. It was a very sad time in my life. She was such a tremendous blessing to everyone, and she was gone from us.

After her death, the Field Council needed to shuffle personnel. The missionary who was in charge of the school in Abbottabad was also a nurse. She could fill Norma's place, but there was no one to fill the vacancy at the school. We were asked to return to Abbottabad so I could take over the school. I did not want to go but knew I should. It would not affect Richard's ministry. He was working in the north, sometimes staying as much as a week in one of the villages there. He could travel back and forth by bus.

We moved back to Abbottabad. When the women in the houses behind me knew we were leaving, they invited me to come for tea. They had spread out a small cloth and had the hot cups washed and the tea ready when I arrived. I was moved to see these poor ladies had wanted it to be special. They had bought some dry rusks from the bazaar to serve with the tea. The children wanted one and the mom said no. They were poor; I did not want to take them, but did pick up one, then later slipped a large part of it into the hand of a little girl.

I think I can say I learned a lot about hospitality from the villagers. They were helpful, kind, like family. I found hospitality to be a part of the Middle East and Asian culture. Hospitality is an ancient custom that may be one of the things lost in our fast-moving electronic age, whittled away by cell phone and iPad communication.

Lessons My Children Taught Me …

As parents, we expect that we will be the one teaching and training our children, not just to read, write and do "rithmatic," but also the things concerning God and the importance of the Gospel and following Jesus. After all, Paul wrote that we are to bring up our children "with the training and instruction of the Lord" (Ephesians 6:4). However, I discovered that we can also learn, or at least be reminded of, very important lessons from our children! I recall two such occasions involving Elizabeth and Jim when they were young and we were living in Mansehra.

"Count your blessings, Name them one by one …"

Our daughter Elizabeth was singing. I smiled at the thought of one so young "counting blessings," and continued with the work of my busy day.

Her next rendering of the chorus again caught my attention:

"Count your blessings, Name them two by two …"

I waited, accurately guessing the words that would follow—

"And it will surprise you, What the Lord will do."

I listened in rapt attention as this seven-year-old continued her play, all the time singing this chorus she had learned in the missionary children's boarding school.

"Count your blessings, Name them three by three …
And it will surprise you, What the Lord can be."

"Count your blessings, Name them four by four …
And it will surprise you, More and more and more."

"Count your blessings, Name them five by five …
And it will surprise you, How the Lord provides."

I couldn't stand it any longer. This was exciting! "Honey," I said, "That's so good! Where did you learn it—at school?" "Yes, Mommy," she replied, "And Mommy, I guess you could go up to a hundred times a hundred!"

Yes, I thought.

Blessings unnumbered and all too often forgotten.
Blessings every moment of every day
Blessings seen and unseen, measurable and immeasurable.
Blessings by day and blessings by night.
Blessings in answer to prayer.
Blessings given by a loving Father, even before we pray.
Blessings at work and blessings at play.
Blessings outside and blessings insider our home …

Like snowflakes they come—silently, beautiful,
        all different shapes and sizes …

Blessings often unnoticed—
        Usually unmerited—
                Mostly received with ingratitude …

And although the years passed all too quickly, and my little daughter is now a mother and grandmother and herself became a missionary, the words she taught me that day are with me still: "I guess you could go up to a hundred times a hundred!"

Yes, I guess we could. Maybe more. It's just that we lose track when we try to count that high!

Another lesson I vividly recall involved son Jim and a cake plate!

"Here's the cake plate Mom. I've licked it clean—there's not a crumb left!"—pause—"But you'll still have to wash it, Mom, 'cause even tho' it looks clean, it has germs on it."

Jim was five. His sister was already in the missionary children's boarding school, but his two younger brothers were at home. When I baked a cake, each boy, in turn, got to lick the pan, or eat the leftover crumbs and frosting. This had been a gooey chocolate cake, so the turn was special; not a bit would be left. He had "licked the platter clean!"

To look at it, one would never know but that it had been washed with water. But somewhere in the mind of even one so young as five, there was an awareness of germs. The outside might *look* clean, but Jim knew the germs were there. The dish had to be washed.

I remember the day so well. It was 1959; we lived in the village of Mansehra, and the children were playing in the courtyard. I had had great fears my glass cake plate would be broken—until Jim reminded me of the need to wash it.

Then, my thoughts had turned to something else: the need to be on the inside what one appears to be on the outside. Paul speaks about it in Philippians 1:8-11, using the word "sincere." He tells us in order to be sincere, we must approve the things that are excellent (not just licking the dish clean but going beyond and washing it in the dishwater)—using discernment.

Jesus said, "Ye are clean because of the word which I have spoken to you." This is how we get the inside clean—our dishwater experience. We let His Word give us the washing that takes care of the "germs."

And so, I prayed –

"Here's my life, Lord. I've tried to clean it the best I could but it still has the germs of sin. It looks clean, but I know—I know my own method of cleaning it is not enough. I am asking you to clean it for me.

And Lord, please help my children to be always as sensitive to the germs of sin as they are to the bacteria on cake plates. Help them to remember it is not only important to *look* clean, but to *be* clean—through the Word which you speak."

Making Do or Doing Without

Many things which we were accustomed to buying in the US were not available in Pakistan. We learned to "make do or do without" but sometimes, the product was a great substitute. We learned to make cakes without shortening or eggs, both of which were sometimes "seasonal" and sometimes in a dozen eggs we might get a boiled one—to make up the dozen, of course—or one or two that did not hatch out the baby chicks. We had a potato slicer and could make good potato chips—when we could get the shortening—and good mayonnaise. Alas, we were never able to make a good "French's mustard~ sigh~ though many of the missionaries tried. English walnuts were sold in the hill stations at the end of the summer, counted out by a thousand, and we always bought a supply of one or two thousand to take with us when we moved down to our stations after the children went into boarding in the fall.

We could also buy wonderful mountain grown apples, mostly Golden Delicious, wrap them in newspaper and keep them for several months. Dates were always available in the fall, and we would buy a clump of ten or so pounds. They were good for cakes and cookies and eating and kept well. Sugar was rationed, but we managed to get enough by asking for special permits to get a little extra. We always asked for double of what we wanted, because we learned early on the ration would be cut in half.

Part of the "outfit" given us when we left the US was a canning set and we also took some jars with us when we went overseas. We were able to get lots of good fruit, so we had jellies and jams and canned fruits for the winter. Cocoa from Holland was expensive, but available in seven-pound packages. One missionary might buy the package and sell part of it to others. We usually did that. We could sometimes buy butter, but used it only in cooking, so we made chocolate cakes, chocolate fudge, chocolate cookies, and, of course, with the peanuts, peanut butter fudge!

The *kaccha* (wet, not ready for immediate use) peanuts were dug and sold in the fall. Each year our family would buy two *maunds,* 180 pounds of freshly dug peanuts, put them out in the sun on a tarpaulin to dry and when dry, pay a lady (our cook's wife) to shell them. They were then stored in a metal drum. Of course, while they were drying the birds, the kids, including the neighbors, all helped themselves, but there were plenty left for us. When dry, shelled, and ready for use, we stored them in a metal container. When we were ready to use them, we first roasted them over a low heat in our tin oven or, if we were able to get some *dalda* (vegetable oil), we fried them. If we wanted peanut butter, and we always did when the kids were at home from boarding school, the kids had to take their turns in grinding the peanuts. They counted and said it took 32 times through the meat grinder. (Their ingenuity soon won out. They decided PBJ— peanut butter mixed with jam or jelly—was just as good and did not require so much grinding.) We also used the peanuts for snacks, for cookies and for delicious fudge, too!

Sagging Mattresses

A few years ago, while lamenting over the mattress that was already sagging in the middle on a new futon, I was reminded of the mattresses we had in Pakistan and especially of the *pinjne wallas.* The memory of some of these simple luxuries still remain, reminding us we are of more than one culture.

I guess the best definition for the Urdu verb *pinjna* is to pluck or to "ping." The word *walla* just means "doer"—the person doing the job in this case. With regard to our mattresses in Pakistan, the *pinjne walla* played an important role.

Our mattresses in Pakistan were made of stuffed cotton. We would order the material in the bazaar, explaining the size mattress we wanted. The material was usually striped, not very fancy nor very thick, but durable. A *derzi* (tailor) would sew up the cover and have it filled for us. We could decide how thick we wanted it. Of course, the thicker, the more comfortable, but also the more expensive. Some beds were made of rope for the "springs," and some of two- or three-inch-wide tape, woven in an over and under style. When attached to the bed, both the rope or tape were pulled tight, but in time, they loosened, and we would have to either have them tied again or tie them ourselves. When the tape or rope was tight, and the mattresses newly *pinjed*, they were very firm and very comfortable. In time, however, they would stretch, and we would find ourselves sleeping in a semi-fetal position, as if in a hammock.

Each year, and sometimes, in between, we would have a *pinjne walla* come to our house. This was a most interesting work! First, he would open up the cover of the mattress. If the cover was worn, or torn, of course we had to replace it, but if it was okay, we could quickly wash and dry it.

The *pinjne walla* would then set up his "instrument" and start to work. He had a very large wooden bow-shaped "tool"

with a string or two attached. He would sit and literally pluck the cotton to fluff it up. What made the cotton fluff up? I have no idea! But soon he had a pile of cotton done. He would then lay out the cover, fill it, then sew it back together. We all luxuriated in having a nice fresh bed of fluffed cotton for our mattress!

A *pinjne walla* hard at work.

152

I am not sorry for those times. I praise God for all that we had or did not have in those days when our missionary motto was "Use it up, wear it out, make it do, or do without!" We cannot ask for more than God has allowed us to have and do!

****

During all those years, I was learning my lessons that God wanted to take the something I thought I was and change it into what He wanted me to be. Today I know He may send us through the fire (or even what might seem like the meat grinder) of adverse conditions, but only then can He make something of use to Him.

It is the "drying" process, the "apple keeping process" when we are wrapped and kept in a dark, dry place and the transforming of the elements of our lives (sort of like the making of cakes and cookies and fudge?) which is also a part of the transformation He is doing.

This I have learned: From the ashes of our sinful self-control and complaining, God would and will recreate something of value for His own use when we allow Him to do so. The Psalmist prayed "purge me with hyssop and I shall be clean, wash me and I shall be whiter than snow." That has been my prayer, too. And so, I pray: *Lord, keep up the good work~*

God Closes a Door

"The Lord Thy God in the midst of thee is mighty;
He will save; He will rejoice over thee with joy." (Zephaniah 3:17)

"Therefore, neither the one who plants nor the one who waters is
anything, but only God, who causes the growth. The one who
plants and the one who waters are equal, and each will receive
wages in proportion to his labor. For we are God's co-workers;
you are God's field, God's building." (1 Corinthians 3:7-9)

Once again, it seemed like the days, months and even years, of our second term in Pakistan had passed all too quickly. Richard and I loved this ministry God had called us to and thoroughly enjoyed the experiences of serving with our fellow missionaries and meeting the wonderful people who God put in our way. Additionally, our children seemed to be growing and thriving in Pakistan. However, all too soon it seemed, we were faced with the daunting task of clearing out five years of accumulated "stuff," packing and getting ready for another trip across the ocean, this time with four children in tow. We were all looking forward to returning home to spend time with family and friends. Richard and I also looked forward to being able to reconnect with the wonderful churches and other folks who so generously supplied our support and enabled us to serve in Pakistan.

Our Second Home Leave

Our second home leave began in November 1962. *En route* to the US, we took a little tour of Europe: Italy, Switzerland, Germany, Amsterdam. We traveled by train and saw many of the tourist sites. That made history come alive for the children and may be the reason Elizabeth eventually became a history teacher. Each night, I would wash out any clothes I thought needed it, but only if I felt sure they would dry by morning. I placed them on the radiators to dry. With just two large suitcases, our clothes were in short supply! The boys made it to the US with just the clothes they were wearing; the rest had worn out on the way!

REV. AND MRS. O. R. THOMPSON
WEST PAKISTAN

Richard and I in traditional Pakistani dress during our second home leave, 1962. This photo was taken for a local newspaper article.

My sister, Evelyn ("Aunt Leny") had found a place for us, a duplex with the Melvin family in Cradock, Virginia. It had three upstairs bedrooms, and a bathroom, with a living room, dining room and kitchen downstairs, a nice backyard, and this wonderful older couple who became like grandparents, fixing anything that needed to be fixed, including the kids' bikes or flat tires. Since we arrived just before Christmas, the generous people of Sweethaven Baptist Church and Pastor Damun Wyatt had decorated the apartment prior to our arrival. What a wonderful and thoughtful surprise!

Aunt Leny and Uncle Howard often cared for the kids so I could go with Richard on some trips. Aunt Leny was a "second mother" to our children, in some ways, closer to them and they closer to her than we were when we were on home leave. She was also a mentor to me, having had the advantage of our mom to give her some guidance. She had a son three years older and a daughter the same age as our Elizabeth. Her advice and help were invaluable with lessons I needed to learn about raising children. When we retired and went to live in North Carolina, it was never home to our children. They always wanted to be back in Portsmouth and wanted to spend time with her. My brother Woodie and his wife Ellie also helped; family members were wonderful to us, and so were our churches.

My sister, Evelyn (Aunt Leny) and her husband, Howard. What a blessing they both were to us!

Missionary children often live a "divided" life. It has its advantages and blessings and its downside. In our case, our children were separated from us when they went to boarding school in Pakistan. They also experienced brief periods of separation when we were requested to represent our work in mission conferences during our home leave. Traveling around, speaking, and getting to know the people who so faithfully supported us financially and in prayer brought blessing and encouragement. It was also an advantage for the churches and other groups to be introduced to other cultures.

Missionaries on assignments rarely stayed in motels. Mostly, they were guests in the homes of church members. Sometimes supporters graciously offered to have the kids stay with

156

them when we were in or near their area and speaking in, or attending conferences, such as TEAM's Annual Conference in Wheaton, Illinois. One such offer was on a farm with a family which had seven children. That added a great deal of work to this loving mother who had to prepare the meals, bandage the *"chotes"* (skinned knees) and settle any disputes. We were grateful for their invitation. On another occasion, within a day after arriving in a home, our children came down with measles. There were no children in that home. It was an embarrassing thing for me, but how could we know that would be the situation? I did not get to attend many of the meetings then.

Although I know of no special problems our children experienced, I think there likely is both a good side and a not too good side to staying with so many different, and often unknown, families. It helped the children to see what other families were like, but I am not sure I would do that today, even though I am not sure why. Perhaps it is the same reason I would not put one of my children in daycare unless it was absolutely necessary. For us as parents, it was probably enjoyable, because it meant seeing old friends and catching up on what was happening around the world.

Our Family Is Complete

It was during this second leave, that our son David was born.

It was like a case of "we went out empty and we came back full." Our first three children were born in Pakistan. Elizabeth, born February 1951, Doug, December 1952, Jim, a small surprise fifteen months later, March 1954. We returned to the US in 1956 for our first home leave and Baby Bobby was born in September; four children in five and a half years. We returned to Pakistan and I thought our family was complete.

Six years passed and we were once again home for our second leave. Right "out of the blue" one day Jimmy said he wanted us to have another baby. I had no idea how a child's desire for our family was important enough for God to grant his request, but He did.

Shortly after arriving in the US, morning sickness began dogging my life. I thought I needed to explain to the kids. I told them we *"might be"* having another baby but had not said anything more. I was soon back in maternity clothes, two outfits. In those days the latest fashion was a skirt with a large round opening to cover the expanding waistline and a top which reached below that special opening.

Jimmy's sharp eye must have been noticing how I was dressed. One day he asked, "Mom, why are you wearing those funny clothes?" I said, "Don't you remember? I told you we are having a baby!" He said, "*No Mom, you didn't say we **are** having a baby, you said we might be!*" What does a mom do with such a perceptive child? God was answering Jimmy's prayer.

As the summer days wore on, I waited for the moment when my "labor" would come full speed and I would go to the hospital for the delivery That moment came the day after we celebrated Bob's 7th birthday, September 25, with a cake shaped like a boot. Aunt Ellie had made the cake because Bob was now the proud owner of a pair of cowboy boots.

On September 25 I knew my waiting would soon be over. Short pains had been the order of the day, but I needed more before going to the hospital. I got the other children in bed and was soon on my way, later in the evening. This was a big baby, lots of "labor" needed to get him out and into the new world he would face.

He was placed in the nursery across from my room so I could go to the window and see him. It was soon obvious he was hungry, and the nurses had the privilege of feeding him. He weighed 9 pounds 6 1/2 ounces, was in the nursery with other newborns but must have caught the eye of "onlookers" because I heard one person exclaim, "Did you see that 9 pound one!" I wanted to say, "Yes, he's mine and we are going to keep him!"

In those days moms stayed in the hospital for a few days to insure all was well with mom and baby. My own mom who had nine children said the two weeks they spent in bed after a birth were the only times she got any rest! Almost from the first times he was brought to me, I noticed he smiled, maybe something unusual for a newborn, but it was as if he were saying, "Hello, world! I am here!"

I don't remember any ultrasound to tell us the baby would be a boy, but he was named before he was born and would be called David. He was named by his great Aunt Zelma who had said her piece after we told her we were expecting our third child, Jim. She didn't think we should have any more! We wondered how she would handle our telling her a fifth was now being added to the family. Instead of being disturbed, she said she had earlier said too much. It was she who welcomed and did so many nice things for our children.

His crib was in our bedroom. My wonderful sister was acting like a mom, watching over me and helping with the other children. I had told her about his smiling, to which she replied, "ha ha! - new mom doesn't know the baby has gas pains." I couldn't convince her until she was upstairs watching him and called down to me, "He does smile!"

Before long the whole family was cuddling him, and he was returning the favor with a happy face. He had three older brothers. Bob, seven years older, always a child I could depend on for behaving, and Doug and Jim who would be sure to "teach him the ropes."

Very soon we were back in Pakistan and the older children were in boarding school. I was on my own with one baby. Alone at home with his dad and me it was interesting to find him able to easily make friends and also entertain himself. The outside interested him, and he found rocks he called "a beaut" and bugs like the very large beetles of the insect world. I think the kids taught him how to tie a string on them and "race" them to see which ones could crawl away the fastest. They were all slow.

He entertained himself or was entertained by his loving siblings. What a joy are families. I am so glad God thought of them to bless our lives!

Highland Baptist Church

When we returned to Portsmouth from Pakistan during our first home leave in 1956, my sister Evelyn and her husband were attending Highland Baptist Church. I was surprised to find the pastor was Rev. Carlton Long; his wife was Evelyn. They were the couple I had known when as a teenager I attended a Friday night Bible Class with them and studied Romans at the YMCA in Norfolk. Shortly after we returned to Pakistan from that first home leave, this was the church that voted to contribute to our support and buy the truck for us.

One of my biggest concerns for our children was that they come to know Christ at an early age. I remember being fearful that I would die and someone else would raise our children and not be as concerned about their spiritual life as I was. I tried to impress on them their need to accept Him as Savior. I wanted all of them to one day have the knowledge of sin "stick" in their hearts and have the assurance they had received Christ. Elizabeth had a sensitivity to sin even though she never showed any signs of being a sinner! She was always obedient.

Doug was a different story. None of the children's stories which had helped Elizabeth understand her need to know Jesus produced conviction for Doug. I prayed for him. A few months before leaving for our second home leave, we got a letter from him from boarding school which said, and I can still quote it, "Dear Mom and Dad, Today I asked Jesus to come into my heart and He did." That was it. Nothing more. We did not learn the details until much later. We were sitting in a small circle of friends in Karachi, *en route* to the US for home leave, when the host asked each of us to tell about our Christian experience.

Here was Doug's story. The verse which spoke to him was Revelation 3:20. A man from an overseas organization, the Christian Sunday School Union (CSSU), had been having meetings at the Missionary Children's School in Murree. Doug's little testimony that night was that this man had presented Revelation 3:20, and Doug had believed it. I was near to tears as I heard what I had waited to hear, not for a very long time, but for assurance that if anything should happen to me, I felt my children were safe in God's care.

While on our second home leave from Pakistan, our children again became active in the youth groups of Highland Baptist Church where Carlton held pre-baptism classes. Elizabeth and Doug wanted to be baptized, and Carlton said they could. But Jim, age nine, also wanted to be baptized with them. Carlton said as a rule he did not allow children that young to be baptized, but after he questioned Jim, he was convinced Jim understood. They were all baptized together. They considered this their church for many years. This church was also very supportive when Doug was attacked when we returned from Pakistan for the final time in 1968.

Camp Joy

During this home leave, I volunteered to help at a summer camp run by several churches while Richard visited our supporting churches and attended to mission business.

Summer camping and kids go together like ketchup on French fries, but sometimes the match doesn't "taste" as good as what we get in the fast-food restaurant. I should have been forewarned as I drove in the dirt lane that led to the site, but I had recently returned from a third world country overseas and didn't think I would be facing a third world country experience in my home area.

It would take a few years before I found that last night of a difficult camping week was worth every single moment in those rustic conditions of that old campground. I would rehearse the story many times to remind others it is not always the more modern, more expensive places in life where the angels in Heaven would find reason to rejoice. Even I did not realize what joy that camping experience would become for me.

It was the first summer of operation for this camp. As I turned off the highway and started down the dirt road, I saw the newly marked sign, "Camp Joy." I noticed fields grown up, no longer cultivated. I wondered who had owned this property. It seemed to have been neglected for a long time, unattended farm-land, just weeds growing behind the fence along the road.

Three small Baptist churches had put their funds together and purchased the site. The debris had been cleared from around the cabins, but there had been no time for refurbishing the little cabins. They were anxious to get started, believing God had opened a door. I was invited to be the "Mom" for little girls, and the missionary speaker for the week. My husband was visiting some of our churches. My sister and her family would keep our small children.

I never knew the history of when nor why this campground was founded, only that these three churches had a vision for a camp ministry. One of the pastors knew my husband and me; his church people in Virginia had been supporting us. The pastors wanted a missionary speaker for the week. I was asked if I could be there to speak and help care for the children. As a mother of small children, I felt qualified for that job, and hoped I could be a missionary challenge to the young people.

There was no one outside when I drove in. I sat in the car for a few minutes, then got out and walked around, just letting my mind unravel some of what might have been in the past. Had it been a place where churches in the 1920s or 1930s met before the dark days of the depression? If so, the grounds would have reverberated with praises as they sang the Songs of Zion and were refreshed with Bible studies and preaching.

I exercised my memory. The picture of a meeting under a grape arbor in a country area of my hometown came to mind. I was about 16 years old at the time, a committed Christian, and very desirous of having that spiritual renewal. Not all God's bless-ings come in a beautiful sanctuary. Some come as we walk through the fields in our lives. I thought of how country people got together to celebrate God's creation and beauty without the need for an air-conditioned auditorium.

Some of the counselors saw me and came outside to ex-tend an invitation of welcome and point me to my cabin. I pulled my luggage from the trunk of the car. I had not brought much, just the bare essentials, a couple changes of clothes, soap and towel, a few extras. I had not thought to include a raincoat and umbrella.

As I stepped up to enter the cabin, I noticed the screen door was off kilter, meaning a squirrel or small animal could also pay a visit. On the inside, it could be pulled tight and hooked. There was no other door. The floor had been swept clean; the lumpy bunk bed mattresses had clean coverings. There was a sense of peace as though God had brought me here for a ministry. I needed that reassurance. The week would be a huge challenge.

It was not the children who would be the challenge. It was the wet weather and the rustic conditions of the old camp. The cloudy, dripping skies would compete for the fun of making this Camp Joy.

The churches had wanted to put together a memorable time for the children. The staff had planned the details, laying out a wonderful program. A week of rain will do a lot to wash the ink off the planning board, and we had it. We could not escape the drips. The rain meant leaky roofs, muddy clothes and shoes, slippery paths as we went from one building to another and wet beds and bedding when we needed to put the children in for the night.

By the time the week was over, I was happy for the assurance I could go home and use the washer and dryer to clean my muddied clothes. The week had been a challenge comparable to any I had living in the third world country. The challenge had been met, and the difficulties overcome, but I was glad I was going back home. I was glad for the washer and dryer at home. My muddied clothes would again be clean.

The little girls and I walked downhill together, trying to be careful not to slide on the muddy wet ground. We all sat on wet logs or benches near the river. Someone had managed to find dry wood and the fire warmed our bodies as well as our spirits. We were thankful it was not raining. We sang the choruses we had been learning all week. Some of the older children spoke and a final message was given. The speaker asked for commitments or recommitments of the children's lives to Christ. Several children made professions of faith that night, tossing a small stick in the fire as a token of remembrance.

As we started back up the hill after the service, a nine-year-old, one of my little girls, caught up with me and said, "Mrs. Thompson, I have never asked Jesus to come into my heart." I felt depleted of energy, just wanted to get the kids to bed and get to bed myself, knowing that in the morning, I had to be sure everything was sorted out, the kids had all their belongings and were packed up, ready for their parents. I was tempted to say you have a good pastor, go home and talk to him! But I knew I could not do that. Instead, I told her as soon as I got everyone in bed, we would talk about it. We did and she received Christ that night. I would not know for some years the part I played in her life by explaining to her that night God's plan of salvation.

When we woke up the next morning, the sun was shining. It was bright and beautiful and both staff and campers were exulting in its warmth and ability to dry us out. We worked together to sort out and pack up our things and leave the cabins in order, then checked to pick up any trash left on the grounds. Parents began arriving and I said goodbye to my little group of girls as they left for home, hoping the memories would continue to encourage their Christian experience. I began the long drive home; happy I was not driving in the rain and that a washer and dryer awaited my muddy clothes. My husband would soon be back, and our children returned to me from staying at "Aunt Leny's," for sure, spoiled a little by all the attention she and Uncle Howard always gave them.

There was a good feeling to know we had finished with an experience of God's gracious care in the midst of what we termed "difficulties." The kids had learned Bible stories and been kept from harm and danger. The rainy weather that had dampened our clothes and bedding did not seem to have dampened their spirits. They excitedly displayed papers and tiny mementoes of what they had made and done during their camp time. Next year, the cabins would be in better shape and with the vision these pastors had, there would be blessing on the future of this Camp ministry. I would not be back at this camp again. We were scheduled to return overseas to Pakistan in the fall.

****

But that is not the end of this story. Fast forward to the mid 1970s.

Pastor Buddy Arnold, whom we had known from the church in Fredericksburg, Virginia, was one of the three pastors who had gotten the camp started. His church had supported us while we were in Pakistan. He was now pastor of a church in Ottawa, Canada. We had been back in the US for eight years due to a medical situation. We had a new commission and were ready to head out for Iran. The invitation to come and speak in the Missionary Conference of the Metropolitan Church, "The MET", in Ottawa, was very special. To meet with this pastor and his wife Gaye was another link of encouragement we needed before leaving the USA.

The conference was a week long, and started on a Saturday night. The featured speakers for the opening were John and Jennifer Brown. John was Canadian. This was his home church. Jennifer was the first speaker. She reached out to everyone in a delightful way as she shared her excitement about the ministry God had given her. Hearing her freshness made me wonder if I had ever come across to my audiences as that enthusiastic about the work into which God had called me. I needed what she had to say. The past eight years had been very difficult. I felt dried out. I needed the renewal this younger missionary was bringing to me. We heard more from both these young people during the week. God had given them a great joy in their ministry.

On Thursday night, the Browns and we were invited to have dinner with Pastor and Mrs. Arnold. Jennifer and I sat on the couch in the sunroom. I asked her to tell me about herself. Her testimony about the work they had been doing was refreshing, providing a new impetus for me and the new ministry to which we were going.

She then asked me to tell her about myself. I remember feeling a little intimidated. After hearing her excitement, I didn't feel I could match it. I had been a primary speaker about missions in many groups, but I sat wondering if I had ever infused in my audiences the excitement about missions that Jennifer was bringing into my life at this moment.

I started by saying there was not much to tell. I ended up describing more about our life than I had planned. I recounted our missionary experiences in Pakistan and other events that had transpired since, telling her about our trails and discouragements. I told about our family members.

Suddenly, she stopped me and said, "You are not going to believe this, you are just not going to believe this!"

I said, "Tell me; I am gullible, I believe everything."

She said, "You led me to Christ!"

I said, "I *don't* believe you!"

She then sang the Pakistani song I had taught the children in the summer camp when the rainy days had discouraged us, "*Raja Yesu Aya*." She remembered all of it! It means "King Jesus has come..." (...to bring us salvation.) How often are God's gentle blessings hidden in what we think are the difficult or wearing times in our lives?

We shared this memorable experience with the mission conference. When the conference was over, I was ready to go to Iran with a renewed vision and a lifted spirit, remembering the testimony of a little girl who came to Christ during a rainy week and a difficult rustic camp situation.

After we retired and were living in western North Carolina, John searched our whereabouts and got in touch with us. It was a surprise to answer the phone from someone in Canada. He asked if I would make a tape to greet Jennifer on her 40th birthday. I very happily told the story about a rainy, muddy week and the sunshine that came about because of taking time that night to tell a young child how to give her heart to Jesus. Any missionary ministry I have had in Christian Camps has been worth the time, patience, energy, and funds, but this one brought a special blessing with even more eternal rewards.

We have stayed in touch. John is now the Canadian General Director of what we used to call the Africa Inland Mission. Jennifer is a nurse, and their sons all have outstanding ministries of their own. There is always a reward for service in God's harvest fields. They await the harvester and harvesting.

Returning to Pakistan

During the Christmas season of 1963, as our second home leave was nearing its end, our hearts were more than ever tuned to the land of our calling, where for millions there was no joy of the salvation offered through our Savior, Jesus Christ, whose birth we commemorated during this special holiday season. The people of Pakistan did not know God's unspeakable gift. Thus, with visas in hand, immunizations underway, barrels for packing ordered, final preparations for our return for another term in Pakistan had begun.

We sailed out of New York in February 1964 aboard the Cunard Lines ship *Carinthia*. While in New York we were able to visit and stay with some of Richard's relatives. It was such a blessing to me as I was exhausted from all the preparations! The trip on the ship was not very pleasant; the ship was not very clean, and the food was not very good. Just as during the return trip from our first home leave, there was a very bad storm in the Atlantic on this crossing and we had the news that a British freighter had sank as a result! Once again, God brought us through that storm, and we arrived in England safe and sound.

We had a lovely visit in England with an almost 80-year-old woman and her daughter with whom we stayed. Her zeal at 80 almost put us to shame. What a lighthouse she was! Although we saw some of the usual tourist sights, I am not great on tramping around just to see sights. Mrs. Rush and the experiences she had during the war were more interesting to me than the British Museum and Westminster Abbey!

The second ship out of England was nicer and we enjoyed it more, but the weather was not very pleasant. There were only a couple of really warm days, and even Port Said, Egypt and Aden, Saudi Arabia were cool. In Port Said, people were wearing winter clothing, and even in January I had not seen that before. We went through a part of the Suez Canal in the daylight hours which is always an interesting experience.

We arrived in Karachi on March 17th but were not able to go through Customs because it was after closing time. We were allowed off the ship and Richard went to find some independent Baptist missionary friends with whom we planned to stay. While he was gone, friends of ours from Rawalpindi, who were now living in Karachi, came aboard. We were so surprised and had a nice visit with them! The next morning, we all got off and went to the Customs office (really more of shed) where we were met by the missionary friends—the Montgomerys. Ruth took the kids which was a big help! Richard and I waited at Customs until the line was almost clear. Kipling's poem, "Rushing the East" takes on new significance when one comes face to face with the subject! One does not rush. After the line was almost clear, they came to us and our sixty-nine pieces of baggage. Some of it was for the school and some for the large hospital in Lahore.

We could not get reservations for the 1000-mile train trip to go "up country" until the next day. We finally arrived in Rawalpindi where we were met by some of the TEAM missionaries who had brought our old faithful '52 pickup truck and Caleb Cutherell with his Land Rover for the trip to Murree where we would be staying while the kids were in boarding school. We arrived with poor baby David crying his eyes out. We had not been able to find baby cereal in either Karachi or Rawalpindi. Luckily the next day we found some tins of Farex brand cereal in Murree. David was soon switched to eating Pakistani-style cream of wheat and buffalo milk! Elizabeth had gotten very sick on the train; thank God for good medicine and she was soon on the mend!

Living at "The Shelter"

In May 1964, our Field Council voted to station us in Abbottabad and a suitable house, called "The Shelter" was found. It was an old, old house built by the British, but adequate for our family. The mud walls were plastered and whitewashed, as they were in all the better houses of that time and may still be, although houses built by the Mission are of much sturdier construction. The poor people did not usually whitewash their homes. The walls

The "Shelter" in Abbottabad, about 1965.

of the mud houses were as smooth as if they had plaster board on them, very convenient, for when a chunk of the plaster fell off, as it often did when it dried out, we could always send to the bazaar and get a couple of men who would repair it at a small cost.

The house was probably built for the British military who were in charge of the frontier. My guess is, it was an officer's home, but I could not verify that. These old houses were few in the city; knowing their history would have been delightful but I knew no one to ask.

The high ceilings in these old bungalows were meant to carry the heat up high to provide more comfort during the blasts of the summer sun. Cement floors, often covered with a rough *chatai*, rope-like, matting, and a tin roof were the order of the day. The living room had a fireplace with some nice wainscoting and a chair rail. The house arrangement left me wondering just how the house was used, by whom, and when. It had been bought earlier by a Christian businessman when it was rented to us. We were so thankful that it was big enough for our big family, which now had grown into five children.

The one scary thing we faced was earth tremors. Fortunately, they were mostly in the daytime, although one took place in the early evening. When the house shook, it dropped down mud chunks. Once I swept up a wash pan full of it.

The designs had been carefully calculated to minimize the heat of the summer sun. Although we were 3500 feet in these foothills of the Himalayans, the summers were still hot and sometimes humid. We always welcomed the winter sun in our mostly unheated houses. It was called "the poor man's heat." When constructed, the NS/EW positioning of the houses was done to take into account the winter cold and the summer heat. A glassed-in sunporch at the back of the house was a warm and cozy place to be in the chill of winter.

It had four large rooms and some smaller ones. It was fronted by an L shaped veranda, with a screened in porch on the short side of the L, and a kitchen on the other side. The kitchen had a 30 inch or so high cement block, about 24 inches wide, with a drain, for washing dishes. Our stove and tin oven were placed on an old table, nearby. We had a *"dolie,"* a screen enclosed small cabinet where we kept the vegetables. The large open drain for releasing the dish water made a lovely entrance for some very fat, large and feisty rats, not mice, and I would hear the sound and run with my shoe. They could jump up very high, but I almost always got them before they got away. There were no traps available.

The front door led into our dining room. Apparently, it had been used by the last owners or renters for cooking. Almost the whole floor was coated in grease! I scrubbed it nine times— yes, nine times-- to clean it and then used a mix of chemicals (with shellac) a furniture maker in the bazaar suggested for going over it instead of the usual painting of it. After a few washings, the "paint" cracked and actually made it look a bit like a marble floor! We had a nice large blue area rug and used white nubby material for drapes for the outside doors and also the door into the bedroom.

To the left of the dining room and adjoining the kitchen was our dinette. There was just enough room for a table, chairs, a small dish cabinet and the big refrigerator.

On the screen porch side of it was our special "guest" living room. Pakistani custom decreed having a "*baitak*" for entertaining guests. It was made into a nice living room, suitable not only for entertaining the western ladies who lived in the area, and came as my guests, but for the *khans* (tribal chiefs and other men) who visited Richard.

On one side of the house was a deep ravine, on the other, a long driveway wound around to the front part, with the servant's room and an old garage building facing it. I recall one time, my son Doug had been saying, "I can drive" this lane, so one day, as we drove home, I stopped the truck as we entered and told him, "OK, you can show me!" He was just 15, and with my heart in my throat—the sides of the lane were heavily wooded—I let him! He made it just fine and became a good driver later when he got his permit.

1965 Conflict

It should surprise no one that conflicts regarding Pakistan's borders would arise since the country had been formed from dividing land from India. Unfortunately, just such a conflict reared its ugly head in August and September 1965 during our third term.

We had some sort of inkling from the local newspapers that something was brewing, but were not sure what, when we went to Mangla to visit another missionary couple for the weekend. We had arrived back in Murree the afternoon of September 6. (We were staying in Murree at the time since the kids were in boarding school.) The trip from Mangla was hot and tiring—about five hours—and we were exhausted when we got to Murree, so we all slept soundly that night. The next morning, we got news that Rawalpindi, 37 miles away, had been bombed. Apparently, the Indian forces had been aiming for the airport, but missed by a few miles. We learned that six people had been killed in the attack. Although we had a couple of alerts following this, there was nothing more in our area. The odd thing was that according to the Pakistani radio and news service, India had still not declared war!

A few weeks later, we learned that there was heavy fighting in the Lahore and Sialkot areas. That was some 250 or more miles from us in Murree, and it seemed Murree was as safe a place as any to be just then. The children could not have been more nonchalant about the matter and continued in school.

We experienced nightly blackouts, so we had been going to bed with the birds! It made me realize how powerful light is; I got such a spiritual lesson and blessing from the thought. The 75-watt bulb was not trying to shine light of itself, but out of every crack it came, and I thought of how we are the light of Christ, and even when it seems we are not very bright lights because of circumstances, still we can shine! How wonderful is the Word of God in dark times!

The ayah who helped me in Murree during that time was from Rawalpindi; she herself was a Kashmiri who came to Pakistan after partition. She was very concerned about her family and she decided to make the move home. Her name was Daryai, but David (about two years old) called her "Dolly." Although she had no children of her own, she really took to David and when she came to say goodbye, she just hugged and kissed him. Afterward, David kept asking "Where's Dolly?"

Our mission had advised us all to stay put, and not to be out any more than necessary, which I thought was the height of wisdom. Although we had heard that persons of our nationality were "persona non grata," we personally had no incidents. Any officers we saw treated us with respect. The parents in Murree held daily prayer meetings and news cast "gatherings" and we made great use of the 12-cup coffee pot my sister had given me!

Our mission had also planned in case we might need to be evacuated and cautioned us what to put in our letters home (possibly being censored) and to be sympathetic to the feelings of all Pakistanis during that time of national crisis. In the event we needed to be evacuated ("evaporated" as one young missionary child innocently called it!), the mission planned to keep everyone together as much as possible, and if the doors to Pakistan were closed, to seek to enter a similar mission work amongst Muslims in another country. Fortunately, that plan never needed to be put into action!

Even after the fighting, travel was somewhat restricted outside of our district; we had to check in and out with the police, which was not difficult, but somewhat time-consuming. Our mission also decided to hold our Annual Conference in October which had been postponed because of the fighting. Since I was Field Secretary that year, I had much work—reports to stencil and mimeographs to distribute—in preparation.

A few months after the emergency, our missionary work—at the hospital, school, and evangelism—were back to full-force! "Behold I have set before you an open door, and no man can shut it" (Revelation 3:8). Not even the forces of a horrible thing like war can shut the door God opens!

Ministry Through Serving

During this term, I had several opportunities to serve in Murree. One concerned the boarding hostel at the school there. God had laid the burden on my heart to help raise funds for some much-needed furnishings for the hostel. I prayed much about it and then sent out letters. After I had sent the letters, I had awful misgivings thinking that we would never get enough funds from missionaries. But God! The deadline to raise the 5,000 rupees (about $1000 at the time) I had set as our goal came and we counted 5, 214 rupees! Praise! The money came in and I asked two missionary friends to help with identifying what needed to be ordered. We contracted with a furniture maker in Rawalpindi to have the furnishings made.

In 1967, the Murree Christian School organized an "International Evening" in conjunction with the Centenary Celebrations sponsored by the Murree Municipal Committee. The event was an opportunity to showcase the international flavor of Murree. In addition to the locals and those from the Christian school, participants included nationals from Germany, Holland, Canada, the UK, France, Ireland and the US. Participants gathered to portray their culture and traditions and sample dishes from each nation.

The vice principal of the school highlighted the various cultural and social activities of the community who had settled there since 1848. He emphasized "international understanding" and the relationship between nations and communities. He also recalled the past contributions and associations of the Christian community in Murree. As one local newspaper article writer stated when writing about the event, "They were all foreigners but not strangers in Murree, as they have lived in this place and loved it just like their own home and, as somebody put it 'sweet home.'"

I had been asked to be on the committee and to head up the food arrangement. It was to be a "potluck" dinner and I had told everyone to please make sure their names where on the dishes they brought, and I would see that they were returned. In the midst of this, I noticed one lovely dish had not been touched. The reason? Lucy Hamm had prominently displayed the word "Hamm" on the front of her dish and Muslims do not eat pork!

For my efforts, I received a kind letter from Mohmmad Arif, the Chairman of the Murree Municipal Committee, which read:

"Today we bow before Allah gratefully that our ambitious and comprehensive programme of the Centenary Celebrations of Municipal Committee, Murree, has come to a successful end. This all-embracing programme which commenced on 23rd June, 1967 with the inauguration of Bagh-e-Shaheedan, drew applause from all quarters in the

174

country and was highly appreciated by all those who happened to attend our functions.

Please let me express my deep appreciation and gratitude for your cooperation and the dedication and high sense of responsibility with which you helped me in organizing this programme. The occasion has brought all sections in this Sub-Division nearer to each other and a new era of mutual understanding, co-operation and good will has ushered in. Let me once again thank you for your contribution to the success of the programme. I assure you that I shall always fondly recall our happy association during this venture."

Ministry Through Education

During this term, I also had several opportunities to use education as a means of serving in ministry. One summer, I served as the assistant Sunday School Superintendent in Murree and in the fall taught English to four classes at the Abbottabad Christian School.

I also counted it a rare privilege to speak to various women's groups. During one women's retreat, a good-sized group of about twenty-five women met together and I spoke on the book of Philippians. At the third meeting, feeling very much constrained to turn the meeting over to prayer, I spoke briefly to the women on the need for consecration from Philippians 3. Who can say what God did that morning? One after another the women poured out their hearts to God for about fifty minutes. There were prayers of penitence, of confession, and many things were made right. Later, when I visited the area and met with these women for a few minutes of Bible study and prayer, it was obvious that God had been, and was still, at work.

On another occasion, during a meeting of the Murree Christian Fellowship, I spoke on Heaven from Revelation 21 and

22. One of the nurses who attended seemed to be intently following every word and looking up each reference. I had also invited our cook's wife to attend. Two of her relatives, who were Muslim, had come to visit just as the meeting was starting, so they were also invited. When the meeting was over, they said they wanted to have the cook's wife come and explain all this to them, for this Bible view of Heaven was such a new view. The cook's wife went a few days later; one woman was very interested, but the other was scornful. But they invited the wife to come again and to bring the missionaries to talk about spiritual things! And while there was no opportunity for my further interaction with these women relatives, the seeds had been planted!

Trekking Into "No Man's Land"

Richard once again continued his treks and made contact with the leaders and men in the surrounding villages. I was fortunate to have one opportunity to see some of this area first-hand during our third term.

Richard in Pakistan, ~1966. I often joked he could pass for a native!

In the outreaches and on the border of Pakistan is an area called tribal territory. It is not under the authority of any government; it is ruled by its own people. Getting into it without an invitation is both dangerous and very difficult. There, the people have authority over themselves, and they rule by the gun. It was never a part of any country.

Dr. Phyllis and Russ Irwin, and their little daughter, had invited Richard and me to go along with them on a medical mission into tribal territory. Russ would drive his VW bus as far as he

176

could, over roads that were usually only traveled by jeep, and we would have to walk the rest of the way. After seeing those roads, there was no question but that this would be a very unusual trip, at least for me. Richard was used to this kind of travel, but I was not, so I was excited about going. We knew we would be staying overnight, but not even a toothbrush went with us, although Phyllis had her medical bag, and we did have a camera!

TEAM's Bach Christian Hospital in Qalandarabad, about ten miles from our HQ station at Abbottabad, had received patients from many miles away, some walking 25 miles or more, sometimes carrying people on rope beds, sometimes on their backs. The hospital system when we were there was to have patients queue up early in the morning, each receiving a number. When there were too many to be seen in a day, many who came a distance would stay overnight so as to be the first in line the next day. Of course, the very sick ones would be seen. Often, the patients were too far gone by the time they came to the hospital, because for various reasons, it was a "last resort" for the families.

Through this outreach, the doctors were sometimes invited to go to the villages, and this was the case for Dr. Phyllis and Russ. One of the men, probably a chief (*khan*) of the area, wanted Dr. Phyllis to come and treat the people of the village because it was too difficult to get them all to the hospital. That had to be significant; it showed the status of the *khan* in being able to offer the invitation, but it also showed the confidence Phyllis had inspired in the man or men of this territory.

On the given day, we left, Russ driving his VW bus as far as he could. At least at one point, maybe more, the road was so

Russ Irwin driving his VW bus up the mountain road into tribal territory. At one point, Phyllis and I got out of the bus to watch!

narrow that we got out of the bus and stood watching, I am not sure if it was because we feared our extra weight might cause the bus to topple or if we felt we would only lose one person if it did go over! How often God protected us in those days!

At some point, we left the bus and set out on foot, climbing over rocky terrain and edging our way along very narrow footpaths which had steep drops down the sides of the mountains. It was about eight miles of walking. When we got into this "no man's land", a "guard" armed with rifles and bullets met us to ensure our safety and took us on into the area where we were to stay, and where Dr. Phyllis would see and treat patients. By this time, I think it was probably late afternoon. I am sure they fed us a meal; tribal people are also hospitable people.

Trekking into tribal territory with our "guards."

The stream of patients began, one after another, with Dr. Phyllis prescribing, or suggesting the patient be brought to the hospital. One of the first to be seen was a small boy. Dr. Phyllis did not think the child would survive the night, and just before we went to sleep, she got the word that the child had died.

It was about 11:00 when she saw the last patients. Then, *charpais*—wooden bed frames strung with woven grass rope— were brought into the same room, and thick cotton comforters were spread over them. We were given comforters to keep us warm. One of the men guarded the door by sleeping on a *charpai* across the doorway.

The next day, we were served some breakfast and we started on our way back, again with an armed guard. Along the way, Phyllis stopped and talked to people who needed medical

Dr. Phyllis Irwin, far left, Richard and I being served tea in the remote, tribal area.

help. At one point, I was dragging behind, probably from the sore muscles I was experiencing! Some of the women grabbed me and pulled me into their courtyard and started talking to me in their language, which I did not understand. I admit to feeling a little frightened, as I knew the others were ahead of me, so I pulled myself loose and using my adrenaline, ran to catch up. My sore muscles were suddenly no problem for me!

The area itself, once we got into it, was beautiful. The corn seemed to be about as "high as an elephant's eye"—at least six or seven feet, with beautiful ears on every stalk. Everything was lush and green, suggesting a wise use of land and good crops.

At a certain point on our return, our escorts pointed out where they had shot two *dacoits* (robbers) a day or two before we went in. This area is heavily guarded by the men.

The pictures we took show us fording a river. I must admit that it felt good to get into that water. We were all hot and stinky from perspiration, and dusty from the dry paths on which we walked.

Phyllis and I fording a river in the tribal area.

****

As I have reflected on those days and reminisced over the pictures, the strange thing is that we were not frightened by all those guns and bullets. We knew it was their way of life, and we and they accepted it. When Richard trekked, all he took was a Bible and an umbrella—and some chocolate fudge, if I could get sugar (it was rationed) to make it. His complaint was that he had to share it and the people all liked it! However, it was his little contribution to their delicious curry and rice dinners, which they so willingly shared.

God is good, the memories are rich and whatever was accomplished, we pray it paved the way for an entrance into the hearts of the people. We will not know this side of Heaven what God had been doing in answer to our prayers.

May the Lord of the Harvest raise up many who will accept the challenge. We know He is doing that, and we praise Him for it. The Irwins' daughter is one of those. She is making a great impact.

The times have changed and our time in Pakistan has only been a memory since we left in 1968, but the imprint on our hearts and minds is still with us. We thank God for those days and that privilege of serving Him there.

Time for School: The Lessons Begin

Just as He did to the Old Testament people, God changed how my husband and I had expected to live, which was to spend our lives in Pakistan. That had been where we first felt God was leading us, but we were allowed to sojourn there for less than eighteen years only. It was a great disappointment when our residential permit was not renewed, and we had to leave. Surely, I thought, God has made a mistake, and I reminded Him of it. We had studied and learned the language and gotten to understand the culture. It was our third term; we were finally prepared to do

180

the ministry to which we felt called. I believed God could and would change the outcome, but He did not.

From October 1967 until June 1968, we were under police surveillance and in and out of court. We would appear when told the case would be heard only to find the judge couldn't make it. When the case was finally before the judge, he said we were accused of being in the country illegally. Richard said that was not correct. We had a legal and up to date visa. The outcome of the case was that we could stay until June when Elizabeth graduated from High School. That was actually a leftover from the British rule. They did not move their families until the school year was over. We would have to prepare for a new future. Faith had just encountered its first real bump in the road.

Compounding the situation with our permits was my health. In August 1967 I became ill while filling in as a "housemother" at the Christian boarding school in Murree and was clinically diagnosed with amoebic hepatitis. Because it was of the amoebic variety, it was not infectious, but it took everything out of me! There were six weeks of recuperation for that and then we moved back down to Abbottabad, where another "bug" hit me— a staphylococcal infection of the intestines! That took another two months of recuperation. December brought a brief respite, but in January I went to the large Christian Hospital in Lahore for extensive medical tests. The doctor changed my medication and steady progress was the result. And in March 1968, I was again asked to return to Murree as a "housemother." The doctor felt the change would be good, and so I went. Although Richard's heart was on "trek" he had to remain in Abbottabad because of our situation. Still, Richard and I praised the Lord for His goodness and His nearness to us in those trying days.

＊＊＊＊＊＊＊＊＊＊＊＊＊＊

It was October of 1967, time to register for our "Extension of Stay" permit so we would be prepared for returning after our planned home leave. We applied and received word that it was not granted. We could not believe it. We had been in the country for seventeen years; they knew who we were, we were sure this must be a mistake. It was not. We were told we had to leave immediately. When we did not, we were summoned into court and charged with being in the country illegally. In court, we said we were "not guilty" because we had a valid visa. Other court days were scheduled. We attended but found them cancelled because a necessary official or paper was not on hand. In the meantime, our Field Chairman, Paul Lundgren, and Richard continued to pursue the matter, even arranging an interview with President Mohammad Ayub Khan and some other high officials in the country, all who were cordial, but said they could do nothing.

The only charge we knew against us was that we were "overzealous evangelistic missionaries," but Richard was also charged with having been on a road that was being constructed, which today is called "The Silk Road." This road had been written about in the local newspapers. It was being built to connect with China, which borders Pakistan. While on that road, Richard had met with the *Wali* of Swat, who had granted him permission to pass through the area. Swat State is a beautiful area where we had a short vacation one year. The head of the state, called the *Wali*, had been to our mission's hospital for his family's medical problems. On one occasion when his son's wife was about to give birth, she came into the hospital just as I was leaving. She knew who I was, and that I had sons. When she was ready to deliver, she knew it would be a son, because I was a good "omen"! (I believe she had a boy, so I must have been!)

Shortly after we were told to leave, we heard of two other missionary families who had been told to leave. Later, we believed we three may have been "test cases." It seems some in the government wanted to be rid of missionaries. Of the three couples who had been targeted, we were in the Northwest Frontier Province part of the country, in Abbottabad; one couple was down south in Sindh Province, and the third couple lived in Karachi. Also, we were under three different missions. The couple in Karachi left immediately. The couple down south knew a high official in their village, the then foreign minister Zulfiqar Ali Bhutto, and he was able to get their permit changed. Richard tried, but was unsuccessful in pleading our case.

We did, however, get an extension of stay; permission was granted for us to remain in the country until after Elizabeth's high school graduation in June, so we began to make our plans, while still hoping things would change for us. Such important events as graduations were honored in Pakistan and work or military transfers were delayed when there was a good reason and schooling was one of those.

In December of that year, we returned from a Christmas celebration the children of Abbottabad Christian School were

Akbar and Richard, ~1966.

having. When we got to the backyard of our house, we saw two policemen, standing and talking to our cook, Akbar, the only one at the house. Knowing we were leaving, and he would have to search for work, Akbar had already moved his wife, Sarvar Jan, and children back to a village to live. It was a good arrangement; Jean Soderman was living nearby and would mentor her.

The police were there to deliver a summons for Akbar to go to the Office of the Superintendent of Police and for Richard to go to the Office of the District Magistrate. Just a few days earlier, we had gotten a postcard from Jean, saying Sarvar was going to be baptized. However, before we got the postcard, we ourselves had known nothing of these plans, since she was not living at our house and we did not know exactly where she was! Apparently, the police had intercepted the postcard and knew all about what was planned. At the Police Station, Akbar was told the

183

baptism would incite a riot and it was likely someone could be killed. Richard was told if it was going to happen, it should happen in some other place where she was unknown; otherwise, there would likely be trouble. Even today, I don't know if nor when the baptism took place.

We were nearing the time when we would be giving up the house. Akbar had left to try to find work further down south, in the Punjab. He wanted to learn to drive a bulldozer. Richard was out somewhere; I was alone, continuing the packing. I happened to look out and saw a nicely dressed young man standing outside. I went out to ask if I could help him. He asked, "Where's Akbar?" Thinking he might be a friend, I said he had moved out, since we were leaving. He wanted to know where and I said I did not know, "down south, somewhere." There may have been another question or two, and then, "Did Sarvar Jan get baptized?" I knew then he must be from the CID—Central Intelligence Department—so I asked, "Are you from the CID? Because if you are, I will answer your questions. We are in your country as guests." He then showed me his ID badge and again asked some questions. I answered what I could. He then started to leave, whereupon I said, "Just a minute; I have not given you permission to go; I have something I want to tell you!" The moment I started my conversation, he must have known where it was going, because he said he did not want to discuss anything more with me. But I reminded him I had "not given permission *(ijazat*, an important social custom)" for him to leave.

It was then that he stood and listened as I told him my story. The best I can recall, it was like this: I said, "If a person comes to me and says he (or she) has a heavy burden of guilt on his back and does not know how to rid himself of it, and how the person has sought but not found peace, I tell them how I got rid of my guilt, of how I found peace." We talked about how many good works we would need to balance the bad ones and how there are not enough good works to do that and how when I came to Christ, I found forgiveness for sin, and peace, and now I no longer live with that burden. There was more; then I said, "If you have questions, I may be able to answer them; otherwise, you have *ijazat.*" He then left, and I went inside the house and prayed for him. I would see him again, but this time, I would know his agenda.

We moved out of "The Shelter" and up to Murree, to await Elizabeth's graduation and our trip back to the US. That first Sunday, as we sat in the Anglican Church where the missionaries met, regardless of their denominational affiliation, I saw a Scottish missionary, Ken, walk in with this CID man. The man and I looked each other right in the eye. I made a slight nod of my head; I felt sure he recognized me. I whispered to Richard, "He is from the CID" and Richard said, with something of a slight smirk, "How do you know!" I said he was the guy who came asking about Akbar.

As we left the church, I caught up with Evelyn, a friend of Ken and his wife Kathleen, and asked if she knew who the man was. She said she did not, but he was a man who had been "enquiring." I said, "He is from the CID." Evelyn thought for a minute and said, "You know, he has been coming to Ken for a long time, "studying" with him, asking questions, but any time Ken mentions baptism, the man says he is not ready just yet! She said she would pass on the info to Ken. We left Murree the day after graduation, which I think was June 8th, and went to Rawalpindi for the first lap of our trip to the U.S. Some friends, including the Zafar Saliks, were there to see us off. It was a sad day for us.

****

At this writing, I can look back and see although the roads were not clear, it was essential for us to keep walking. I needed to learn that faith is trusting God to do His work in His own way. When we do that, it becomes the substance of things hoped for, the evidence of that which may not immediately be seen but is promised to us. To be able to trust God and not be disappointed when the answer does not come, or when the answer is not what I wanted, is true faith. On several occasions, God dealt specifically with me in answer to my prayers when I poured out my heart to Him for something that seemed right to me. But God did not always answer my prayer the way I wanted it answered. At other times, He answered in a unique and wonderful way, and I was encouraged in my faith.

I was once again reminded of one of the verses given to us by the dear elderly British missionary lady we met aboard the ship on our first trip to Pakistan.

"The Lord Thy God in the midst of thee is mighty;
He will save; He will rejoice over thee with joy."
(Zephaniah 3:17)

It would become my "security blanket" during those years. God was in the midst of us. He was mighty, He would protect us; we would attempt to live so that He could rejoice over us because of what He wanted to do through us.

But we would not see for many, many years the fruit for which we yearned. Today, we know there *was* fruit although it is the younger missionaries who were able to harvest it. Heaven alone will someday reveal what God was doing by giving us these experiences. God is different from us. He is Infinite, illimitable, able to do "exceedingly abundantly above all we can ask or think." He has done that for us.

A Season In God's Waiting Room

"Many are the afflictions of the righteous,
But the Lord delivereth you out of them all."
(Psalm 34:19)

"For if you forgive others their offenses, your heavenly Father
will forgive you as well." (Matthew 6:14)

Seventeen years after learning the language and feeling culturally secure, our extension of stay permit in Pakistan was denied. We were told we had to leave the country immediately. Devastated, in and out of court and under surveillance 24/7, we worked to get the order changed. Doubt began digging a trench in my faith. I wondered if my faith had been built on a sand hill. I could not understand why God should choose this path for us. 'Midst tears of sadness and goodbyes, we made plans to return to the US.

The Return Journey

Richard made the return travel plans while I packed up our house. He had spent his early years in India and had been around the world more than once. He had also seen so much of the world in his Navy days in the Pacific. He wanted his children to be able to say they had been around the world, so he planned the trip with stops in Bangkok, Hong Kong, Japan, and Hawaii. We had missionary friends in some of those places and received a warm welcome as well as a place to stay.

The first lap of our trip was by plane to Bangkok. We had decided on this route so our kids could see the other half of the world, but we also wanted to see Disneyland. They had saved up money for that. As we flew over Viet Nam, I think it was, we got a good scolding from the stewardess. It was monsoon time, and the weather was terrible. The plane was bumping along and the "KEEP SEAT BELTS FASTENED" sign was staying on, but David, not quite five, had to go to the bathroom. Finally, he could not wait any longer, and we both got up to go. The stewardess immediately confronted us. I tried to explain, and she just said, "Well, hurry, and get back in your seats and put on your seat belts!" We did.

In Bangkok, we took a very interesting boat trip up the river and saw little houses, built right on the river. Most had a pot of orchids or some other flowers on the little pier at the back of the house. When we got to the end, there were masses and masses of phalaenopsis and other orchids, covering a trellis. I said I wanted my picture taken there, since it was the only time I would ever be "covered in orchids!" My picture was taken under that trellis, but I have no idea where it might be now~~sigh! I have loved orchids since I was 16 and my brother-in-law, Fred, got one for my sister, my mom and me when we visited one Easter. That night in Bangkok we saw a great show—maybe magic or something like that? Can't remember, just that it was great!

We were standing on the tarmac in Bangkok, ready to board the plane for the next lap—Hong Kong—but Richard could not find the tickets! Needless to say, it was a little scary for a few moments. There we all stood, watching as Richard searched through his pockets and his briefcase. After some minutes and while the plane waited for us, the elusive tickets were found, and we boarded the plane for Hong Kong. There we would meet missionaries and see an ancient Chinese land and people who were not only enduring, but so resourceful.

We stayed in a little "high rise" apartment, very reasonably priced and very clean, and the people who ran it were so cordial. While out for a walk, we met missionaries from the Evangelical Free Church; they were sitting in chairs out by the river, and we visited with a college friend who had a boat ministry. His boat was tied up on the river and was really like a little auditorium inside. He used it for his meetings. He gave us the name of a family we were to meet in Hawaii, but that is another part of the story!

Along the noticeably clean streets, we saw tiny shop cubicles with most anything one could want, while outside the shop, there might be a lady sitting, cooking the family meal over a single burner stove, and inside, the youngest child or the baby being watched over while family members worked in the shop. The people were all so ambitious, so busy. When we heard the tailors in Hong Kong were noted for their fine and fast work, one of the things we did was search for cloth. Dad and Doug had suits made and Elizabeth and I had dresses made. These tailors measured perfectly, and I think they sewed all night, but everything was ready on time and fit beautifully.

In Hong Kong, we boarded the American President Lines ship *ss President Wilson, en route* to Japan and from there, to a day in Hawaii. We saw in the distance "the rock" called Guam and then, the Waikiki Beach, where we were welcomed with leis.

In Hawaii a friend of a missionary met us, wanting to take us to her home for a meal. The kids wanted to stay and play on

On board the *President Wilson* on our way home from Pakistan, 1968. All our travel to and from Pakistan was aboard various ships ... it was a good thing none of us were prone to seasickness!

the beach. I still gasp when I think of that day. It is one of two times when I know without a doubt the angel of the Lord was watching our children. I did not know this lady's home was at a distance and they were left there with no money, no food and no way to get in touch with us. When we got back to them, they were hungry, exhausted and must have had some fears, but we were again together. It was an unforgettable lesson for this mom.

The other experience had been during a summer jeep trip up to Thandiani for a break from the Pakistani heat when Elizabeth, Doug and Jim were still young, maybe eight, ten, and twelve. We thought we were right at the top of this high mountain, maybe a couple turns away and the three older kids wanted to get out and run up the rest of the way. We thought it was safe and let them out. After several turns on that crooked road and not finding them, I became very concerned. One last turn and there they were! What a relief! We and the other missionaries had spent at least two times in that high mountain hangout without fear, but this summer would be a reminder of God's every present care. At the end of our stay and just as we had packed up and were leaving, one of the caretakers came to tell us a leopard had killed a horse the night before, just a short distance from these mountain cabins. Our ever-present Father God had been our watchman all those days and nights, but especially as our three small children ran up that mountain alone!

Our Joy is Overshadowed with Sadness

We arrived in Norfolk, Virginia in early July 1968, greeted by loving family and friends, covered in the warmth they provided us by their love and supplying every need, a house in Portsmouth furnished with food in the pantry, even some clothes for the children. The sadness of leaving Pakistan was left behind. It was a very joyful occasion. We knew we had to eventually make plans about our future, but it was not immediately important.

My mom and dad were at the airport. Dad, age 87, had been very ill, but had recovered enough to come with family to welcome us home. Someone said he had wanted to see us safely home. Maybe so. The memory of those first weeks in the US are somewhat dimmed. There was so much to adjust to, so many things to think about. I did try to get out to Mom and Dad's a few times, but looking back, I wish I had gone more. That is always the way when we take a backward glance at life. It is the memories that sometimes hurt us.

Shortly after I got up on August 16, the doorbell rang and there was a lovely bouquet of flowers from my husband, sent to celebrate our 19th wedding anniversary. We had breakfast and

My dad and mom on their 60th wedding anniversary, Dec 1967 just a few short months before my dad passed away.

then my sister, Evelyn called and said Mom had caller her to say Daddy had quietly slipped away. Earlier, Daddy had talked about dying and Evelyn had said something to him, which sparked a reply something like this; "Oh go on! I am old and worn out and tired, I am ready to go." Even with the many hardships he had endured, he had lived a good life.

He had "taken to his bed" those last days after we got back, and Mom kept a constant check on him, but that morning, after checking on him, she had gone out to feed the chickens. When she came back in, she immediately realized he had left her, quietly, without a struggle, without saying a word. He just went to sleep in Jesus.

I wonder now, if he had things he would have liked to say to me, had I gone out more often. I don't think I had any idea he would go so quickly after we got home to the US. I had not seen my parents as often as I should have during those hectic weeks. It is a regret I live with and review sometimes. Old age does that to us, I guess. I am not sure if it is the right thing to do.

I have asked God to reward my parents for all they did for me, for us as a family. We were never hungry and never neglected. We had all the necessities if not all the things we may have wanted. We will see him again someday. We will be together with both sets of parents then. What a wonderful assurance!

Lessons on Forgiveness

When we arrived in Portsmouth, we anticipated resting our weary heads, enfolded by family love while we planned a new future. Little did we know that deeper waters awaited us, waters in which we would need to swim to avoid going under. We had not yet adjusted when the greatest tsunami to challenge our faith would strike suddenly. Just six weeks after losing my father, we would face our next time of sadness, much deeper sadness than we had ever known. It would demand all the faith and forgiveness we could muster.

In Muslim countries, boys have more freedom than girls. The two older boys, Doug and Jim, made friends easily. They were especially at ease in conversing with the intermingling dialects spoken in our area of Pakistan. Doug was fourteen when he got his first bike. After learning the rules, we let him take some short road trips, up and down the foothills of the Himalayan Mountains, where we lived. Once when he got tired riding uphill, he hitched a ride with a Pakistani driver in a delivery truck, threw the bike in the back and they visited as they rode back to our city. He got home safely. Our kids felt free in Pakistan, could speak the language, enjoyed the people. We knew nothing of the racial tension in Portsmouth in those troubled years of the 1960s.

****

The house was quiet, still dark, as I crept down the steps the last Saturday morning in September 1968. I was anxious to have some Bible and prayer time before the family woke up. We had been back in the US less than three months. I was still recuperating from an illness, not up to par physically. The weeks before leaving Pakistan had been strenuous. Within the next few hours, I would need to see that everyone had breakfast, prepare Richard's clothes and pack his suitcase, and make a trip to the grocery store. He was catching a plane in the afternoon, going to Mission Headquarters in Chicago.

The days ahead would be busy. I would be alone, caring for the daily needs of our five children. They had been in school since the early part of September. Portsmouth, Virginia was home to me. I had family nearby. We had returned twice, each time after five years, but this time, it seemed everything was changing, all so "new" to us as we were integrating back into American society and school. I needed the reassurance of help from the Lord. I wanted to commit again to Him for His strength and guidance (Psalm 48:14).

The overstuffed old living room chair in this rented house had become my "altar," comfortable and comforting, as it held me in its faded slip covered arms. It was there I sat and read each morning, then kneeling in front of it, sought God's guidance for the day.

I was still on my knees when I heard the boys waking up. Three of the four were involved in a pillow fight, laughing, trying to "best" the other. I stopped praying and went to the kitchen, got breakfast ready, then went upstairs. I reminded the boys I was going to the store and if their rooms were cleaned, they could go with me and pick up their model airplane in a shop where it had been left for repair. My little speech was ignored, the pillow fight was continuing.

Richard was still in bed. When I went to call him, he said he woke up with a bad headache and wondered if I could go to the store for aspirin as soon as possible. The boys had gone downstairs to eat breakfast, their rooms still in a mess. I dressed and prepared to leave. They were not ready when I was. I told them they would have to wait, that I would take them in the afternoon when I took their dad to the plane. I could do the grocery shopping and they could pick up the model airplane at that time. I made a quick trip to the store and got the aspirin.

The airport was about 20 miles away. Friends had given us an older car. It was fine for local driving, but my sister Evelyn did not think I should drive it that far over a route I did not know. Her husband Howard volunteered to take Richard to the airport. I drove my husband and our two older boys to my sister's house and the two men left a short while later.

Doug, almost sixteen, and Jim, fourteen, were playing catch with the football in her back yard, not anxious to leave. They had bikes at my sister's house and asked if they could stay awhile longer and ride them home. They could make the stop to pick up the model plane. They were good kids. The route home meant riding along the main street of our city, Portsmouth, the only way to get to our house. I had no idea it would not be safe. Jim was the one closest to me when I gave them the dime "in case you need to call me." The dime, like "insurance money," was something we always gave them. He put it in his sock so as not to lose it. I said goodbye to my sister and the boys and drove away.

Sometimes we all feel time is the essence of life. On my mind was what had to be done that day. Not waiting for the boys that morning was a decision I will regret as long as I live. The life of our family would be changed forever and the tears, so many stored in God's bottle (Psalm 56), would be a constant reminder of that Saturday in September. God would wash our eyes with tears many more times in the years that have followed.

A short stop at one store, a longer one at the grocery store and my errands were complete. As I neared our home, I noticed Bob, age twelve, waiting in the driveway, no bikes in sight. I immediately felt uneasy. The minute I stopped the car, Bob said, "You're meant to call the hospital. There has been an accident and Doug is hurt." I ran into the house, tried phoning, but the hospital was not answering. I left immediately, telling Bob to keep calling and take care of David, age five. I drove as fast as I could to the hospital, hoping to see a policeman who would help me, but none was in sight.

The hospital was located on High Street. It was the only way to get to our house, a short distance from where our sons had been attacked by ten black boys who had gathered on the street corner. Doug heard one of the boys call out, "Here come two honkies! Let's get 'em!" One of them lassoed Doug, catching him around the neck with a nail-embedded rope. Another, using a bicycle chain, made a direct hit across Doug's eyes, cutting into the middle of his left eye, across his nose, and in the bottom of his right eye.

The incident took place three months before he turned sixteen. He had been waiting for that day so he could get his driver's license.

When the gang of boys later appeared in court, they testified under oath it was an unprovoked attack, that our sons had not done anything to incite them and cause the incident. They did not know our boys. Their anger was directed at white people, they said, without any further explanation. Our two sons had come along when they had the lasso and chain in their hands, and they used them to lash out at this first opportunity. We knew nothing more of what was causing their anger.

It may have been a kind of innocence which blinded us to how different our country had become. Shortly after the boys were enrolled in school, Doug was walking home alone when a small group of black boys grabbed him. He had just bought a lock for his school locker. They thought the box in his pocket was cigarettes. He told them he did not smoke. They demanded he take it out. They pushed him and left. It should have been a yellow flag signal, but it wasn't. We were about to learn the meaning of racial tensions and uncontrolled anger in America, something which at that time we had not experienced in Pakistan.

Jim was riding behind Doug and was unhurt. Doug dropped his bicycle and fell in the street, crying out, "Jim, they have blinded me!" Jim asked the boys to help him, but they laughed, as though it was a joke. He tried to flag down cars but was ignored by the drivers. After a few minutes, three sailors stopped, and the boys ran away. Jim crossed the street and used the dime to call the police. The store owner had seen what happened but had not come to help. The police came. With the help of these sailors to whom we will forever be indebted, Jim got Doug entered into the hospital. He was waiting when I arrived and related the whole story to me.

Doug was still in the ER. An ophthalmologist who "happened" to be in the hospital had taken care of Doug but had already left. While I waited, I made quick calls to family and churches, starting a prayer-wide circle which quickly went around the world. Shortly after I finished the calls, the ER attendants brought Doug out of surgery. His white T-shirt was spattered with drops of blood and dirty where he had tried to wipe his eyes with his dirty hands. Both eyes were bandaged, but he was awake.

On our way to his room, I asked what happened. Both sons had told me an identical story. I knew I could trust them for the truth. They were riding along the street when they had come upon the gang on the sidewalk. They had a moment of apprehension, but there was no way to avoid the attack. They were on the street, obeying the rules of the road, not on the sidewalk.

We knew nothing of the racial incidents of the 1960s. We learned about the seriousness of them that day. It was ironic that this should take place on the main street of town, the only way to our house. What we did not know, but others did, was this section of the main street had been a source of problems and trouble, due to be torn down and rebuilt. The reconstruction started a short time later. In later years, I was told a new development did not help matters, the problems persisted.

When I finally reached the doctor by phone, I could not believe his words, "I doubt your son will ever see again!" I was alone. A sense of helplessness enveloped me. I couldn't reach my husband until 11:00 P.M. He had been met at the plane, taken to a home, then to a meeting. Communication in 1968 was not as easy as today.

My biggest concern was how I could reassure my son. I had only one resource, prayer. God's presence was with me.

A local newspaper reporter called immediately. There had been many articles written about us during our seventeen years of ministry, so our names may have been familiar to him. The first article about Doug was front page news in Sunday's paper the next morning. When I was interviewed, I said I could forgive these boys because God in Christ has forgiven us. Dozens of other pieces of communication followed, letters of sympathy, written to the editor, and progress reports about Doug. It seemed unheard of that a missionary should have undergone such a trauma.

Many people did not understand, others did not believe me. At one point I was told someone thought I was having a breakdown from the incident, but I knew I was following Scripture, that it was best to forgive. We cannot live, really live, with unforgiveness. It is like a bad cancer. Jesus said, "If you forgive not men their trespasses, NEITHER will your Father in Heaven forgive you" (Matthew 6:18). This was an atrocious act. The Judge later said something like "the intent of this crime was to harm, to hurt or to kill." Another court official said forgiveness was what stayed the possibility of racial rioting.

Because he was not yet sixteen, I was allowed to stay with Doug most of those days and nights. On Thursday night he asked me, "Mom, am I going to be blind?" I wanted to say no, but I knew I could not. I knew I had to say, "Doug, you may be. But we can live with blindness and no one ever lives with bitterness." Doug came to understand that, but it took several years before my husband could get over it.

What? A handsome, innocent young man having to live his whole life with blindness? It stirred up the emotions in the community. We did not have adequate insurance coverage. Mr. Bernard Griffin, an African American, was one of the civic leaders. He contributed monthly a sum of money from his own pocket and other African American community leaders and church people followed his example. In addition, Christian Broadcasting Network, headquartered in Norfolk, Virginia, started a fund to help with medical expenses. While many agreed, expressing gratitude for my words, others in the community expressed how they would have retaliated. I asked one man what good retaliation would do. It would mean only that two wrongs had been committed. It would not change what had happened.

Had it not been for God's loving tenderness in forgiving me, and His strength and presence in this time of trouble, neither could I myself have believed what I had said, especially those words about forgiveness.

The fast-food hamburger rage and TV were new to Doug and our family. Hospital food was not that appetizing. People who came to visit often brought Doug a hamburger and a milkshake. Some left money so we could go and get what he wanted. While the bandages were still covering his eyes, we played a game. He had to tell from the feel of the change and give me the exact cost before I would go out and buy the hamburgers and milkshakes. He learned quickly how to denote the quarters, dimes, nickels and pennies. When the milkshakes were stacking up in the fridge, I knew he understood what he was facing.

TVs had been installed in the patients' rooms, but the patient had to pay before it could be turned on. The bandages were taken off on Thursday. I arranged so the TV would be ready for him. Within a short while, I saw he was not watching it. He told me he could not see what was showing.

Richard returned home. It was a hard day for my husband. Doug was released a few days later. A tremendous amount of human and some financial support was given to help with the needs and, I suspect, to encourage Doug. One of the classes for which he had signed up in school, was typing. His teachers gave him a new typewriter, the latest model like the class had. Doug was musical. He had played the trumpet in Pakistan but needed one here in the US. Someone gave money for that. Once home, he imitated Herb Alpert, much, I suspect to the annoyance of the neighbors, but they never complained. There would be medical and educational costs. An account was started by a group of businessmen. It was a tremendous help. Much love and prayer support was poured out on us. My family members helped with the care of the other children. I owe a large debt of gratitude to my sister. She was always like a "second mother" to them.

No one believed the boys responsible would be caught and punished, but Jim had seen the color of the athletic shirt and its number on one of the boys. The Monday after the incident, a black police sergeant located them in their school, and they were charged. Of the ten boys, the two who wielded the lasso and bike chain were ages thirteen and seventeen. They were tried in court and convicted. Some of the others testified about what happened. When a pro bono lawyer called to say he needed more time to prepare the case, I asked if he thought he had a case. He reminded me everyone is innocent until proven guilty. I said, "Not in this case!" I told him I knew my boys were innocent, but these boys had confessed to their crime.

The thirteen-year-old received a two-year suspended sentence. He was released into the care of his grandmother. When the judge of juvenile court asked me to speak, my kids said I gave a sermon! But there were many "amen" voice responses from the mostly blacks who were attending. For the seventeen-year-old, there was a hearing. He remained in jail until the trial, held in February, at which time he was sentenced to eight years. Of that, he would have to serve two years and seven months. I was subpoenaed and again asked to speak. I told the court while forgiveness on our part was essential, society must do the judging and pass the sentence. I said, "No one wants to step outside the door and fear being attacked."

People in the community, both black and white, agreed about how wrong and cruel this act was. The District Attorney told my niece the city had been anticipating serious racial problems in another part of town. He said it was the attitude of forgiveness which probably prevented further problems. Today, I believe the community responses were used by God.

The judge allowed me to have time with the older boy. Tears were streaming down both our faces as we talked. He apologized, saying he did not know there were people like us in the world. I told him a jail sentence did not have to ruin him, to serve his time, that while both he and Doug would have to change what they had planned for careers (athletics for him and aeronautical engineering for Doug) it did not have to totally destroy their lives. I gave him a Bible. Inside, I wrote verses about God's plan of salvation and "This Book will keep you from sin or sin will keep you from this Book." I told him to read it. His sister was at the trial.

199

She was so distressed. Later, she contacted us, wanting to do something, anything which we needed to have done. She did artwork for a Children's Hospital. I let her draw pictures of children around the world which I used later in speaking about missions. I do not know what happened to the young man after he served jail time.

Each time Doug had to see a doctor after he was hurt, I had been with him. When his doctor determined he needed to go to Chicago to see a specialist, it was decided his Dad would go with him. I wanted to go, but we had other children and there was no money for the flight. The Lions Club heard about it; a member came by to say they thought I should also go. They gave the airfare money: my family took the children. With no idea how long we would need to be in Chicago, nor where we could stay, we found God had "gone before." A family was willing to take us in; the Mission had a car we could use. We had been told to expect a three week stay, but ten days later, Doug was discharged.

I watched and could almost feel the intensive bright light probing as the instruments were used to stabilize areas where his retina was torn. The work was successful: the Mormon doctor charged no fees for this specialized surgery. The night before we left the hospital, I laid out a copy of the newspaper article telling why we were there. The next morning, there was a note from the young orderly who had cared for Doug. He wrote, "I had no idea who it was I was caring for. I am so sorry to hear of this."

At first, Doug's doctor thought he should be enrolled in the school for the blind. After getting to know him, the doctor made the decision that would not be right for Doug, that he should go back to his classroom, which he did the second semester. While he was healing, he had homebound instruction. He even passed the test for a restricted (daylight) driver's license. Richard and I never thought he could do it—but Doug said he knew he could, because he had prayed about it. Faith. What a thrilling possession!

The local papers were very interested in writing about Doug's injury and recovery. These photos appeared in the Virginian Pilot.

****

Doug's is a story of triumph; he overcame in the real sense of the word. He persevered, even with this serious handicap and is a wonderful son, husband, and father. He has been very dedicated to his work, done required courses, and accomplished far more than many who have full vision and more resources. Possibly the only thing he has missed out on in his life was that he could not play sports. He had to do that vicariously, managing teams for his children. He was a victim of that incident, but he has never acted like a victim. His great personality makes him a delight to all who know him, more so when they know his story.

He and his family live in Maryland. His earlier aptitude for taking apart the toys and bringing them to me to put back together—something for which I had no ability—paid off in his chosen field of computer technology and telecommunications. He has a wonderful gift for figuring out how every new toy works. Richard and I liked to joke about how we didn't need to call a repairman when we needed help with our TV or phones, we called Doug. He was always able to get us out of our dilemma—doing it by telephone!

At this writing, Doug has lived with a visual handicap for over 40 years. Thankfully, his other eye, although badly damaged, has had enough vision for him to live a very normal life. As a family, this terrible happening is like scar tissue when it is pressed. It is still soft in memory, but we have all come through with a deeper understanding of the meaning of forgiveness for both physical and emotional pain. His Dad struggled a long time before he could express that forgiveness. I think we can all say now the meaning and need of forgiving others is necessary if we expect to be forgiven. The Creator and Sustainer of the universe traced it in the heart of the "inner man," in our spiritual engram.

****

The years passed quickly and with them, our nest emptied out. Our 1968 family is now grown, with families of their own. We have grandchildren and great grandchildren. Like many writers who have half-finished articles and books, I have half-written stories; this was one of them. Why have I waited to publish it? Do I simply want to use the cliché, "Jesus is the answer"? That has no weight if we don't know the question. In my deepest feelings, I want others to know the story of God's grace in a world torn up by the arrows of the enemy. I also want them to know the Divine Warrior is on our side.

I want to remind the reader Abel, like Doug, was an innocent victim, that Cain killed his brother Abel out of jealousy. I don't know the motive of those black boys, but I suspect jealousy of some kind was rearing its ugly head. We are thankful Doug did not lose his life, that God has preserved enough of his sight so he could have the joy he has, and is to his family, in a world that often mocks goodness.

From the beginning of time, a fight has gone on between good and evil. When that truth takes hold of us, we know the world has not changed. It cannot change itself. Our human nature is lopsided with evil. Destructive behavior has always existed. When retaliation becomes revenge, the idea of forgiveness may seem foolish, but it is what Jesus taught. I wanted then, and still want to live by that maxim. I have written this story in the hope that if or when others are faced with a choice, they will exercise forgiveness.

Jim, who was with Doug when all this took place, is a doctor. Bob who waited to tell me and had to phone the hospital to tell them I was coming, is senior pastor of a large church in North Carolina. The memory trace of pain for our daughter who was away in her first year of college is still just below the surface, still hard for her to talk about it. David, just five at the time, has a clear memory of what happened, but sees his brother's strengths in his successes. Occasional other remembrances still surface, but the bottles don't get as many tears in recent years. We have been through deep waters, but they did not overflow, through the fires of adversity and found they did not consume us (Isaiah 43). God's grace has been sufficient, "A very present help in trouble" (Psalm 46:1).

I would not be truthful to say all has been forgotten because all has been forgiven. Forgiveness and forgetting are two different things. It was a tragedy inscribed on our hearts with a pen of iron. However, I believe we recognize it was **forgiveness** which brought us peace and serenity. With God's grace and help, the spirit of triumph has prevailed over the spirit of evil. Over and over, we have been reminded God was there for us.

The Psalmist said,

"Though I walk in the midst of trouble, thou wilt revive me:
Thou shalt stretch forth thine hand against the wrath of mine enemies,
And thy right hand shall save me.
The Lord will perfect that which concerneth me:
Thy mercy, O Lord, endureth for ever:
Forsake not the works of thine own hands." (Psalm 138:8-9, KJV)

Missionaries at Home

After our initial months of rest when we returned from Pakistan and the initial crisis of Doug's ordeal, we were busy contacting those churches and groups which had supported us. Sometimes we felt like little children, wanting to raise our hands to make sure God knew we were still there, sitting, waiting for Him to lead us out. On other days, the ministry there at home became so great and rewarding, we knew He had not forgotten us, and we were filling an important place.

Richard was appointed as a Special Representative to the Mission which meant he was on the road a lot. In that capacity he represented the Mission in churches, colleges, conferences and wherever there was a need. He anticipated being able to interest young people in full time service for the Lord. Although we had not given up our hope for an overseas ministry, it seemed that, for the moment, there would be a "semi-colon" in our lives.

In February 1970, Richard made a trip to Trinidad and Venezuela with TEAM. He arrived in time to see an event called "Carnival." It was an indescribable event in the lives of those who participate. The word means "leaving off the flesh," and it precedes Lent. It was a very ostentatious affair—costumes, drinking, "religious" exercises. He was impressed—with the need to get to them the true word of God! Many go into debt for the costumes alone. Tattered and torn costumes and litter on the streets the morning after were a grim and mute reminder that "Carnival" was over for another year.

I had had my first taste of being in education when I was in charge of the small Christian school in Pakistan. Our support money was in short supply, so I applied for a position with the public schools in Portsmouth doing homebound instruction. This involved going to a student's home to tutor them since they were not attending regular classes due to emotional and family issues or other extenuating circumstances. It was an "education" for me in what was happening to America's young people. Two thirteen-year-olds I tutored were pregnant, one young man was an excellent student but was reluctant to leave his mother who I suspected was an alcoholic, and one young lady had taken an overdose of drugs right before I arrived at the home and I had to drive her to the hospital.

From there, I had some long-term teaching experience when in 1971 I got a job teaching at Alliance Christian School, which had just opened in Portsmouth. Education became a part of my "ministry." I remained at Alliance for the rest of the time we spent in the US.

Sometimes teaching the English classes and one Bible class at Alliance (grades 7-12) was tiring, but I loved the whole bit! He who knew my every need knew this was the way to get me to concentrate on Himself. Teaching at Alliance also provided me the opportunity for one of my great passions: writing! One Christmas the Drama Club presented an original choral reading that I had written— "Born to Die"—which traced God's plan for mankind from eternity's "beginning" when Christ was the Lamb, slain from the foundation of the world, to His triumphant return and reign on this earth. Another year, my 12th grade students and I wrote and produced a play about Christ's birth and second coming called "History Recycled."

Although God had closed the door to us doing missionary work in Pakistan, Richard and I found ministry opportunities where God had placed us. It was rich and rewarding work, but our hearts remained burdened for people overseas who had not heard the Good News of Jesus Christ and we longed and prayed that God would open another door.

Our Emptying Nest

Just before Doug's injury, Elizabeth entered her freshman year at Columbia Bible College in Columbia, South Carolina. She wrote of being happy in such a Christ-centered college. After completing her studies, she had planned to enter the University of South Carolina to concentrate her studies in the field of Communications: Radio, TV, Journalism, etc.—with an aim to entering Christian service in that area. During the summer of 1970, she spent a wonderful, busy summer as a junior missionary in France. Jim, sixteen at the time, also spent time in Europe that summer with the American Leadership Study Group—a group of high school and college students selected from schools throughout the US by Clark University in Massachusetts to spend the summer studying in European universities. It was a wonderful opportunity for him made possible by a family friend who was a teacher.

During her second year at Columbia Bible College, Elizabeth began dating and became engaged to David Harris, a young man she had previously known from Highland Baptist Church. David had previously graduated from the University of Virginia and then felt God's call to become a missionary. Therefore, he entered Columbia Bible College to complete required Bible classes. It was there that he and Elizabeth became reacquainted and in June 1971, they were married.

Doug also graduated from High School in June 1971 and began college work at Tidewater Community College, while working part-time for a lumber company. The following year, Jim graduated High School and decided to attend Wheaton College in Illinois. Shortly after Jim left for college, Doug decided to transfer to Moody Bible Institute in Chicago and spent a year attending there.

About this same time, Doug was becoming seriously interested in Renee, a lovely young girl in the church youth group. After he returned home that summer, a friend working with telephones asked if we thought Doug would like to try that as a career. When Doug heard it, he jumped at the chance, but I said, "Whoa! We need to pray for three days!" The answer had to be given after the weekend. That phone job was made for Doug. He learned the business very quickly. Jarvis Telephones became a company after the breakup of "Ma Bell" telephones. Doug was required to be on the job any time a phone went out. It was the quick responses which promoted the company—and Doug.

Soon after getting established in the job, he and Renee decided they wanted to spend their lives together. After a six-month period of waiting, both families gave their blessing. They were married in June 1974. Renee has been the soul mate Doug needed, a wonderful wife and mother.

Another exciting event in June 1974 was watching Bob, just seventeen, but 6'1" and supporting a mustache, walk the high school commencement trail at Alliance Christian where I was teaching, and then give the valedictory address on the need for Christians to busy themselves with the Lord's work. This was even more a satisfaction and sense of accomplishment as we recalled that when he decided to change schools that year (he had previously attended the local public school), he would have to pay his own tuition, which he had done faithfully by working part-time in a nearby department store. Shortly after graduation, he left for Clifton Forge, Virginia where he helped rebuild Grace Bible Camp. After that he began classes at Columbia Bible College to study for full-time Christian service. After graduating CBC, Bob and his bride Linda began decades of shared ministry in local churches. Bob later earned both masters and doctorate degrees in theology.

Four generations, 1974. Back row, L to R, Jim, Bob, Richard, David Harris, Doug. Middle row, L to R, Aunt Zelma, Mom, me. Front row, L to R, Dad Thompson, Emma, David, Elizabeth holding baby Christina.

That same year, Elizabeth and David attended orientation classes preparing for service in Belgium with the Greater Europe

Mission. They, along with baby Christina, our first grandchild, were planning to leave as soon as their support was raised; they left for Belgium the following year and eventually would serve there for ten years.

During this timeframe, Jim also called home requesting prayer and guidance for his future. He was still at Wheaton College and was a conscientious, and excellent, student. He had worked as a pharmacy technician in Central Dupace Hospital to help with college fees. He was planning to enter the pre-Med program in the fall. As we discussed his future, his primary concern was the huge financial consideration of medical school. We said, "Don't worry—we did not have the money to enter you in college, and God has brought you this far. He will meet the needs if He wants you there." I had just heard Wilbur Nelson on his program say, "Small things borrow greatness from their connections." We would just have to continue borrowing from Him who owns the cattle on a thousand hills! At that time, Jim's desire was to one day "bury himself someplace overseas where they need medical help." Our answer? God calls the signals. We ourselves were proof that the Christian does not direct his own life. We were blessed to attend his graduation from Wheaton College in June 1976 where he graduated *magna cum laude* and was planning to enter medical school to pursue his education in medicine. He entered Loyola Medical School in Chicago in the fall of 1976.

Dad Thompson's Passing

We were once again faced with the passing of a parent when Dick's dad, Dad Thompson, died in 1974. He had pastored most of his adult life but for the last few years he and Emma lived in India he was involved in other ministries. He had a part in developing **Sat Tal,** a place of rest in India where workers could go to relax. It was then time for his retirement.

After returning to the US in the early 70s they lived in NY where Emma worked in the NY office of the Methodist Church until full retirement came for Emma in 1973. We were living in Portsmouth at the time, and they moved here "to be near the grandchildren," they said. They found an apartment very near us. Dad was not able to get out very much, but Emma remained active in a local Methodist church and did volunteer work at the Wesley Center.

Emma and Dad Thompson.

Richard and I were by Dad's bed with Emma when Dad Thompson took his last breath. Emma moved into a Methodist Retirement facility in Asheville, North Carolina until she died in 1980. Her body was brought back to Portsmouth and Dad Thompson and Emma are both buried in Olive Branch Cemetery, not fifty feet from my parents' graves, yet they had lived in two different worlds.

A Wedding Does Not a Marriage Make

Missionary couples need a special closeness that is not always possible. Daily concerns often cloud the intimacy husbands and wives need for sharing. Some couples have problems with managing money, or children, or one wants more "space" or more time with friends. Alcohol, pornography, bad habits and a myriad of other differences surface as the years pass. None of that was the cause of the feeling of distance between Richard and me, but the stress of problems we faced in the ministry did take a toll.

Doug's injury and my willingness to forgive those responsible was another of those events which placed stress on our relationship. At the time, I did not know Richard had been unable to forgive. While he traveled as a Mission Representative, I worked to supplement our income. We were still a couple, but not together in the closeness we had known. The physical separation and difficulty in easily communicating (no cell phones or e-mail in those days!) contributed to the feelings of distance in our relationship. I wondered where it would end. He may have thought it would. We had a nice little vacation with counseling in another state. Two hurting people do not find it easy to listen to a counselor who may never have walked their road. I felt there had to be something more. I started with making sure my own heart was right with God.

I searched the Scriptures to determine what pleases God in the husband/wife relationship. Both Paul and Peter in the New Testament and many examples in the Old Testament gave me ideas. I tried to make my husband the center of our family, to "keep short accounts"—to hold no grudges, to apologize when I did anything to upset him, even if I felt it was not my fault. I once wrote a note and left it on his pillow to be discovered when he got home from a trip. I prayed, asking for wisdom. I took care of family matters, did not ask him to do anything if I could get it done. Initially, it did not seem to make a difference. It seemed I was at fault for anything which went wrong. I tried not to disagree. While I know I made mistakes, God heard my prayers.

Several years passed. Then came the day and one much unexpected moment which lives in my memory. Richard had battled the twists and turns of his life for a long time. He told me he had finally found peace. He realized he had to forgive Doug's attackers and seek God's forgiveness.

The roadblocks for God's work in our lives were removed. We began to grow together in a new way. The wilting vine of our love was watered with tears and came back to life and continued growing. Our love in those years was different, but stronger than it was when we stood at the altar. Since that day when Richard opened his heart to God's forgiveness, I have come to understand the strength of Matthew 6:15. Forgiveness is like the refreshing springs of water which give life to a dry land. Many marriages can be put back together when there is forgiveness, and it may be the heart of a lasting marriage. Coupled with prayer, it is what makes the difference, because "a wedding does not a marriage make." Only a willing couple can do that.

So, what causes problems that can lead to breakups and can a marriage be restored? The answer to the first part of the question is "many things" and the answer to the second part is yes, they can be restored. I know that. The road may not be lined with roses, but when God puts it back together, He uses good sealing wax, but only if the couple is willing.

****

My life has not been free of care. At every turn, there have been new challenges, new depths to explore faith, new determinations to follow the Living God. Would I exchange my life for the life of those who have lived more elegantly? Never. God has been gracious and loving through each difficulty. It is Jesus Who has led me all the way!

It is said of the refining process when nuggets of gold are turned into something of greater worth the gold is heated to remove the dross. Cannot God do with His children as the goldsmith does with the nuggets? That is what I see when trials and difficulties come our way; God is removing the dross, the superficial in our lives. He is changing us into His own image so that we can serve Him.

Our Short Sojourn in the Land of Esther and King Ahasuerus

"Teach me to do Thy will, for Thou are my God;
Thy Spirit is good; lead me into the land of uprightness."
(Psalm 143:10)

The long June afternoon stretched out as far as the miles of the barren mountains over which we were flying. The pilot announced we were flying over Mount Ararat and I excitedly looked out the window, but it was more of the same—sun burnt hill after hill. The scene did not change when we were told to fasten our seat belts for landing in Tehran, Iran. Was this what I was coming to? How could I, who love greenery so much, endure years of this? Eighteen years in the lush, green foothills of the Himalayan mountains, eight years of living in a moderate East Coast climate, and now barrenness. My heart sank.

The airport was stiflingly hot and extremely crowded. Somehow my light blue dress with matching shoes and purse, chosen to insure me a fresh look on arrival, seemed a farce. Nothing could remain unwilted in that mid-summer heat.

Friendly folk met us, and we inched our way through unbelievable traffic. I was old enough to know that my acceptance—and my family's acceptance—of this new land would depend on me. With such a beginning then, it seems unbelievable that leaving that land just a few short years later, would produce such heartache. We learned to love Tehran and a hundred of the things about it.

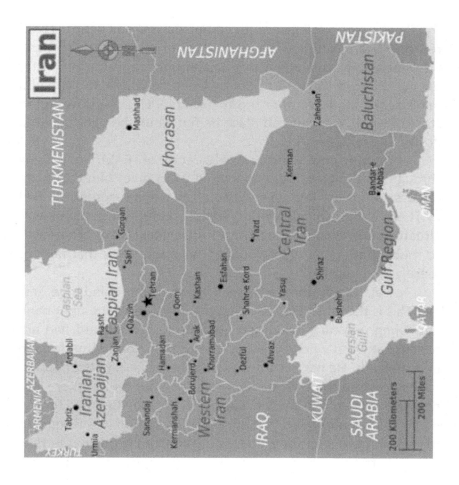

213

Our Sojourn Continues

After eight years in the USA, we began to think about returning to an overseas ministry. Elizabeth was married and she and her husband, David, were making plans to go as missionaries to Belgium. Doug was married and working in telecommunications. Jim was in Loyola Medical School in the Chicago area and Bob was at Columbia Bible College, planning to go into the ministry. David was finishing seventh grade. Richard had been a TEAM representative, but he was never a "front man." He was restless. I had found a place working in education; that became a ministry for me. Richard traveled to South America, where TEAM had a ministry. He made another trip to Trinidad. Like the dove in the story of Noah, he found no place he felt would be right to settle down.

Dr. Mortenson, the General Director of TEAM, was passing through Washington, DC, and invited us to meet him there and discuss our future. We did and had a few hours together. He told us TEAM was opening a work in Iran, and one young couple was already there. Would we be interested in going there? There was so much that we thought would be favorable. Was that faith or merely presumption?

Isaiah said, "thine ears shall hear a word behind thee, saying 'This is the way, walk ye in it, when ye turn to the right hand and when you turn to the left" (Isaiah 30:21). Richard had not heard that word when he visited the work in South America and in the Islands. He had returned saying there was plenty of opportunity for me since they needed teachers, but he felt there was no place for him. We knew it was not in the plan God had for us.

As we continued to pray, we believed God was leading us to Iran, and it was exciting. Four of our children were now settled, either married or in college. David, our youngest, starting eighth grade, could go with us. People had been faithful in supporting us, and we thought the Iranian language, though very different, would not be as unfamiliar as some other language might be, because the Urdu language of Pakistan is made up primarily of Persian and Arabic.

214

It was October 1975; we made plans for a Spring departure. There were many details to attend to, selling the house we had purchased, packing up, decisions about what to ship. What lay up ahead would have left me pondering the choice had I known about it, but God in His loving ways chooses not to reveal much to us, and thankfully, He cared for the details along the way as He led us through some "tunnels" with very little light shining up ahead.

I began to study the Bible book of Esther. When she was chosen to be the Queen for King Ahasuerus, Esther did not know what she would be facing. Like us, she surely would have been excited, but unlike us, she had no idea what it would mean to become a beauty queen and establish a relationship with a man she would scarcely come to know before her life was in jeopardy. No marriage counseling classes here! How much did she know about the king's exploits? About his divorcing his wife Vashti, about the richness of palace life? Ahasuerus ruled over 127 provinces, stretching from Ethiopia to India. When he celebrated, he did it royally. First, he invited people to come to the palace. The description of the palace defies our imagination. Would we still find that opulence there 2,500 years later?

Thus, in 1976, with son David, we began a short sojourn in Persia, Esther's land. We studied language and made friends with Hebrew Christians. I taught in the English medium, multi-national Iranzamin International High School, while also doing graduate work from the Michigan State University extension in Tehran. Living in Iran was neither like living in a village nor visiting in a palace. It was different but it had something of each.

Arriving in Tehran

After a brief stop in Belgium to visit with Elizabeth and family, we arrived in Tehran to mentor a very talented young couple who had gone out about a year earlier and were experiencing some problems. We left the US in June 1976, but by the time we got to Iran, the die was cast, and the couple were returning to the homeland. There was not much I could say or do. Thankfully, they were later to get help and their family problems were straightened out and they went back to another field. As for us, we went under the umbrella of another faith mission now known as Christar.

I cannot recall with whom we stayed when we first got to Iran. It may have initially been with someone from Christar. In one letter home, I wrote of the difficulty of sleeping with heat and noise for our first few days after arrival. Apparently, the place we stayed for the first few days in Tehran was located on a street which was used by big trucks, which were only permitted to travel at night, so all night long they travelled. When they got in front of the house where we were staying, they would honk, because there was an intersection ahead and they wanted everyone to get out of their way! We slept in an upstairs room where the doors opened onto an upstairs porch overlooking the street. There were no screens anywhere in evidence, but there were very few flies and mosquitoes, miracle of miracles!

Kundan Massey and family lived in north Tehran. Kundan had been my language teacher in Pakistan. It was a delight to meet him and Iqbal, who were serving as the area leaders of Campus Crusade for Christ. They had a son our David's age. They offered us a room in their house while they were travelling through the end of August. It was really a blessing since before then—after the location where we initially stayed upon arrival—we had been sleeping on the living room floor in an already crowded apartment with other missionaries!

We were on the go from the moment of our arrival. The missionary couple who we intended to mentor departed soon after our arrival but left most of their belongings behind. Therefore, it fell to us to take care of moving, and storing, their belongings and cleaning their apartment to return to the owner. Afterwards, we had to sort through the items and dispose of the things they did not want. I must confess that at times I was angry and critical with this burden. Several months later, during a prayer meeting, the person in charge asked us to spend time in praise to God. I felt that the Lord was speaking to me to praise Him for this couple. I could not think of anything to praise Him for in that situation, as I felt really worn out that I had had to pack up and care for all their things when I felt they were really capable of it and should have done it before they left. As I sat, meditating on it, it occurred to me that I was wrong, and there was much to thank God for since we had not had much to do in the way of shopping for appliances and had benefitted from their having bought those things and left them. So, I did thank the Lord, and afterward the burden was much lighter!

We got busy house hunting, first by phone. Rents were extremely high, but there was another problem which should have alerted me to the real face of many of the people. When I phoned about a rental, the first question was, "Do you speak French? Persian?" I had to say no, and the reply was always the same, "I don't speak English," perfectly spoken but followed by a hang-up.

With the high rents, we had to wait to see God do the impossible! When I told someone that our mission normally allotted only $250 a month for housing, they looked at me in utter disbelief and shock! After consultation with our mission secretary in the US, we eventually found a place for $1,000 a month in north Tehran, the lower floor of a large house, owned by a banker.

First Impressions

The identification of the area was unusual, to say the least and made travel an interesting experience. Addresses were very specific, because Tehran was very unorthodox in the way the area had developed; alleys, streets, sections were all part of an address. We had no car and the other missionaries were at a distance from us. The main method was to go by taxi, a somewhat complicated affair, because we had to know exactly where we were going. The taxi filled up with people going the same way, and sometimes we had to make a transfer. The drivers were very helpful. We learned their signals quickly. With a nod of the head which in America would be a yes, they told us they were not going in that direction!

Perhaps because we were new and did not read well enough or did not yet understand the culture, but we did not appreciate the driving at first. It seemed that there were a million cars for the four million people who lived in the city! To our unaccustomed eyes, it appeared there were no laws regarding traffic. Some roads had no lane markings, and even when there were, no one seemed to pay them any mind. It was defensive driving all the way, and the driver that had a six-inch lead was in the right, even if he cut in front of you. But no one seemed to get upset about it! Occasionally (often) someone would decide to make a U-turn in the middle of traffic. There were dozens of accidents every day, but few were serious. Soon after arrival, we were involved in an accident when someone turned right in front of the taxi we were riding in to make a left turn, and we just sheared off his left fender as neatly as if we had cut it. Luckily, no one was hurt.

During our time there, the city was building at an unbelievable rate and construction was everywhere. In one letter home, I wrote of being fascinated watching the construction of a new building. They used mud and straw with a bit of cement for a three-story building as mortar. This was then covered with a lovely façade on the front of tile or marble. There were few individual houses; most were apartment complexes, one house joining another.

There were no lovely residential areas with grass lawns and flowers. Water was precious. Seeing the parched earth all around—it was gray, rocky, but not solid rock, and dry—brought about in our thinking of the spiritual parallels. We were told that the ground was fertile; it only needed water to make things grow. Might it be that the same is true from a spiritual angle?

However, there were some lovely parks around. On one occasion, to celebrate David's thirteenth birthday, after the Masseys returned, they drove us about 50 miles north of the city for a picnic in an apple orchard along the road. On one side were located the brown barren mountains, with lush greenery only

218

where water touched the earth as it cascaded down from the high mountains. On the other side of the orchard and road was a mountain stream. To see water was such a welcome sight in Iran! If you look at a map, you will notice that rivers, or other bodies of water, are few and far between. It is a hot, dry, dusty land, even on the plateau.

Along the side of the streets ran open, but rather clean, drains, about 18 inches deep and 18 inches wide, called *jubes*. They were often full of running, not stagnant, water. We were told that they were accessible if you wanted to wash dishes, clothes, vegetables, or take a bath. We understood it was the water supply for many people. Yet we were told we did not need to boil the drinking water, and no one we knew did. I didn't know the source of the drinking water in our apartment.

There were many kinds of stores and most items were available (unlike our situation in Pakistan); most of them made in Iran. Imported goods were very expensive. Because of the hot weather, most businesses closed from 12-4. Shopping was done in the mornings.

A few months after arriving, we bought a freezer. Many people had told us about the necessity of freezing or canning food for the months of January through March when supplies got low. I experimented to find out what would keep nicely. In addition to meat, I froze fruits and vegetables, even some baked goods.

The first few months after arrival, we were also busy learning the language. A few weeks after we arrived, we signed up for our language courses, four hours each day. We found that we could read some of the Persian words. Farsi is very different, yet similar, to Urdu; the differences caused us problems. Although the script was the same as Urdu, we had to change sentence structure and add a bit of a French accent. When we first arrived, David would go to the *kuche* store (a little neighborhood market) for me and would use his hands as much as his mouth to communicate!

Our second year there, Richard enrolled in a different language course. He studied with the Academy of Languages, while I continued with the regular missionary course. Richard went to school three nights a week for two hours each night. During that summer, I was busy taking the required series of tests to complete the first course but did not complete the final exam because I was sick. And then when I started teaching at the Iranzamin International School, I was not able to complete any more language studies.

Giving Our Children Wings

Shortly after arriving in Tehran, we learned Doug's eye that was cut during the incident in 1968 was causing so much pain it would have to be removed. I wanted to return home to be with him. He said no to that, it was not necessary, he had a lot of support—his wife, her parents, and our family members. There would be nothing I could do that others could not and would not do for him.

My ego suffered a drop. During most of these years, his Dad had often been out of town, involved with Mission business. I had always been the one with him, the spokesperson who said we could forgive, who was with him in the hospital, in court, at the doctor's office. I wanted to be with our son, but now, I was "not needed"?

It was then I realized as a parent, a mother must give her children roots and wings. Doug had both, roots in our family, and wings so he would not have to remain in the nest. He did not need me, or us. This had always been God's plan. The roots had been our part. I was thankful they were strong, and the wings had fully developed. Renee would help him "fly." She called us after the surgery to report that all went well. Doug was in good spirits and good hands!

Iranian Experiences

The religion of Ancient Persia was Zoroastrianism. They believed in four sacred things: earth, air, fire and water. Islam had conquered the country by the seventh century A.D. When we first arrived, the ruling Shah wanted a secular country where every religious group could worship, but the religious Muslim clerics opposed that. Their opposition would eventually result in the removal of the Shah and increased tension and rioting in the country.

There were Armenian, Assyrian, and Hebrew Christian churches, as well as Tehran Bible Church and a Southern Baptist Church in Tehran. The Christians in many churches worshiped on Friday since the Muslim weekends are Thursday and Friday instead of Saturday and Sunday. The Jews worshipped on Saturday and the Armenians worshipped on Sunday. It was confusing to us at first. Apparently, years ago it seemed the better part of wisdom to do this, since in a Muslim culture the Christians had to work on Sunday.

We were first invited to visit the Southern Baptist church. Following the English service there was a Persian language service. We stayed for it and were surprised to find ourselves able to understand some of the songs and Scripture, though admittedly not much! Afterwards we went into the fellowship hall for punch and cookies. Imagine our surprise when we met one of the Presbyterian women missionaries who recalled meeting us in Murree in 1967! It is indeed a small world.

We also visited the Tehran Bible Church, a lovely large group of internationals, very good Bible teaching, but we decided if we wanted to learn the culture, we needed to worship in the Hebrew Christian Church of Tehran and entered into many of their activities. It was a good experience except for one occasion involving David.

This occurred when a Persian celebration was taking place. I was told it was a fun thing, no religious connections, just a cultural affair. David and I went. There were games and food. For one game, there was a large fire, and the kids were lining up, challenged to jump over it. David wanted to do it and I let him. How silly can one mother be!

All were successful in jumping until it was David's turn. He jumped and would have made it except a man was jumping from the wrong side and hit David in the head, knocking him out, fortunately, on the edge of the fire. I ran and picked him up in my arms. I don't think anyone realized what had happened, and no one offered to help me. He came to but was bleeding from his mouth. I took him into the nearby bathroom, but there was no towel, no water. Someone came to my rescue, and we got him to the emergency room clinic for treatment. The clinic was not far from our house. The blood from his mouth was likely where he had bit his tongue or jaw when he was hit. The man later apologized for trying to run the wrong way.

There was one other scare involving David when we were there. He wanted to try skiing one winter. The nearby mountains were popular and the cost of renting the skis and getting a little instruction was not much, so we went. He caught on quickly, had a great time, skied all day without eye protection. I knew nothing of that need. Later, that night, he woke me to say his eyes were hurting. We went to the emergency room and again, he was treated and survived that incident. Fortunately, I don't believe there was any long-term damage.

Visiting the Place of Esther and Mordechai

During the spring of 1977, we were blessed to visit the city of Hamadan where the mausoleum of Esther and Mordechai was located. This happened as part of an eight-day, 2000-mile trip to visit four mission stations in the north and west part of Iran with another missionary couple who invited us to go along. One of the stations was at Hamadan, which was about six hours from Tehran. At the mausoleum we had prayer in a still used tiny ante room and wept as we rehearsed God's dealings with his own people in ancient Persia.

Everywhere in Iran the past lives on and on. We walked the King Cyrus Highway and traveled on Darius Street. *En route* we saw sculptures in stone dating back over 2300 years. It was really awe inspiring! But Iran is really desert wasteland, barren in so many places. I guess you could say in many places all they had is oil and minerals! There were places of lush green growing things and some beautiful wild tulips and wild poppies. In every village, the houses were mud (but village life seemed very different from what we experienced in Pakistan). Some villages had dome-shaped roofs on the houses which was new to us. We could picture the events of Cyrus (500 B.C.) and Darius' time, for in many ways, life had not changed that dramatically.

We did see one village where some changes had been made: it was a Christian village. Although very run down, we visited in one mud hut that was very interesting. It had four rooms and a courtyard, with a little room on the side in which they had an underground oven. The portion with the four rooms had screen doors and Persian rugs on the floor in the sitting room with pillows to sit on (very little furniture). In the kitchen was a kerosene refrigerator and a bottle gas stove and a "swing-like" contraption with a goat skin tied up (much like you'd tie all fours of an animal to barbeque it). The skin contained yogurt which was shaken back and forth to separate the cream to make butter from it. The curds would be dried to use in food or eat dry. It was something unreal to see modern appliances next to that—must be centuries old—method of butter making! And all this in an almost totally mud house and village!

Hospitality Ministry

Hebrews reminds us not to forget to entertain strangers because some are "angels unawares," sent to us from God, such as in Abraham's day (Genesis 18). Abraham practiced the servant-hood required of hospitality. It is also how the servant found the right wife for Isaac. In the New Testament Jesus, His disciples and Paul all received a welcome at the hands of others, many times a family and often women busily caring for others. Paul admonished the Philippians to help those women who had labored with him in the Gospel.

I did not know hospitality was what my mom was teaching us when we grew up. I am sure she did not see it that way, rather just a way of life, a very valuable lesson. She fed all who were at our home when it was mealtime and wanted or needed something to eat. For me, that meant it was not unusual to have colored people at our table. On one occasion she was sewing choir robes for a church group. They arrived to check on them at lunchtime. Mom was not expecting them, but they were invited to sit down and share whatever simple thing she had prepared, probably a pot of green vegetables or beans and cornbread.

The people in Iran, much like people in other places in the Middle East, place a high value on hospitality. Just as we experienced in Pakistan, we had many opportunities to use our own hospitality as a ministry in Iran, not just to visiting missionaries, but to our Iranian friends and neighbors.

Hospitality had been a two-sided experience for me; providing hospitality to others in our home and receiving the hospitality of others. In Iran we had visitors from several different countries, American, European, and African. Each added something different to our lives. One couple from Scotland invited us for our first taste of delicious quiche.

Iranian hospitality was displayed on several occasions when our Iranian neighbor sent Persian dishes to our house. One occasion I recall her sending a big bowl of the famous Persian soup. It was very rich and made with yogurt, beans, rice, fresh vegetables, and spices such as coriander, parsley, fennel, and mint. Another occasion she sent a yellow rice dish which she called "halva," similar to a Pakistani dish, with rice, sugar, slivered almonds and decorated on top with cinnamon, almonds and ground pistachios. My language teacher told me the Muslims make that dish and distribute it when they have received a special favor or blessing from God. Although it is intended to be distributed to the poor, it usually just goes to friends. My feeling was our neighbor wanted to make friends and she knew I wanted to sample Iranian food!

One occasion for me to extend hospitality was when I hosted a bridal shower for our assistant pastor's bride to be. A friend helped me make a special cake and the bride to be received many nice gifts. We had each person bring something to eat—a special recipe. Although it was not a surprise party, she was surprised. She was English and apparently, they didn't have such showers in England. However, all had a good time.

The summer of 1977 was especially busy with hosting many visitors to our home. Among them were Bill Johnson, Bruce Rasmussen, Graham Duncan, Stan Brown, and Jonny and Joel DeHart. Each one had arrived hot, dusty, dirty, and tired from the long trip overland, but still glad to be going by bus because of the cost and because of a strong desire to see the world before settling down to college. Bill Johnson had just finished Wheaton and gone to India to see if he could get into medical school there. Because of the high cost, he instead went to Pakistan, met some people involved in making rugs and felt that was what God was leading him to do; therefore, he was returning to Pakistan with the hope and desire to help Christians in Pakistan with the rug exporting business. Graham had been in Pakistan helping at the Bach Hospital and then was going to a university in Scotland. Stan had been at Wheaton but was then planning to take courses at DuPage College and hoping to get into the University of California to study linguistics. That summer we also hosted the Clemenger family for a few days. They were a former missionary family who was then living in Phoenix and had been helping that summer at TEAM's Oasis Hospital in Buraimi.

During Christmas 1977, we invited our Muslim landlord and his family, and our Iranian next-door neighbor and family for Christmas Eve dinner. They stayed until about 11:30 p.m. The neighbor's family, who had not been entertained in our home before, was very gracious in their comments, saying it was the most wonderful visit—one of the best times he had ever had in his life. An Iranian formality to say such a thing? Perhaps. They say many such things, but we preferred to believe they were sincerely speaking from their hearts, as we enjoyed it also! We gave them

Christian Christmas literature and gifts. We prayed for them and enlisted our family and friends back home to pray as well that God would open their hearts and minds to His truth.

That year we were invited to Christmas dinner at the home of a young British couple who had gone all out to entertain five American guests and one young black Christian lady from Ghana. The Ghanaian was a special friend of ours; we had met her when we first got to Iran. Her government had sent her to Iran to study insurance. We were blessed to see her grow so much spiritually in the time she was in Iran. The young British couple had also been our friends since we arrived. They had been there on a two-year contract, which had just ended. They were a dedicated Christian couple whose ministry had meant a lot to many people there.

Our Ghanaian friend at our apartment in Iran.

One New Year's Eve, we entertained four single girls, three of whom were missionaries. It was a fun time, but none of us were prepared to stay up to see in the New Year!

An occasion of hospitality also highlighted the different way our cultures viewed time and dates! Our neighbors had invited us to spend the Persian New Year with them. When the lady invited us, I brought her into the house and said, looking at the calendar, "This is today (naming each day), and you want us to come on this day?" I thought I had it all worked out. I got home on Monday afternoon about 6:00 p.m. and Richard said, "I checked with the man next door. It is tonight we go there!" The difference was that their day started in the evening, and New Year's, while always March 21, varies on the calendar. Another example of this confusion: we had read in the paper that clocks would be advanced one hour to take advantage of daylight-saving time, beginning at 12:01 Friday night. To us, that meant Friday, but to the Persians it meant Thursday, for Friday began at 7:00 Thursday evening! It was so clear then, how Christ could have been in the tomb three days: before evening on Friday would be one day, Friday to Saturday evening would be two days, and he rose on the third day, Sunday morning; the Persian would never question the terminology!

God Provides a Solution

Before leaving the US, we had to make some plans for David's education. It was decided to home school him, so I taught David for his eighth grade, using the Calvert system. David did well in his home schooling, memorized some poetry, including "The Cremation of Sam McGee." Tehran had both hot weather and very cold winters. We had some fun with that poem, even if theologically, it is very wrong. In the story, Sam dies and goes into the fire. When someone opens the door, he calls out to them to "shut the door, it is getting cold in here."

Home schooling brought on a new set of experiences. David had made friends quickly with the neighborhood children. He usually finished the daily work quickly, but I did not have access to other materials for study. He would go outside and play. Before long, the neighbor boys wanted to skip school and play soccer with him. That changed when I decided not to allow him to be out until they were already home from school.

I knew we would have to face how to handle David's schooling after eighth grade. I did not feel competent, nor did we have the resources for the Math and Science and foreign language he would need for his continuing high school years. The other missionary children had gone to high school in Tehran, but that was before the influx of Americans, of which there were supposedly 40,000 living in Tehran. There was an American school for their children. I soon found we could not afford for David to attend there and did not know what plans to make. But God! He always has in mind our next step when we are trusting Him, even when we cannot see where it is leading.

Late in the summer of 1977, through a contact with the Hebrew church, I was asked if I would consider teaching English, in a large high school, Iranzamin International School. I would be paid a nice salary, from which we could pay David's schooling. The school was started by a group of Hebrew Christian businessmen. The medium of instruction was English, using the International Baccalaureate System (IBS). Farsi was taught, with studies for Armenian and Assyrian Christians as well. Classes were limited to about 25 students. The faculty was made up of American, Iranian, French, and German teachers.

The Headmaster was an American who had gone out as a missionary teacher in the American school but left to help start Iranzamin. The Headmistress was an Armenian Christian lady. Instruction-wise, I made some mistakes, but I soon had an appreciation for the IBS educational system. These students were taught to write. I thought some papers were so well done I showed them to the department head. When I went to show them to the headmaster, his secretary told me the student probably had his father's secretary write them! Incidentally, a few of the students applying in their junior year for college in the US were sending in these samples of their work and being given scholarships on that basis. Even so, these students were exceptional, much better prepared than the ones I had in our local schools in the US.

I enjoyed the camaraderie with the faculty at break time and learned a lot from the discussions, which often centered on what was happening in the world, or in Iran or in their personal lives. When the French teacher saw I had bought a certain kind of cheese, she told me I should never buy that unless it was made that day!

To get to school, David and I often rode the school bus. Although it made for a long day (we boarded the bus at 6:30 in the morning and didn't get home until 5:00 in the evening), it was a good way to get to know the students. Almost every afternoon, someone would tell the driver where to stop and get the large pieces of hot bread, baked in an underground oven by slapping the flattened dough onto the side of the hot wall. Those ovens were dug out of the ground and lined with clay, which had hardened, and heated by a fire in the bottom.

I intensely disliked the chairman of the English department but tried to be civil as his subordinate. He made a habit of either calling me to his office to discuss something, usually unimportant, delaying my being in class when the bell rang, or coming into my room. The day one of my students joked about his flirting with me, I told them they had better not ever say that again. At my first opportunity, I went to the headmaster and reminded him I had a husband, and I did not want that kind of gossip about me. I am more aware today of how the enemy is more like an ant than a snake in some situations, in that he sneaks in every tiny crack to try to destroy our Christian testimony. My students knew I was a Christian, as well as the teachers with whom I sat in the lounge. For the most part, it was a lovely group of colleagues.

The building was laid out in an Iranian style with a courtyard in the middle where students gathered during break time. There were 53 nationalities in the school, which had a class for children ages three through grade twelve and there were classes for two years of college, similar to a community college education. New young people to attend high school were coming in from different countries. Many knew little or nothing of English. They were given six weeks of intensive English study, then main streamed into the classroom with an English dictionary and one from their own country. We were required to study two Shakespearean plays a year. Knowing how difficult this would be for them, I sat at the typewriter and virtually rewrote those plays in a brief way so they would know the essence of the plot and could answer questions on an exam. It was a very pleasant experience.

One exciting episode during the time I taught at Iranzamin was the visit of Queen Fara Diba, the second wife of the Shah of Iran, in September 1977 for the 10th anniversary of the school. She was a very beautiful, elegant lady and very interested in all that was going on in the country. The night before she visited the school, it was thoroughly searched, including turning over and emptying of flowerpots! The Secret Police were looking for hidden bombs and other things that would endanger Her Royal Highness. All staff and teachers had to go through security the morning of her visit. She seemed very much at ease, and except for the fantastic amount of security, you might have thought her to be just another parent or guest.

Queen Fara Diba's visit to Iranzamin International School, Tehran, Iran, 1977.

There was a cake to celebrate the school's anniversary, which she cut, but not before it was also checked. Just as things were getting ready, I noticed a man with a long knitting needle in his hand, and sure enough, he poked it through every side of that cake! She peeked into some classrooms, but not mine, but we had a good look at her as she walked down the halls. When the students and staff sang the Song of Peace (Finlandia—"This is my song, O God of all nations …"), we heard she had tears in her eyes. We farewelled her by singing the national anthem, in Farsi.

Michigan State University was sending out professors so we could work on our post graduate work. The school was willing to pay the costs. I had wanted to do an MA degree. I signed up for two classes and one independent study on the bi-cultural experience of children. It was an introduction to how part of the world lives, in contrast to our American way of life. For that preparation, I talked to both children and staff. There were students who had lived around the world without ever knowing their grandparents and family members. One was a lovely Filipino girl. She had lived in several countries but knew almost nothing of her family heritage.

I can't recall who went with me to those classes two nights a week, but there was a group which left from school. We had to cross six lanes of Tehran traffic, three streets at the time. I did not think their courses of study were as difficult as I had at Bob Jones University, but I did feel I learned a lot. I was in classes with people who were superior to me in their education, but I ended with a 4.0 in them and a pass in the independent study.

Preparing my lessons for school and the lessons for my classes, in addition to the washing, ironing, and cleaning, was taking a toll. I was trying to keep up by cooking and freezing meals on what was Iran's weekend, Thursday and Friday. I often baked a chocolate cake and iced it, only to find my beloved had eaten the icing, leaving the cake!

Even with the difficulties, there were additions as I worked in the school. There were several opportunities to speak of my faith. On one occasion, it was interesting to suddenly see a number of kids begin to wear a variety of crosses. And the principal, in a private conversation, indicated we were free to start a prayer meeting if we felt it was the place to begin! If I could bring those kids to the Lord, help them to be bold in their own witness, and maybe someday start a Bible study, I felt it would be worth every aching bone in my weary body!

I was acutely aware that an enemy lurked behind every activity we did for Christ in that land. A fresh study of Daniel was so vivid to me: Daniel 7:25 speaks of one who will rule, who will change customs and times and will "wear out the saints." In chapter 10, Daniel speaks of being in mourning and tells how when (angelic) help comes, this angelic help mentions having been in battle with the "prince of Persia" for 21 days. The prince of Persia still rules and seeks to block every move we make for Jesus Christ. I continue to pray for an effective witness in Iran.

Richard's Adventures

I think Richard struggled with finding his footing in Iran. He kept busy with language studies and assisted in the missionary offices and participated in the Persian choir at our church. However, I think he missed trekking the mountains of Pakistan and visiting with the khans. Therefore, I was grateful for the times he was able to travel in Iran, even when I could not accompany him.

One such occasion was in late October 1977 when he and David hiked up one of the nearby mountains. When they got to the top, there was a place to stay; they were tired, and the weather was terrible—rainy and snowy further up, so they decided to stay the night up there. They had thought they would be home by 6:00 p.m., but as I watched the miserable weather all afternoon, I knew they would not! About 8:00 I got a phone call saying they had a dry place to sleep and some food, and they would be back the next day. When I say, 'I knew they would not be back,' I anticipated they would be sitting under a rock someplace! I really could not sleep all night, wondering if they would be cold or hungry. The next day, about 10:30 a.m. they straggled in. Richard had so badly bruised his feet that he had to stay in bed a few days! I had advised him to soak them—and I guess my training must have come from some place other than Loyola—for it was the wrong thing to do! But he was soon up and at it again. However, it did make him have to cancel the Esphahan trip he had been planning with David's scout troop; he was going to be the chaplain. He had hiked in tennis shoes—an obvious mistake.

Another occasion occurred in the spring of 1978. Richard was asked to accompany a professor from Damavand College to the city of Kerman, located 1,000 kilometers to the southeast of Tehran. They traveled there to determine whether there were opportunities for ministry work there among the few Christians in Kerman, who were largely Anglican. Kerman was located on the edge of Iran's Baluchistan province, which bordered Pakistan's Baluchistan. Richard's father, a Methodist missionary in India, had that region as part of his responsibility during the 1920s and 1930s!

Short Home Leaves

After being in Iran for almost a year, we learned that our son Jim and his fiancée Vivian were planning to get married in June 1977. While this was welcome news, it also saddened me to know that we did not have the funds for Richard, David and me to be able to attend the wedding. Richard and I had decided that David, 13, should go alone to the US to represent us. He had very much missed his US family since we had been in Iran. Accordingly, we made his travel plans, trusting God to meet this large need.

Do you believe in miracles? I mean the kind that in reality might be considered "unnecessary" answers to prayer. Such a miracle came to our lives at this time, showing us God's power to love. Someone, who wished to remain anonymous, sent a prepaid ticket so that I could also attend the wedding! I could not believe the good news. Just three weeks prior, as we prayed about David's travel, Richard suggested we pray for such a miracle! While David and I were in the US, Richard remained in Iran and was planning to minister to a group of boy scouts in camp near the Caspian Sea.

Since we had made David's travel plans before the ticket for me arrived, he would fly, by himself, to Belgium to visit with Elizabeth and family for a few days and then continue on to the US. The airlines had promised to take care of him, but I also asked the Lord to lend them a hand!

The next year, in the summer of 1978, we were approved for a three-month home leave; this time, all three of us would be able to go and visit with family and friends! Although it was just a short home

Emma, Aunt Zelma and Mom during Bob's wedding, 1978. Three wonderful and Godly women who meant so much to me!

leave, we all enjoyed it very much including attending son Bob's wedding to his bride, Linda.

There is something to be said about beginning an anticipated journey. Only the unattached and untied want to remain when the visit is over. Tehran was home, and as such, gave us a longing to get back. That sentiment will not be understandable to you who have not lived away from loved ones. We loved every minute being with family and loved ones; we shared their joys and prayer requests, but when the summer was over, I knew we belonged in Iran—by God's appointment and His loving calling.

Therefore, we returned to Iran at the beginning of September 1978 to a country in turmoil. We had been told at the airport in Amsterdam on our return trip, that a curfew had been imposed in Iran. When we arrived, all seemed quiet and calm, but tanks and the military were in evidence everywhere.

Iranian Revolution

The turmoil in Iran that would result in the revolution and the overthrow of the Shah, intensified during the fall of 1978. During October there were outbreaks of violence, demonstrations, and some impassioned pleas. Anti-American feelings were beginning to be expressed. Truly, we knew not what the future held, but we knew Him who held the future! What a wonderful assurance there is for the believer in Christ that we could be happy and have peace at that time of turmoil!

David and I continued in school as if everything were calm and certain. Our students had been warned about not participating in demonstrations, and not to miss school because of scare tactics. Although our school had not had any incidents, other schools had. The Community School in Tehran had rioting all around them in the city and they were losing students every day—they were transferring to other schools or going out of the country. One of the teachers at that school told me they felt the effects of the tear gas when the mobs were being dispersed. And one morning they found graffiti written on the walls: "We kill all

Americans!" Iranzamin International School was far enough out of the city that they would have to make a special trip to come there. It was unpredictable where and when they would appear.

Who were "they?" At that time, no one seemed to know for sure. They were accused of being pro-Shah some of the time, but those were also peaceful demonstrators. The rest were anti-Shah, out for demanding a pure Islamic state. Many were school kids, and of those, many were girls; some were college age young people. I had heard of one school where the demonstrators went into the classes of small children, frightening them.

Those were tense times for everyone, Persian Christians, non-Christians, and foreign workers. Rioting was breaking out all over. Everywhere there were strikes. One day one thing would be closed, and another day it was something else. Our bank went on strike for almost two weeks. Fortunately, just as we were running out of money, they settled and reopened it. But that would not be the only problem with the banks and money.

One very evident change was that we almost never saw any women in veils except for black ones. When we had first arrived in Iran, the women wore white-flowered ones, or none. But when the revolution started, it was strictly black. Even tiny girls were robed in black. It was rumored that any schoolgirl not wearing black would be attacked. This did not happen in our school, but rather in the public schools.

There were a few incidents involving Americans and we were told to keep a "low profile." Our school nurse, who was married to an Iranian, was on her way to school when they encountered a mob. The driver told her to put a scarf on her head and to duck down in the seat. The mob pushed the car into a side alley and left her and the driver drove off quickly. On another occasion, the bus for an American company was *en route* home with three men onboard when it had all the windows broken out, but no harm done to the men.

Also, during that period of turmoil, our landlord had asked us to either move, or pay an extra $300 a month rent. We started packing up but had no idea when or where we would find a place.

We planned to sell everything we could and try to find a smaller, furnished apartment to cut costs. However, the situation with the demonstrations soon became so tenuous, that a move was overcome by events and the necessity to leave the country. And while I was able to send home a few precious items (such as my wedding silver, pictures, and a few sentimental trinkets), and a missionary friend was able to pack up more valuables and send them to us after we left, most of our possessions were left behind.

Decision to Leave Iran

Adding to the stress of the ongoing unrest was the situation with my official papers and permits. My passport was set to expire in November and all my official papers (residential and work permits) were also set to expire on that date; David's name and permits were included on mine while Richard's were separate. I received a new passport in October, but it did not include a new Visa, therefore I was told to keep the old passport with me. Unfortunately, there was no way to renew the Visa or my residential and work permits because the Iranian offices had been on strike for several weeks. With the political situation intensifying, it caused a great deal of stress and anxiety.

During this time, I was also having a serious medical problem, but the clinic where I could be checked was in the middle of "downtown," the center of the revolutionary activity which was quickly spreading. Besides being unsafe to travel, the electric power in that whole downtown area was unstable, no one knowing when and if it would be on and clinics able to operate. Sometimes it was the water which would be turned off, sometimes the electricity, sometimes both, so my doctor was unable to have any kind of schedule.

One morning while teaching I began to feel dizzy. With perfect composure, I said something like this to the class: "Mrs. Thompson is not feeling well. I think my blood pressure is getting low. If I should faint, please do not panic, stay in your seats but one of you call the nurse." I may have named someone. Students in Iranzamin would have probably obeyed. Fortunately, I did not faint, but I knew it was time to leave Iran.

Therefore, with the unrest intensifying and my medical condition, it was decided I should take David and go to Belgium to be with Elizabeth and her family and return to Tehran if the situation improved. Schools had been closed off and on since September. Getting out was no easy thing to do. Not only was there a shortage of money at the banks, but flights on all the airlines were filled up.

It was early in December 1978. No one was really sure what was going to happen in Iran. Even the President, Jimmy Carter, thought it would all blow over, but one of the teachers in my school had told me, "They want him (the Shah) OUT and they are not going to stop until he is gone." She was right.

The Tabernacle Church of Norfolk had given funds for us to buy a car. It was in the bank, but we had been unable to get it. The banks were being cleaned out by depositors leaving. It was said that as much as fifty million a day was being taken out of the country. We needed that money in order to pay for airline tickets if and when we could get a flight. With the airlines overcrowded, it seemed impossible to know what to do. But God!

One day we decided to go to the bank rather than call, as we had been doing. It was a good move because whereas we had been told they had no money, when we got to the bank, we were told some money was arriving during the morning. We sat down to wait, were second in line, and we got our money. I had had to put money into an account run by the government, like Social Security, I think it was, and of course, that was never recovered. On our arrival in Amsterdam and Belgium, I would find no one wanted Iranian riyals. The exchange rate was only about half of what they had been worth.

Our next step was to wrap up the final details and try to get a flight out. I had taken a leave of absence from the International School where I was teaching; a lady who had been substituting had agreed to sub for me until I could get back. It was exam time, so I made out the exams and set up a schedule for her.

Luckily the airline had two tickets available. Although David and I could leave, Richard would remain behind, coming later for a short visit in Belgium before returning to Iran. We were hoping that the situation in Iran might improve, and David and I could join Richard there again. When the Ayatollah came in, we knew we would never get back.

God Watches Over Me

David and I arrived safely in Belgium on December 4th. Elizabeth was able to get an appointment for me with her doctor. He checked me and said I needed immediate surgery "to save my life." I asked if he could not give me something so I could get to the States. I said my son is in medical school and I would like to be with him. I recall very well what he said, "I can give you something, but you may not make it there." That negated any intention of my idea of leaving! The little operating room in that hospital was being cleaned up after another's operation and I was being prepared for surgery.

They had the blood transfusions I needed—five units of them—and the operation was successful. Both David and our daughter were waiting in the hospital with me and came to see me. As I lay waiting on the gurney, I recall praying, "Lord, when I wake up, it will either be in this hospital, or in Your House, and it doesn't matter which. I am Your child and want your will." I was not afraid of dying if that should be my lot. What a wonderful reassurance is the absence of fear when we dare think of death, the final earthly call for everyone. I had received Christ as my Savior; I had the blessed assurance of the only acceptable representative before God's throne of judgment, Jesus.

I did wake up in the hospital; the doctor's comment was he had made a very low cut so that I could still wear my bikini! I thought to myself, "O yeah? I am 50 years old! I don't think so!" I had the good care of the hospital personnel, daughter Elizabeth, son David and son-in-law David Harris, along with the loving visits of Elizabeth's two girls. Richard made a short visit then returned to Iran.

Two days before Christmas, I said good-bye to a wonderful group of nurses who had been very good to me and was discharged. Although the language in the hospital was French, which I did not speak, the language of love was the communication there where I received excellent care! The long recuperation (the doctor had told me six to nine months) had begun.

By early January, I was allowed to travel and returned to the US to complete my recovery, straight into the loving and welcoming home of my sister Evelyn and her husband Howard. I stayed with them in Portsmouth, Virginia and enrolled David in a Christian boarding school, Ben Lippen, in Asheville, North Carolina where we hoped he could make up the work lost during the previous months of uncertainty.

Richard eventually returned to the US, in February 1979, on one of the two last flights out of Tehran arranged by the US State Department. He and about 125 other American passengers stayed at the US Embassy the night before the flight; they slept on the floor, throw rugs, and blankets and made do as they could. He said they could hear gunfire nearby.

Two Pan Am pilots offered to fly out any people left. The airport was closed; they flew without the advantage of radar. The pilot said, "Welcome to Pan Am and America." There was a tremendous cheer when they took off and it was quite an emotional experience.

Once again, we were reminded that "here we have no continuing city" (Hebrews 13:14).

****

I find nothing in the Scriptures about a "toidle in my goidle." What I know about the turtle is that it moves slowly. As a child, I was always the slowpoke, so maybe I can relate to it. Better yet, I think I can relate to why God made such a creature. In the Scriptures, God rarely is seen to be in a hurry. I have found He

239

sometimes girds Himself in silence. The taunting of my childhood has enabled me to see meaning when I read such Scripture as 2 Peter 3:9 which speaks of God's patience with us.

The other day I watched as a gaggle of geese flew over our house, squawking as they moved ahead, all following the leader in formation, turning when he turned. I thought of how wonderful it would be to do that in our walk with God, without the squawking, which we sometimes do when we don't like what is happening.

We need the girdle of faith to be able to trust and not be afraid. Our Leader knows where He is taking us on the flight. God has a plan for our lives. When we let Him have control, He will work out His will. For that, we can praise Him, but His will is not always easy and certainly not always ours, not the easy way, sometimes a "dry and thirsty land where no water is" and we cry out for God to show Himself to us. Job had a bitter complaint. He said, "When I lie down, I say, 'When shall I arise and the night be gone? I am full of tossings to and fro unto the dawning of the day...'my days are spent without hope" (Job 7:5-6). Within that year of trial, he found the grace God gives and said, "He knows the way I take, and when He has tried me, I shall come forth as gold" (Job 25:10).

Although our time in Iran was short-lived, we will never forget seeing Mordecai and Esther's mausoleum. And Richard saw the ruins in Persepolis from the time when Alexander the Great went through and ravaged the area. Iran has a LOT of both world and Bible history!

Iran was left behind, but not the memories. They are still with us. God opened another door, and we would trust His will for whatever He had for us.

Our Time in the Desert

The wilderness and the desert will be glad,
And the Arabah will rejoice and blossom;
Like the crocus
It will blossom profusely
And rejoice with rejoicing and shout of joy.
The glory of Lebanon will be given to it,
The majesty of Carmel and Sharon.
They will see the glory of the Lord,
The majesty of our God. (Isaiah 35:1-2)

God throughout history has used the desert as a training ground for some of his choice servants. The lives of such men as Moses, Jacob, John the Baptist, and Paul, to say nothing of the whole group of the children of Israel, were all placed for a period of learning and retraining in the wilderness—the desert. So it would be with Richard and me.

Our next sojourn was in the United Arab Emirates. My interest in desert Bedouins like Abraham and the patriarchs was tweaked. They had riches but did not live in palaces like the oil sheikhs today.

Ministry in the Desert

In consultation with the Mission about our next assignment, we discussed two possibilities. India was our first choice, but it seemed doubtful we would be able to get a visa for there. It was decided we would go to the Oasis Hospital in the United Arab Emirates (UAE) and try there to get the visa for India. If it worked out, we could go back to the UAE, get our few

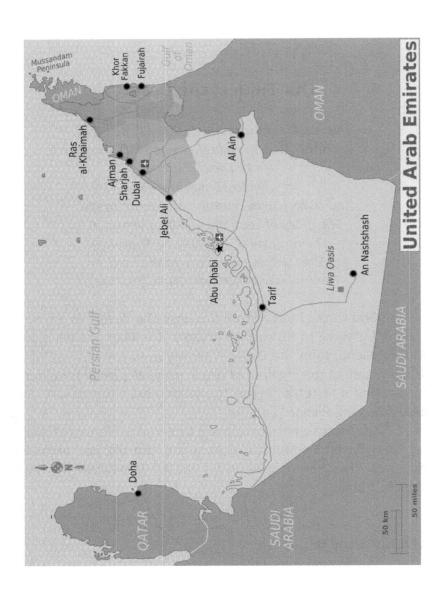

things and go to India. If not, we would stay and work in the UAE.

We arrived at the Oasis Hospital in October 1979. Most of the hospital personnel spoke Arabic or English, but a number of the patients who came for treatment were Pakistanis who came to the Gulf to work as laborers. They could not speak either language. My husband would be assigned as an interpreter for them. I would do whatever was needed, work with the children, clean houses after someone moved out, visit patients who spoke the language of Urdu. In other words, just "do whatever my hands found to do." I had no particular assignment and was free to use my time as a "helper."

Before settling in, we made a quick trip to India, but after visiting the various stations and talking with the leadership, it did not seem likely we would be able to work there. India was not very accepting of missionaries at that time. Our sojourn there was short. We returned to the UAE and settled in.

Oasis Hospital

Oasis Hospital was located in the desert city of Al Ain. There was nothing but desert and a few adobe dwellings when the hospital was started in December 1960. In those early days, the trip inland was by camel or jeep and took seven or eight hours traveling over sand dunes. By the time we got there Mercedes

Front entrance to the Oasis Hospital, Al Ain, UAE. 1984.

cars and new cement construction replaced the adobe huts and Bedouin tents had changed the look of the area.

We were told that when the hospital was first built, the water table was 35 feet down and was "sweet" (fresh) water. But because of the towns' growth, when we arrived, it was 185 feet down and still they could only find saltwater. Therefore, all clothes washing, dish washing, and bathing had to done in salt-water. Sweet water was brought from some distance away; it had to either be filtered or boiled for cooking and drinking. We brought it to our houses in five-gallon plastic containers.

We had a nice, small, living place at the hospital com-pound—two bedrooms, a living room, a kitchen and a bath. It was furnished with all the basics: an almost new queen bed, dressers, couch, chairs, buffet, dining set and cooking and dishware; all we needed were linens and they were loaned to us. We usually ate breakfast in our house and took lunch in the common dining area with the other hospital staff; it was inexpensive and saved work in the middle of the day. We would then eat supper at home or accept an invitation out.

The staff at the hospital, about 140 when we first arrived, were about half American or Canadian and half ex-patriates from mostly India, Pakistan, Egypt, and Syria. Richard, serving as Personnel Manager, had varied duties including helping the doctors interpret needs of patients from Pakistan and Iran.

First Impressions

The weather was lovely, most of the time. Because it was a dry heat, it was not really that uncomfortable, even when the temperature was 105 degrees! And in the evening, it would some-times feel cool at 85 degrees.

It seemed the desert winds blew continually. Usually it was a gentle, cool breeze, but sometimes it was a whirlwind or a stronger wind, and then we had a little sand around the door of our house. Because of the shortage of fresh water, there was little vegetation of any kind, mostly limited to date palms, acacia trees,

244

desert brush and an "octopus-looking" cactus plant. Camels and goats roamed about, nibbling at any available green they could find! The hospital had planted a type of tree that thrived on salt-water.

Because of the building in the city when we arrived, what paved roads there were in town were being dug up for sewer or gas, water, or electric lines it seemed. After seeing Europe's carefully laid out old towns, it was hard to believe that one would last long because the buildings did not seem to be well built. But then, I suppose, things don't decay as fast in the desert.

We could buy just about anything we needed in the bazaars in Al Ain. While food was not cheap, it was no worse than prices in Iran, so we were used to it. Many of the shop keepers were Pakistani or Indian.

Soon after arriving, we were invited with other hospital personnel to call on the family of the local ruling sheiks. We were cordially received, and I had my first taste of Arab food—roast mutton. The "table" was spread on a plastic cloth on the floor (to cover the Persian carpet) and huge trays brought in. There were bowls of fruit and various bowls of sweet dishes. The lamb gravy was poured over what appeared to be layers of very thin rolled bread with the leg of mutton on top. The meat was very tender but seemed bland and with no spice. To me, the food bore little similarity to the dishes of Iran or Pakistan.

Growing Desert Cities

Al Ain, called the "garden city of the Gulf," was both beautiful and a desirable place to live with a growing population. The city is about two hours' drive into the desert from both Dubai and Abu Dhabi, which are port cities. As the city grew, so did the need for help.

Among those taking advantage of better wages overseas were Filipino workers who arrived weekly. One unofficial estimate was that there were 5,000 working there by the end of

1988. They came in all capacities. And they became a ministry group for us.

One Easter Sunday night, we had a special service for them, and about a dozen came. That was our first get-together with Protestant believers who could become the nucleus for a new church group like the one that was forming in Abu Dhabi. Dr. Oscar Baldemor, a Filipino working with the Conservative Baptists in the Philippines, saw much potential in these two city ministries and spoke to both groups.

Another group of foreign workers we were able to minister to were from South Korea. During the time we were in the UAE, there were about 500 working in Al Ain. They came to Oasis Hospital for treatment and became acquainted with Richard. Once we were invited to a Korean Independence Day dinner. They were so friendly and tried to make us feel welcome; we considered it a privilege to be invited! Two of these

Richard and two young Korean engineers who became like our sons and often came for meals and Bible study.

young men, engineers who came to our church, often came to our home for meals; they became like sons to us.

****

God meets our needs in many wonderful ways. The important thing is to develop spiritually by concentrating on God. Our spiritual development is in direct proportion to our concentration on our Lord—every moment, every day, every week. This is practicing the presence of God. The desert was a wonderful training ground with these groups of people!

One winter the weather had been cool and there was rain—a lot of it. Tiny seeds sprouted and grew. Who knows how long they had been in the sand, just waiting for water! There was a beautiful greenness and life on almost every dune. One old Bedouin said he had never before seen it so green. The potential for life was there; all it needed was water. The seeds were just waiting.

Then spring came and the searing wind was blowing heat across this greenery; daily, it withered and died. The temperature reading 114 degrees in the shade. Power failures caused some concern (one lasted 24 hours). This affected us greatly in the heat of the day. As long as we had power (for air-conditioning) and water, life was tolerable, and went on without interruption. But when the power was cut for only 24 hours, we were almost overcome by the hot temperatures.

God continued to bless the various international ministries in the UAE. The "seeds" were "sprouting" and needed lots of water. The hot winds of adversity had come in the past; they would come again. We prayed that our roots would go deeper and deeper so we could become a shade for the new little plants!

Water for the Seeds

Education, both teaching in schools and Bible teaching, has been my life's desire and work from God's calling me at age sixteen. My mom said she always knew I would become a teacher because I would gather younger children around me and "teach" them. I don't remember that, but I do believe it was a gift from God, however small and incompetent I was and am, to teach. I have found people who wanted teaching and ways and means to work with them.

After settling into the routine of the Oasis Hospital in the UAE I was out shopping when I met two young Filipino girls doing the same. I started a conversation with them and invited them to

One of the ladies in my Filipino Bible study.

come for Bible study. There were rules for their being away or in another person's house, but we somehow got around those. They were able to begin meeting with me, sometimes in their apartments where they served me delicious Filipino food. It brought about the blessing of friendship. Others were coming to church. They later were able to form their own worship.

Marj Longjohn became one of my mentors for my UAE lifestyle. I was like the "new kid on the block." I had a lot of experience, but it was all among a different culture group than that of the Arab Bedouins. I don't believe God took me there to work with them, but rather to find those of other cultures who needed and wanted to know Him. Every group of people is different. It is the Holy Spirit Who teaches and guides and helps us know how to relate. Friendships formed with the hospital staff still are a part of my good memories. I was doing "hospitality work" and if I cooked a large enough meal, I would invite a tired nurse to come help us eat it. We never knew who it might be, but it formed the basis of friendship. Ruth Rutherford, wife of Andrew, one of the missionary doctors, befriended me, and there were others, too many to name but for whom I still thank God.

Marj Longjohn was not among the medical staff. She and I joined together in a ministry of Bible studies with the international community, many of whose husbands worked for the oil company. That brought about an invitation for us to speak to a group in Abu Dhabi. My message was in three parts, "Knowing God as Father; Knowing God as Son, Knowing God as the Holy Spirit." I recently found those files and was grateful to God for having allowed me to become a part of this ministry.

We were meeting women who were working in the UAE. One was a lovely Christian from Barbados. She did not feel qualified to teach but had leadership qualities and we got that Bible Study started. When emergency treatment for Richard made it necessary to return to the US for an extended period, a missionary nurse took over that class. When I returned, she wanted to keep it and I found other opportunities.

Ladies' Retreat, UAE, 1984. What a blessing they all were!

One of those was meeting Elizabeth Wilson from Canada. Her husband was a doctor with the government hospital. We met when they came to church on Friday nights. I soon found a dear friend who had been deeply involved in Christian ministry with women in Canada. We started a group of women by inviting them to come together and tell us about life in their country. Each week a different one would prepare a dish so all of us could have a taste. At the end we presented a short devotional. I can't remember how long this lasted but John and Elizabeth blessed my life in more than one way.

Our Ministries, Hospitality and Friendship Coffees

We attended worship services on Friday nights and Bible studies other times. We also attended the Arabic services on Sunday and Richard conducted Urdu and Indian language services on Thursday evenings. Richard also served as the chairman of the Evangelism Commission.

Richard's ministry was often with the many Pakistani Christians in the UAE. Here they are on Easter morning walking around the hospital complex, singing psalms and hymns about Christ and the resurrection. It was a blessed day!

Richard thoroughly enjoyed his work as an interpreter in the hospital which kept him pretty busy. Richard spoke Urdu, Pushtu and Farsi; not being medically trained, and not having studied as much in Pushtu and Farsi, it was not always easy to translate! Still, the doctors and patients were so grateful for his services. At the time, there were a large number of Somalis who lived in the UAE and came to our hospital. Fortunately, there was an elderly couple who formerly worked in Somalia who could interpret for them. I could

Richard and one of the many Pakistani men he ministered to in the UAE.

250

relate to the need for interpreters since it was a similar situation to what I experienced when I was in the hospital in Belgium and there was no one who understood what I wanted!

I also assisted at the hospital in various capacities. When people from western countries came to the hospital, I would prepare meals for them. This provided opportunities to invite them for lunch or dinner which then provided opportunities for sharing about Christ.

On occasion, I was called to try to translate. Once I was requested to translate for some Baluchi women. Baluchistan borders Pakistan and the people came to the Gulf for work. One young woman was delivering and was in convulsions and the male doctor was going to have to do surgery. When I got to the maternity ward, these women just pushed me out! I went to get a Baluchi woman who lived on the compound to accompany me. By the time we returned, the baby had arrived, but the doctor had had to deliver it. (Ordinarily, only our nurses, who are midwives, do deliveries.) For some reason, the old women wanted to kill the baby! They said because a man had delivered the baby, it had to be killed. Can you imagine? It is okay to kill, but not okay for a man to deliver a baby!

On another occasion, I helped with the delivery of a little girl. The mother had a rather hard time, and all I could do was comfort her, but the baby was big and healthy looking. When I complimented the women (who stay in the delivery room!) after the birth, they said, "Take it, she is yours!" They were not always happy about the birth of girls!

One year, I was requested to present several messages at the Christian Women's Convention in Dubai where we had about 100 women attend. Most of the women who attended were expatriates from other countries. These women seemed to have a hunger for knowing God.

Just as in Pakistan and Iran, hospitality continued to be a wonderful ministry area for us. Since our ministry staff often changed with some going on furlough and new arrivals, we often held farewell/welcome potluck dinners. We often had other large fellowship gatherings and teas for which I would often prepare food. These were incredible times of fellowship and encouragement. And it seemed there were always guests who came for lunch or tea. Since Richard was chairman of the evangelistic committee, the men involved in the Sunday night services would often come by for tea and discussion. On one occasion alone, we had eighteen guests from three different groups! Most often the guests were Pakistani or Indian. We found

Hospitality continued as an important part of ministry. Entertaining guests in our backyard in the UAE.

this was an excellent way of bringing people into our home, and often the talk turned to something spiritual, which was our first love.

I had made some new friends and decided to invite them over for what I called "friendship coffee." Most were not even church goers, so I used that time to reach out to them. When we want to speak about Christ, we have to start somewhere. Most were westerners and thus, came from "Christian" cultures, but in fact, they knew nothing of the forgiveness of sins and peace.

Spiritual Equipment ... A Lesson in Humility and Keeping My Eyes on the Lord

While performing what some might consider the "menial" jobs of assisting with patient meals and helping to prepare and clean apartments for new arrivals, I recall one occasion where I was reminded of the importance of humility and keeping our eyes on the Lord.

The writer of Hebrews wrote that Moses "endured, seeing Him Who is invisible ..." (Hebrews 11:27-29). That was the Word which came to me as I crossed the floor, tray in hand, on my way to take breakfast to a patient.

It had been a particularly trying day. It made me the prime target for the enemy, who loves to lash us when we're tired and/or busy! There had been four jobs to do that morning: taking breakfast to a patient, setting up the apartment for people coming in (getting linens from another apartment, making beds, cleaning and putting dishes and pots and pans in the kitchen, dusting, etc.), making Kool-aid for the get together that evening, and jotting a note to the Hospitality Committee (of which I was a member) requesting help for meals and laundry for a fellow missionary sick with jaundice. All was finished by noon and I rushed home to get lunch for Richard. I also needed to prepare the patient's supper; her lunch would be prepared by the hospital staff dining room.

Feeling weary but satisfied with myself for getting done all that faced me ("a job well done," I told myself) I crossed the compound just after 1:00 to attend our field council meeting. I thought that meeting would be complete by 5:00 when a fun-food event was planned for all the hospital personnel.

Council business was not finished at 5:00, and the decision was made to come back together at 7:30 when the fun was over. A long day!

I went home to pick up the supper for the patient. There, lying on the table, were the two copies of the committee announcement I had earlier placed in the missionary mailboxes, asking for help for the jaundice patient. They were our only bits of mail for the day, mute reminders I had angered or offended some-one. This returning of announcements—what was it supposed to signify? Was it an outgrowth of the movement in the homeland where one returns unwanted mail to the sender? I didn't know. That was not the first time it had happened to me in our com-pound. Shortly after arriving, I had taken responsibility for start-ing a Bible study for women missionaries and had my Bible study notes returned to me. But somehow, today it was too much. It felt like a slap in the face—two of them, for there were two notes—a "mind your own business!" And I didn't think I deserved that kind of treatment, since hospitality *was* my business. Fur-thermore, what I was doing was being done at the doctor's sug-gestion and for a loving, bedridden fellow missionary. It hurt. I vowed I would resign from the committee, which, while essential to the smooth running of the compound, is a menial, thankless job. "In any case," I told Richard "I will never again agree to be on it. I've had my turn!"

I felt I could have excused the world from doing such things, but there was no excuse for my fellow missionaries to act this way.

But that was not to be the end of the day's discourage-ment. The next thing was "Did you forget to send lunch to the patient?" "No," I said. "I have never been involved with either or-dering or sending lunch meals, except on Sundays or holidays."

I knew why the latter bothered me; at the heart of the matter was a kind of pride I had built up through the years to do well, or, at least, to the best of my ability, any job given me. I wanted my accountability record to show a favorable response to work entrusted me. It is also no doubt a part of my competitive spirit, and maybe even involves some defensiveness, but the overriding desire is like Hezekiah's (2 Chronicles 31:21). At any rate, the question lowered me; I felt "down."

The next morning, Richard woke before I did and was al-ready having his quiet time when I opened my eyes. His first words were "Honey, I think the word of the Lord for me to give to you is 'Keep your eyes on the Lord, not on people.'" And that was the thought that led me to Hebrews 11:27.

These matters among fellow believers are commonplace, almost routine in some places, and not at all unusual. I am sure I too am guilty of both sides of the coin—offending and being offended.

At such times the accuser of the brethren (for so he is called in Revelation 12:10) sees an opportunity to work through a Christian's tongue or actions. The person involved reacts with forms of anger or lashing out, retaliation—getting even—a refusal to share in the burden of the work, etc. Then, the enemy has won the battle "without firing a shot!" He does not even have to launch a major campaign.

If I internalize—go the internal route—and refuse to do anything because of unfavorable comments and criticism, am I not aiding and abetting the enemy? I once heard someone say, "The test of your character is, what does it take to stop you?" If we can be stopped by such words or actions, we surely cannot do some of the work God has entrusted to us. And I am reminded that God's children are no more immune to being affected by such hurts. Our eyes of faith must be on something other than the incident. Both cause and effect are deadly spiritual warfare weapons when thus used by the enemy. No doubt many of God's would-be choice servants are put out of commission when they are faced with either side of the battle: When they see people and not the Commander.

Our eyes are either closed or wandering away from our Leader. In such cases of "closed" or "wandering" eyesight, we are no better than the one we are criticizing, who has, also, and perhaps in a moment of weakness, allowed the enemy to work through their life.

Lord, let me keep this word about Moses before me always, so that the actions and deeds of my fellow believers do not throw me. They, like me, are susceptible to slips and, like me, need to be forgiven. One more thing, Lord. If nominated to do a menial, thankless job, help me to accept, seeing with my eyes of faith how You once took a towel and washed disciples' dirty feet, even though You got criticized for it. And that it was a menial, thankless thing to die on the cross for others. The jeers and criticism that day is still, two thousand years later, a reminder for Your children.

The Desert

Swirls of sands, layering the dunes in finely carved edges, serve as the canvas on which a Master Artist has painted an occasional tiny, dotted oasis and a few barren hills with craggy juts and steeps. A whale of rock lounges on the horizon. To the casual observer, this appears to be a land God either forgot or left off in his redecorating after the mighty flood waters swept across it thousands of years ago. These are the sands of the great Arabian Desert.

For thousands of years they lay as barren, unwanted—except by a few Bedouin tribesmen—wasteland, heated by the sun to temperatures in excess of 140 degrees, seemingly unworthy of the world's consideration. The overwhelming mass of tiny grains held none of the beauty of fairer, greener lands. The Arab warrior, using his ship of the desert, fiercely guarded his prize possession. Like one that is in conspiracy, the sand lashed at the newcomer by blowing in raging fury at times, making the visitor feel unwel-

Desert Bedouins in the UAE.

comed and ill at ease. Water for slaking the thirst was at a premium, and still is today. The stark barrenness seeming intent on drying out its would-be dwellers mentally, physically, and

256

spiritually. The image of harshness that greets those who dare to visit is matched only by the reality.

But the desert is changing. Ribbons of highway lace the coastal areas. Although the ship of the enduring desert still has free rein, he often pads across busy highways, only to become victim to a late-model Mercedes Benz or some other automobile. His bones are left to dry and bleach, mute reminders that another way of life has invaded the ages old domain where the kaffiyeh and dish-dash, the traditional Arab dress and headpiece, once held sway.

Money, once a very scarce commodity, is not the lord of the desert. Oil rigs become weekday homes for men who drill off-shore; fancy hotels provide accommodation for businessmen and anyone else who can pay the price. The money has brought un-dreamed of changes to the dunes. The salty water of the sea is being transformed into a potable substance which waters man, beast and a myriad of beautiful flowers that line the highways and provide gardens—little oases—reminiscent of King Nebuchadnez-zar's day. Where desalinated water is not available, other means are being explored, not the least of which is the possibility of bringing in an iceberg or two. Still, there is sometimes not enough to go around.

The Bedouin has learned to adapt to his unique circum-stances. His coffee cup best describes his reverence for the com-modity: it is about 1.5 inches or slightly larger in diameter, and about the same in depth. Into it, the hospitable host or mother in the family will pour a few drops of cardamom flavored liquid. In days gone by, the problem of thirst was equal to the problem of poverty. Water was sacred. Oh, not the sacred kind of sacredness; rather, it was the kind of sacred that forbid it being used for any-thing unimportant. Sand and the left hand were used for ablu-tions. The custom has its visible counterpart today. It is still ex-tremely impolite to receive or give anything with the left hand. One uses the right hand for every clean act.

If the differences above the sand provide interesting re-flection, no less do the differences found under the sand. Hidden from human view in the Eastern part of the Arabian desert, one finds an array of curiosities. There is the fossil field, which holds petrified sea and plant life atop and underground. For the palate of the archaeologist, there are tempting mounds, tells, to be examined. For the novice, there is something else; for it painted a picture to me that best describes life in the desert. Beneath the sands of this desert, hidden from human view, "grow" tiny crystals of silica. In form, some resemble roses, whence their name, Desert Roses. No two of them are alike, obvious proof of a creation predicated on the work of a Master Designer.

Digging for them might initially seem like a fruitless effort: they are not in every location. Having found them, one must work carefully, for they are fragile. Thus, it is the seeker will sift the sand through his fingers. As he does so, the sunlight catches on a bit of the mica embedded in them, and the reward is forthcoming. There is sure to be a whole hill of sand waiting to be sifted, and a few dozen roses waiting to be lifted from its resources.

I think I enjoyed this search because it was so much like finding friendship in the desert. When language, custom, culture, dress and a hundred other barriers seek to prohibit communication, the onslaught of discouragement is bound to be the outcome. Yet, as we lived among these people, we found love to be the catalyst. Their ways were not our ways, and it is we who had to change.

Lessons the Desert Taught Me …

I did not go to the desert to look for driftwood. In fact, I did not know there would be driftwood in the desert. In reality I don't suppose it is really driftwood. It is wood worn by the elements and time: a venerable substance. From the moment I saw some of the pieces, I fell in love with them. One had been eaten by termites. Termites in the desert? Yes! Other pieces looked hand rubbed. No doubt the wind and sand had combined to act upon them like a finishing tool would, making the wood soft and slick.

These pieces had obviously weathered the storms of hot dusty dunes where temperature rise in excess of 140 degrees and may drop to freezing at night. I picked up one piece which impressed me. At one time, it had been a part of a sturdy tree, strong, virile, able to provide shade for a weary, overheated traveler and his beast. Survival in the desert is predicated on the availability of water. It must have somewhere, somehow, found a source. Desert vegetation must endure the bite of the camel, the gnawing of insects and the climatic conditions that dry out body and soul. This now dead piece of wood had endured this and more.

Its lines showed an elegant stamina lacking in my own life. There was an arc of strength (no doubt a limb had been bent by some outside force) that plunged downward and then rose majestically at a determined right angle. This branch that had won the battled had a split in it which had apparently later healed, for it was not visible nearer the top. Evidence of many other difficult circumstances were there: knots, broken twigs and tinier branches that had struggled and been supported by the main one had all been a part of what I supposed this to have been—a thorn tree. I placed my find in the jeep and carefully guarded it as we headed home.

One day I was asked to prepare a refreshment table for a marriage seminar the church was to have. A tea table needs a centerpiece, but they were scarce. I would have to make my own. But using what? It was then I remembered the driftwood, now being preserved in my courtyard.

As I worked with the driftwood, I saw the parallel so clearly: marriage is like that! There are broken promises, like broken twigs; there are some splits that mend and some that don't, and there are graceful and beautiful lines when the whole is viewed.

I pulled out a small piece of plywood I had found on the construction site nearby. The driftwood would have to undergo one more piercing—a nail—to steady it. With hammer in hand, I struck the blow. It did not yield easily. The wood was tough; it had been grown in adverse circumstances.

With small invisible wire, I wound silk flowers in and out and around the wood. They were a pale coral pink and cream in color, stalks of greyish-green leaves beautifully complemented and drew the piece together. An almost real silk butterfly added the final touch. The whole became a reminder to me of the varied circumstances of married life.

Marriage is a beautiful garden which must be carefully tended if it is to produce anything of worth. It must be weeded, watered, pruned and watched over. Left to itself, it will, like a lovely rose, revert to its wild state. One aim of marriage is to bring beauty out of difficulty.

More Desert Lessons

The topography of the area of Al Ain shows three "soils": a clay-like substance called *sabka*, sand, and rock, which is mostly sediment or limestone. None of this is ideal for growing flowers or vegetables. A lot of labor, a water source, fertilizer, and constant digging are essential ingredients for even the smallest measure of success. But oh, the joy, when seeds take root!

The spiritual parallel is just as obvious. *Sabka* will crumble into dust when it is stepped on. It might be a picture of those born into Christian families who have never availed themselves of Bible teaching and who do not stand up for their Christian principles. The sand, always shifting, might be likened to the transient population. Like the sediment rock, left here for centuries to harden, are the Islamic peoples. Islam is perhaps the greatest counterfeit to Christianity. It is, in any case, a challenge, since so many of its religious concepts are similar to those of Christianity.

But there is also igneous rock here, rock that was formed by the pressures of fire, rock that is hard, firm, not crumbly.

Josie was like that. She was a Filipino nurse at the university there, who came to our home for weekly Bible study, then reached out and taught others who were weak in faith. She underwent a time of testing while we were there. During that testing, she gave testimony to her faith, telling why she could not do as she was being told to do. Her supervisor then told her she should resign. At first, she was crushed. In time, however, she saw this as an opportunity to return to her own country and enter Bible School. Josie did return to the Philippines, and we heard very little news of her after that.

Desert Blooms

Flowers have been my love for most of my life. As a child, I followed Daddy around the field where we had the nursery plants we sold. I asked and learned the name of each one. In Pakistan, we had a gardener; in Iran, I planted a few in the tiny yard outside.

In the UAE, I had the good fortune to meet a gardener from Baluchistan who was in charge of the state nursery. We had to get permission to buy the flowers, but I did and had a palm tree growing in the back yard, along with a beautiful pink and an orange bougainvillea growing on the back wall. Fresh water was in short supply when we arrived there in 1979. They had to be watered and cared

The Baluchi gardener's family, UAE.

for. We wanted to get some shade trees beside our carport to help keep the car we had out of the hot sun, but I feared the shade trees we got would grow too slowly.

I missed caring for them when we left in 1985. Back in the US, I have grown flowers and even a few trees from seeds. I think I have been given every kind of flower I ever saw and wanted, from the ordinary to the exotic. I have never tired of walking through a nursery, nor my own back yard.

The backyard "garden" at our house in the UAE.

* * * * * * * * * * *

My husband and I agreed that the real "garden" is what was planted in our lives—our children, beginning back in 1951 when Elizabeth was born. We thought she needed a playmate, so we were thrilled when Doug was born in 1952. Jim's coming 15 months after Doug shook us up a bit, but how else would they have managed to pull off such mischief without Mom and Dad knowing it (or was Dad a part of it?) if they had not had each other? Bob was not a willing participant to their schemes, but sometimes got blamed for what he did not do. David was like a new toy for all of us.

We were, and I remain, so proud of our children, what they have done and what they have become. What a wonderful life we have had, and what proud parents they made us.

Answered Prayers … But Not Always as We Expect

One of the stipulations for approval to travel to the UAE was for periodic medical check-ups for both Richard and me. When we first traveled to the UAE in 1979, our youngest son, David, remained in the US to attend Ben Lippen, an evangelical boarding school in Asheville, North Carolina. He later transferred to Wheaton Christian High School in Wheaton, Illinois.

In the summer of 1981, we returned to the US for Richard's check-up, and also to attend David's high school graduation. On arrival, David told us he had decided to stay out of school for a year before entering college. I had a lot of reservations about this decision; I felt he was too immature to be left alone, but I was helpless, except to resort to prayer, which I did.

I asked God to allow us to remain with him for the year he wanted to stay out of school. Later, I had an addendum to that prayer: I prayed that whatever decision was made would not be because of what I wanted. (I did not want the problem of convincing my husband or Mission it was of God.) But I also prayed it would not be because my husband wanted to return, or the Mission expected us to return. I feared if we left David and my reservations became realities, I would never forgive myself. I had too many thoughts of the time David had already spent, under the authority of others and without us, and I felt he needed both his parents in those teen years. Thus, I wanted God, the all-wise One, to make the decision.

One week before we were to return to the UAE (our bags were packed and tickets in hand; I had resigned myself to this being God's will), the Mission's Medical Office requested Richard have his routine tests done. They were negative, but the ensuing problems were grave; he came close to death from a bacterial infection as a result of the tests. It took months to recover. Permission to return was withheld; neither of us had made the decision. Although my prayer was answered, it was not in a way I expected or wanted. It was awesome—somewhat frightening—to see what God had done. Instead of three months, we remained in the US for one year.

****

The answer to my prayer and the privilege of staying with our son was not an occasion for a gleeful, victorious celebration. Rather, it produced in me a more awesome reality of God and His government in the lives of His people when they pray. It had momentarily left me a missionary without a "mission"—sort of like one sent on an "errand" who finds on arrival he has forgotten the original message or has not brought the message with him. "Resting" in the coolness of the "cellar" without a specific job (or jobs) to do did two things for me. First, it pushed me into an empty room without windows and doors (it felt like) where I had to spend time thinking, while being unable to act. When I tried to do something in my own strength, it seemed only to create a problem for those around me.

The second thing it did was to reenforce the knowledge that this is God's world; He can do whatever pleases Him. When I made Him Lord of my life, I gave Him the privilege of bringing into it anything which was necessary to mold me into the image of His dear Son—to *conform* me to that image. If what He is doing in my life brings about some suffering, I may find comfort in what the writer of Hebrews says about Jesus:

> *"For it became Him, for who are all things, and by whom are all things, in bringing many sons unto glory, to make the captain of their salvation perfect through sufferings"* (Hebrews 2:10).

And again, in Hebrews 5:8, of Christ it is written:

> *"Though He were a Son, yet learned He obedience by the things which He suffered."*

What then, is God's purpose in sending us, or allowing us, to go down a path of suffering? I believe it to be the same purpose

God had for His own Son, when Christ took upon Himself the form of a man, thus identifying with man so that none could ever say God did not understand what His creation goes through.

That brings comfort to me.

A Brush with Death

When Richard was told he should have the medical tests done before returning to the UAE, we did not anticipate any problems, since he had had these tests done two years previously and they were negative. He entered the hospital on September 22 and the tests were done the next morning. Although the tests were negative, on the morning of September 24, he began to experience chills and an elevated temperature, which continued all day.

That evening the temperature "spiked" to a very dangerous one hundred and eight (108) degrees! He was immediately placed in ice bags, and put into intensive care, where he remained for 48 hours. His blood pressure also dropped dangerously low while he was in that critical condition. The hospital care was excellent, and I might say, lived up to its name "intensive!" The case was something called "gram negative septicemia" which is the invasion of bacteria into the blood stream. Dr. Darvish, the urologist, a highly trained doctor who had also taught in the University Hospital, said he had never seen anything like that before.

One week later, Richard was on the road to recovery and released from the hospital. Does God answer prayer? As I sat by Richard's bed during those critical hours, I knew from past experiences that He DOES, but I took the opportunity to reaffirm my faith in Him and His promises, asking that this part of His PLAN for our lives might be totally according to His blueprint.

Thus, we were delayed in returning to the UAE. That in itself presented some unique situations which necessitated waiting on the Lord for His provision. Not the least of which was the basic need of housing. Our prayers for that were answered when we found a small two-story, two-bedroom town house in a suburb in Glendale Heights, Illinois just three miles from the TEAM office.

We nicknamed it REHOBOTH (see Genesis 26:22): "There is room" enough for the three of us so that David could stay with us; earlier that summer we could not find a place big enough and David stayed with others. It was a wonderful blessing to be together and have David with us. We thought he had missed us the past three years we had been in the UAE! We found some furnishings and were all set for Richard's recovery.

While there were many needs to pray for during that time, one of the most urgent for me was for patience! It fell to my responsibility to make some of the decisions and handle matters which Richard had handled in the past. Thus, I solicited my family and friends for prayers for wisdom, discernment, and guidance! Was God real in those days? And sufficient? Yes, yes, YES!

Although we were delayed, it was neither our plan nor desire to "sit still"; rather, we began to visit the many nationalities around us. Among those who we daily rubbed shoulders within the supermarkets, drug stores, libraries, and shopping malls were Indians, Pakistanis, Iranians and other Asians and Middle Easterners. We prayed that God would lead us to those to whom we could minister in Bible classes and other ways. Our next-door neighbors were Indians; names on rural mailboxes indicated there were many others in the immediate area.

An article in the local paper at that time told of plans by a Muslim group to purchase a school in a nearby suburb. The Islamic religion would be taught, since part of the reason for the school was a growing concern that their children were growing up in such a secular society. At that time, there were over 700 million Muslims in the world (about an equal number to nominal Christians), and Islam was (and is) on the march. The church must not slowdown in their witness and evangelism.

Did you ever wonder if your witness for Christ really counted? We all want to *think* it does, but sometimes we aren't too sure. While in Illinois, we met an elderly Iranian couple who were such dear people. We witnessed to them in a combination of Persian and English. Then we found an Assyrian Christian couple and his mother, from Iran, and put them in touch with the elderly couple. The wife received Christ through this encounter! And although her husband knew quite a bit about the Bible and we often discussed Scripture when we visited, we had no assurance that he had received Jesus as Lord of his life.

Visiting in the apartments around us made us aware of how the world had come to our doorstop. In one section, we found more than 50% of those living there were from another culture and/or language. It reminded us that being a missionary is being where God wants us to be when He needs us to be there (Read 1 Kings 18:12; Acts 8:27). Still, it is not always easy to understand why God needs us to be in a specific place at a certain time; it is absolutely necessary that we go, or remain, as best suits His purpose. We had to rest in that assuring thought.

Still, it was hard during those days to not sometimes feel like a missionary without a "mission."

****

During Richard's illness and hospitalization, I wrote a letter to friends, but when I went to xerox it, I failed to remove the copy from the copy machine. A lady named "Dorothy" found it; in returning it, she enclosed a note to tell me she was touched by what I had written, so decided to tell me so. She was a Christian too and was going through some trials. Her letter was most likely the reason I hung on to my writings; here was someone else who understood. My answer to her letter was written some months later, but not before I had absorbed something of the traumatic time through which we were passing. Here is what I said, and felt, at that time:

> "What can I say about myself? About our activity or lack of it? To have been a doer all my life makes my present existence almost unbearable at times. I suppose I fall in the category of one who likes "Lights, Music, Action!", whereas God wants me to—momentarily, I trust—be like a flower bulb

which, by its nature, must spend time in the cool of a dark, damp cellar just so it can bloom. When the proper conditions are denied the bulb, it cannot flower when springtime comes. Job says, "If a man die, will he live again? All the days of my life will I wait until my change come." Just so, if the grain of wheat falls into the ground, must it not die that it can live again and bring such life with it that it can feed many more than the single original grain?

Perhaps that is the lesson being taught in the classroom of my heart at this time. But I sadly fear I am failing the course. I do not like sitting in this classroom. I do not like "being." I want to do. Do what? Why can't I wait, like Job reminded me, patiently wait, until God effects the change and again places me in the sunlight so I can bloom? I don't know!

Or do I?

Is it an unwillingness to like quietly, waiting on him to perform the miracle? Perhaps.

Long ago—and now it seems long, long ago—I prayed Philippians 3:10-14 as a prayer. I pled earnestly to know Christ. Not "know Him" in the traditional sense as the church teaches, but to know Him in the power of His resurrection, the fellowship of His sufferings, to be made conformable to His death.

Such a "knowledge" is too deep for me! If I am to know Him that way, I would have to become a person identified with His death, thus totally and irreversibly dead to self, identified with sinners, identified with (but not part of) sin, and recognize myself so to be.

Do I really want that? Yes, I believe I do. The church today needs people like that. There are so many of us who are happy with our own class of friends, our own social status, our own identification, our own plans. If God is to answer our prayers, He must first, it seems to me, bind us up, bind us in a dark cellar, do something to immobilize us. Only as He immobilizes us will we stop long enough to meditate on Him. It is only after the quiet period that He can grant us strength to bloom, and blooming will surely require strength.

Does all this sound a bit melodramatic? I am sorry if that is so. It comes from a heart that has not always responded as it should have, from ears that have been deaf, from eyes that have seen only self, from lips that do not know how to praise. My dear sister, we live in a world that is desperately in need! The Indian couple next door are in need. And yes, there are some even closer who are in need—our families.

A few years ago, I heard a sermon in which the speaker said if we would know God as Philippians 3 teaches, we should take that verse and turn it around, using the last phrase first, and the first phrase last. Thus, it would become essential to be conformable to Christ's death before I can know the power of His resurrection. Perhaps that is why just now I feel "bound up" and unable to do what I want. Jello must be mixed in hot water and then allowed to get cold before it takes the form of the mold, before it is made "conformable." The "hot" places and then the "cold": an orderly process must be followed? Is there a lesson in this for me?"

Return to Teaching and Learning

After Richard's illness and recovery, we returned to the UAE in October 1982. I was requested to begin tutoring kindergarten during the first part of 1983. There was a little portable school on the hospital compound, and I tutored a few students. I received a nice note from one of the student's mothers who indicated he had been having a hard time with the method of teaching reading at the English-speaking school in Al Ain. He would get a sick feeling and did not want to go to school. She thought that if I had not taken him "under my wing" as his teacher during that period of time and patiently taught him phonics, he would probably have disliked school forever!

Because of my background and love of teaching, I also served as the co-chairman of the Vacation Bible School. One year (1983) we had about 40 children enrolled, half western and half Asian and Middle Eastern. All week we had been grappling with the language problem (some children went to an English-language school, but the little ones did not). What do you teach a toddler who knows very little English? Also, in the class were children of several nationalities, so there were cultural differences as well as language

Vacation Bible School, UAE.

barriers. But with the Holy Spirit's help, a lot of patience and love, and the use of pictures and flannel graph materials, we ended Vacation Bible School feeling that it was a profitable beginning for these students.

In the fall of 1983, we also began a Bible Education course. The courses were for all languages, and we believed it was what we could and should be doing. I was busy with copying and collating the course for ten books which was a lot of work back then, believe it or not. The entire course book was about an inch thick. It was an excellent method of Bible study.

Additionally, Richard and I both returned to our language study of Arabic.

The Lord Makes a Way

When Richard and I returned to the UAE in 1982 after his illness, we had left David in Judson College in Elgin, Illinois. He was not happy there and soon left, with a girl, to go to Danville, Virginia to Averett College. Our older kids thought I should come home, that David was having some rather serious problems and needed me. Richard, the Mission in the UAE and the Mission representative who was visiting from the Home Office in Wheaton all said, "You have to let him grow up!" and very strongly disagreed that I should "run" home to him. One reason was that it involved money for the trip, and we had none. I gave the decision to the Lord. I prayed He would make a way. I had even made the rash statement that it would not matter to me if I gained the whole world and lost my son.

On the morning of the day the representative was to have lunch at our house, a doctor friend who worked in the Government Hospital dropped by. His wife and I had been working together with expat women, and had shared many personal matters, of which this was one. They were Christians and their own son had gone through a similar time, so Elizabeth understood my feelings, and had probably shared them with John. John's first question to me that morning was, "Why don't you go home and take care of this?" I said there were many reasons. He asked if money was one of them? I said yes. He said if he and Elizabeth

271

were to give me the money for the trip, would the Mission allow me to go. I said I did not know, but I would find out! He said they would finance my trip if the Mission and Richard gave their permission and blessing.

The discussion came up over lunch. Without telling the men anything about John's offer, I asked why they were so against my going home to be with David; both were noncommittal. "Is it money?" I asked. Both admitted that was a big part of it. I then asked if I had a ticket, would they give me their blessing? Almost without any discussion, both said "Yes."

That was Tuesday, late October 1982. I was on the plane on Thursday and remained with David for three months. While there I had so many amazing experiences of God's provision. Someone lent me a car; a friend from one of the churches which supported us was traveling in the area. He heard I was there, somehow got in touch with me and put me in touch with an orthodontist, where I stayed for two weeks, until I got a room in a home of a lady who rented it furnished to me for a nominal sum. It had a 2-burner stove, a small fridge and a TV. I got a job as a substitute teacher, which helped with the finances, and had wonderful opportunities to share my faith, even to having the privilege to speak about Islam and the Middle East in the Political Science classes at Averett College.

During that time, I saw some changes in David, including a job with The Hartford which started his career in business, and felt there had been enough of a turnaround that I could go back to the UAE and trust God to continue the work He had begun. Those changes continued and today I see a young man sold out to Jesus. I cannot say what would have happened had God not worked out those circumstances. God is no man's debtor; He has the resources we need when we are walking with Him.

Visiting in Palaces

I am always fascinated by the way God moves around His people. We do not know His purposes but as we travel His roads we look back and see the winding, sometimes narrow paths He has led. On a few occasions those paths have opened into wider spaces, opportunities, and experiences we had not dreamed of. I had grown up in a village, lived in villages in Pakistan and although we lived in the environs of Tehran in Iran, the section was like a village all its own.

After we arrived in the UAE it was a new venture. I was privileged to visit in some "palaces." Although they did not compare with what is seen in Europe and other parts of the world, even here in America, it was a new beginning, a radical change brought on by oil money. The tents of the past were replaced with "palatial" residences, houses and gardens, work and workers, a dramatic change in the desert sands—such became the order of the day.

British companies had been the proprietors of the oil fields. With the seven emirates coming together in a united front, the United Arab Emirates became a country in its own right. One of the leaders, a sheikh and son with a heart for the medical needs of the people became a benefactor for his people. He helped make health care possible when he met the Drs. Kennedy and invited them to come to Al Ain, his beautiful "oasis" city, still in its infancy for what was to come in the future. The foundations of our TEAM hospital were laid in 1960. The Drs. Kennedy and nurse Gert Dyck became the nucleus of our hospital but very quickly others joined them, learning the Arabic language and the customs and ways of the people. The hospital was flourishing when we arrived in 1979. The languages used were Arabic and English but many from Pakistan, India and Iran were flocking there because of the need for workers in the growing oil economy. We were there to work with those who needed an interpreter. Richard fit the bill and I took on any job where I could help with the need.

Gerry Longjohn was team leader. Neither he nor his wife Marj were medical, but both spoke Arabic and had gotten immersed in the ways of the people. Muslim men are allowed to have up to four wives. The wife of one of the rulers lived near the hospital and Marj took me to visit her in her local "palace." She was a very gracious and lovely hostess. The inside of the home was nicely furnished but not excessive. On this my first visit, we had a meal Arab style, sitting outside on a blanket on the cement verandah. Although Marj had to interpret for me, the visit was as lovely as if I were a new-found friend. On another occasion I asked if she would like to have me take pictures of her children. I believe she had five, another connection since I have five. I was taken inside to an unfurnished room where the faces could be seen clearly against a light wall background. I had the pictures developed, took them to her on our next visit and she seemed pleased.

What is it but the Spirit of God who brings about friendships? I never learned Arabic but somehow a friendship developed. I was very surprised when I received from her a large money gift, Riyals 4,000. I told her I could not accept it as a personal gift, but it could be used to help a Pakistani family who needed money for their hospital bill

I found the people to be generous. The rulers seemed willing to share the country's wealth with the people. They were soon encouraging the young to become educated. I read upon graduation a large amount of money was given to help them get started in their careers.

There was another memorable visit in the home of a wealthy family. This lady's main sitting room was all in cream color with gold trim on the woodwork of the couch and chairs and the same color carpet on the floor. Sometimes the Arab women had dresses made by the tailors but which they didn't want or no longer used. They passed on some to the hospital staff. One was a good fit for me and when we visited her the next time, I wore it. I have a photo of myself sitting in one

Me in my fancy "new dress" while "visiting in palaces" in the UAE.

of those chairs, wearing my "new dress" and looking like this missionary was "sitting in the lap of luxury."

The same sheikh who was due a lot of credit for getting the doctors to work in Al Ain sometimes invited the staff for lunch. He was a very tiny man, very friendly, and the table was always a long one set with every kind of fruit and a meal with lamb and rice. He never stayed long but one day I asked if I could have my picture with him. He grinned and agreed, then took my hand! My face turned red, and it shows in the photo.

The sheikh hosting our hospital staff for lunch. My red face in the photo with the sheikh when I was bold enough to ask for a picture with him!

Leaving the UAE

Again, we would have to leave a country we had come to love before we wanted to. The UAE government required people to retire at age 60, and Richard could not get his permit renewed when he reached that age because we were not considered "essential personnel," such as a doctor or nurse might be. However, that was not the only hurdle we faced.

For a short while, we had a measure of hope that our work permit (including visas) would be extended, and we would be permitted to continue what we felt had been a rich and growing ministry. Both the Labor Department and Immigration approved the request for renewal. When the request went to the third department—the Investigation Department—it was refused. We had done what they had specifically forbade us doing, i.e., we had engaged in "missionary activity," sharing our faith with others. This was not permitted in a Muslim country like the UAE.

More than likely it was Richard's ministry and witness to the Pathans and others from Pakistan and Afghanistan. He had had some wonderful opportunities with these people. But we also had very good opportunities with other ex-patriates, including westerners and Filipinos. We prayed for fruit among those who heard during the six years we were there, as well as the two Filipino girls we met who were in Bible school in their own country preparing for full-time Christian service.

Thus, in November 1985, we left the UAE and returned to the US to start on the next leg of our sojourn.

****

Once again, we were in what Joyce Landorf calls "God's waiting room." The same harvest fields were still white; the laborers were still few. The walls of the waiting room ought to be familiar by then, but the shades are down; the lights still dimmed. Waiting on the Lord is sometimes like we imagine crawling through a tunnel might be—once you are in the middle, there is no turning back! All we can do is to remain alert and watch for the light at the end.

As we sat in that "waiting room" time sometimes seemed to drag, while at other times it raced by. There was time to reflect on the past and use the past as a measuring stick for the present while we also meditated on the future. There was time to observe and hear what was going on around us. Is that why Scripture admonishes us to "wait on the Lord," to "be patient," to "be still and know" that He is God, to "listen for" His voice?

In the *past*, God (to that point) had given us thirty-five years of experience in four countries: Pakistan, Iran, the UAE and the USA. The *present* (at that time) was a blessed experience, visiting with family, friends and supporters. The future seemed to be unfolding before us—not by some person's "word of prophecy," but by hearing facts and seeing figures which make us aware as well as alarmed. We dedicated ourselves to prayer as we considered our options.

Abraham was 75 years of age when God called him. Moses was 80 years old when he led the children of Israel through the wilderness. Paul spent 18 years after his conversion in preparation to do God's work. So, too, we looked to the Lord for the strength for a brand-new ministry, even though Richard had passed the 60-year mark!

Unlike Abraham, we were not going to an unknown place. Unlike Moses, we did not have a large following. Unlike Paul, we were not scholarly. But like all three, we felt God's leading and the urgency. And yet, it would not be a new ministry, but rather a new location. We trusted God to put us into a ministry amongst Middle Eastern and Asian people in the US.

While in that "waiting room," God had given us a beautiful spot where we, like the Psalmist of old, could observe His beauty. We initially settled in Etowah, North Carolina to await direction for our future.

The God Who Understands

"The harvest is truly plenteous, but the laborers are few" (Matthew 9:37)
I chose you before I formed you in the womb;
I set you apart before you were born.
I appointed you a prophet to the nations. (Jeremiah 1:5)

When it comes to missions, God uses people. The people provide the necessary prayer support and finances. It has been said often, "Some can give, and some can go, but all can pray." Jeremiah 1:5, Psalm 139 and a host of other verses remind us that God has planned a purpose for each person born. We believed God planned for us to be missionaries, but we could not have been that without the support and prayers of God's people.

There is no way I can describe how many times we have been blessed by those who could and did give, some beyond what they had, perhaps, but others who gave of their means, like the lady who gave a lovely ring so that we would have money to return to Pakistan. We never knew who she was, or I may have questioned her. It was given in a designated offering. Another dear, older friend who was lying on her death bed asked that her fur coat and her wedding rings be sold, and the money given to those same funds.

These gifts did not come to us directly; the funds were sent to our account at the mission. This "giving" to missionaries and causes has caused critical remarks and some people have expressed that they think of missionaries as those who "do not work for a living." That is an interesting thought, but when put under the microscope of God's Word, we must all admit that it is God

Who has endowed everyone with enough to give away. The Psalmist says God owns "the cattle on a thousand hills, the wealth of every mine..." Psalm 50. Haggai 2:8 tells us the silver and gold belong to Him. If He chooses to use His wealth to see to the needs of those who are proclaiming His Word, can he not do so?

Last, but by no means the least, is the way God always financed our many needs and our trips. It was by churches and individuals who believed in the Scriptures: Jesus' last command to His disciples was "Go ye into all the world and preach the Gospel..." At one time, a church was sending in support in the amount of $600 a month, believing with us that God had indeed called us to go. Individuals gave, some as little as $5.00 a month. We gladly received it, remembering "the widow's mite" as told us in Mark 12:42-44, a blessing to the giver and to us. We knew God doesn't need large gifts; He needs willing hearts and people who will go into the harvest fields, now ripened. Early one morning a fellow missionary stopped by our house, *en route* to another city. He told us God had laid it on his heart to bring by the envelope he was handing us. It contained 25 Rupees—a little over $5.00 at the time. I don't know how he knew that we were not going to make our money get us through the end of the month, but this amount would make it possible.

Our Log Cabin: "Bethany"

In the 1980s, Richard and I began to face the reality we would be retiring before too many years would pass. There is a missionary retirement place in Florida which only requires the missionary to bring suitcases; all else is furnished. Since we had very little savings, that seemed a good possibility, even if far from home, my "roots." Then our friends, Dave and Irma Jean Storr, wrote about the property they had purchased in Etowah, North Carolina. They wanted to develop a sort of Christian ministry there where students from Tibet and India could come and have a place to stay and be ministered to. They gave us a lot on which we would build a log cabin. Richard's Aunt Zelma had passed away, and unbeknownst to us, had through the years put aside a little for us. She was sure we would "never have anything for retirement." (Later, Richard's Uncle Olin and Aunt Theresa's, and Uncle Clarence and Aunt Mary's wills had a tiny bit more.) Dave Storr found a log package for us to begin; it was 24x32 feet, but by building into the side of the hill, we could have two floors about the same size. He was unable to finish off everything before we returned to the US from the UAE in November 1985, but the top floor was about ready. That began the building of our log cabin. My Mom had a gift waiting for us, a beautiful storm door for the downstairs entry, and a microwave oven. We had, or were able to find some used furniture, enough to furnish the cabin. (Sadly, the Storr's Etowah dream never materialized because of circumstances beyond human control.)

Some months later, my brothers Bennie, Woodie and Jack came onto the scene. They planned together to finish the lower part of the cabin, the part which was dug into the side of the hill, into a lower floor apartment. Bennie went to his friends and Sunday School class and got them to donate—again, unbeknownst to us. He brought a very long trailer of stuff to do the job, around those curves and over those mountains, I think it was almost 400 miles! We had to be away that week, and the three of them worked day and night to get it done. They finished just as we got there.

Richard was so worried about the finances, he could not/would not even face them. I kept saying, "Our credit is good; WE CAN GO TO THE BANK!" As it turned out, the anticipated thousands of dollars it would cost were added up to one small bill of only $200.00. It was Unbelievable! Thus, we had a lovely little downstairs apartment. My brothers put a lot of sweat equity into that house that week and Richard and I were forever grateful! We now had a cabin to which we could have family and guests come, and they did. Our total costs in dollars for all of this was in the neighborhood of $38-40K.

The cabin was both quiet and restful; our nearest neighbors were down the hill and across the way—probably close to a quarter mile away. The cabin was about three miles from Etowah. The small town of Etowah is about halfway between Brevard and Hendersonville and about 30 miles south of Asheville and overlooks the Blue Ridge mountains.

Looking at Ministry Options

After returning from the UAE and while living in Etowah, Richard and I looked at options for a future ministry. We had considered several things: going to Trinidad where TEAM was starting a new Muslim ministry; going to England where another mission was beginning a ministry with the many Muslims there and had invited us to join them; and going to the Newark/New York area where "Friendship International," an arm of International Missions, was working with Muslims. We worked with them for two weeks in the summer of 1986.

All those options were good and viable; however, as we prayed and thought and talked and visited, we caught another vision for ministry: the Washington, D.C. area. What a challenge had been laid before us!

There were 60,000 Muslims scattered about the D.C. area, with very little being done to reach them. They were to be seen everywhere, working in fast-food shops, walking on the street, buying in stores. They owned many businesses, some of the land, and one of the largest banks. They were building mosques and Islamic centers and schools. There was a secular radio program, aired in the D.C. area, in the Urdu language.

There were also thousands of Hindus. Along with successful businesses, they had newspapers in English and Hindi, in which they pushed Hinduism. A Christian Indian brother shared his scrapbook of newspaper articles with us. Here were a few of the captions:

"Find Out How You Can Make Washington, D.C.
the Spiritual Capital of the World" (This, when a
new Vedic, or Hindu, temple was erected.)

"Adopt a Cow" (The cow is very sacred to Hindus, so this might be compared to our "Adopt a Child.")

"Hindu Ritual at Home"

"Diwali Lakshmi Puja" (*Puja* is worship for Hindus. This meeting was to be held in a school in Kensington, Maryland. There were several articles about such meetings being held in public schools.)

"Ganesh Chaturthi" (Festival of Ganesh, the elephant-headed Hindu god with a human body.)

The Indian Christian brother who shared this information was very burdened for his own people and wanted to reach them for Christ. He also told us the Indians were buying a 24-hour TV station and building a replica of the Taj Mahal in Orlando, Florida. These things could happen because of our "freedom." Would such freedom lead us into bondage? These false ideologies were growing at a phenomenal rate. We found many in the D.C. area who were concerned about what was happening.

Said one pastor, "I believe Washington, D.C. is the greatest mission field in the world." Another older, very mission-minded friend suggested mission boards send their retired missionaries and those unable to return to the field into key US areas to begin work here.

Those were just some of the experiences we had as we surveyed the area. But the people with whom we met confirmed for us there was a great door opened there in our capital. Of course, there would be adversaries!

If we were to work in the D.C. area, our financial needs would be great. The cost of living there was very high, and we would need more support than we currently had. We had a serious financial deficit in our TEAM account, brought on in part by the use of a TEAM rental car and the moving of our household goods from overseas. The figure was about $1600.00 and was one of the very few times we had a financial crisis we could not correct on our own.

Further, TEAM did not have any work in the US and did not plan to start any. TEAM was founded as a mission operating only overseas and we honored and thanked God for their vision. However, in order to comply with the IRS and ease the tax burden for those who wished to continue our support, we would need to link up with another mission organization.

Thus, in the fall of 1986, we began work with Friendship International, the American arm of International Missions, Inc. We were still with TEAM for financial purposes but were on "loan" to Friendship International.

Working with Friendship International

In January 1987, we moved to Columbia, Maryland and rented an apartment to be closer to our ministry work with Friendship International. That also made it possible to see a little more of Mom and the rest of our family in Portsmouth. We still had the cabin in Etowah and sometimes travelled there to work on the place or just as a "getaway."

Our co-workers in D.C. were a young couple who had just joined Friendship International, John and Michele Marion. John was a gifted young man, who, while in Washington Bible College, had a burden for ministry for Muslims in the US.

How do you get settled in a new place? You start with prayer, and then wait on the Lord. We visited a church in the area and found they had a "Compassion Corps." We were told we should specify our needs and those dear people responded, one couple helped us find our way around and introduced us to another group seeking to help people in need. Furniture arrived and with it came names and addresses of Christians involved in other ministries who could acquaint us with the area. God was working in and through His people and we rejoiced to be a part of it!

283

Within our apartment complex was the Muslim Charities Organization. Richard made contact with them. In the nearby mall, we saw and met Indians who worked there. So many people with whom we could identify! We felt the Lord of the Harvest was calling and prayed that we would be good reapers!

While in Columbia, we met with over 30 young people who were actively interested in reaching out to Muslim people in the area. Our delight was dimmed by the ever-present question, "But what is that among so many?" There were approximately 60,000 Muslims there, an "unreached people." If Muslims were to be reached in America, Christians who live next door, who meet them, and who work with them will need to be actively involved; it is not a one-man job! We found many churches who readily admitted they knew very little about Islam.

It was also a wonderful experience to find people in Columbia praying that God would blanket the area with Bible-believing Christians. The area had a high concentration of professional people who were very interested in "upward mobility." But there were also those who were interested from the spiritual point of view ... UPWARD mobility! We praised God for putting us there and providing us the constant joy of exhorting, encouraging, praying and "feeding" younger Christians!

We often had many meetings and contacts with churches to inform them about missions, Islam and how to reach out to Muslims. We felt more and more that was to be a part of our ministry in the area. And we were blessed to be able to minister to others who were themselves in the ministry.

One such individual was a research scientist who lived near us. He was a Hindu convert, born in India, and led to the Lord while in college in the US. Shortly before we arrived in Columbia, he had a new encounter with God and decided he must either go forward or go back into Hinduism. He had Christian friends but found no one to give him spiritual (and other) direction. During the years we lived in Columbia, we spent countless hours with him. God be praised, he was reaching out in a way we never could and grew wonderfully in the Lord. He led several individuals to the

Lord, followed up on them, and started a very excellent Bible study in his home. He sometimes expressed his desire to be in "full-time ministry" and to be "there." We reminded him that he had a wonderful ministry with people we could never reach. He often told us of our part in his spiritual life.

Isn't it interesting how God puts us in the place of His choosing when He wants to minister to someone, and we are willing to be moved? And all the while, God is also conforming us to the image of His Son!

More Links in the Chain

We met several Pakistani Christian families living in the area. One of them, Nathaniel Din, was a language teacher in Murree, Pakistan when we were there over 20 years previously! Our meeting again was not a "mere coincidence." Surely, it was the Lord's doing!

Through Nathaniel, we met his younger brother, Samuel, who was also living in the area and was a Pakistani Christian. Another link in the chain! Samuel's first wife had died in Pakistan, and he was left with three small children. Shortly after remarrying, he moved to the US and his new wife was expecting. Medical conditions were a concern and she had to be hospitalized for the last month of the pregnancy. After much prayer, we rejoiced when a healthy son was born! We all felt he was special and was named Nabeel Joel (Jehovah is God). Soon after, there was a problem with the baby; he was not gaining weight and might need additional medical tests. I tutored the older children two days a week after school. They were wonderfully adjusted considering the trauma of their short lives. We prayed for wisdom and guidance as our families grew together in friendship and the Lord. Although they were not Muslim, to whom we felt called, Samuel had Muslim friends and contacts. Perhaps God wanted to use us in Samuel's life and Samuel in the lives of his Muslim friends. A few months later, God answered our prayers for Nabeel—he was doing better and did not need the additional tests!

As we counseled and witnessed to people, we saw them grow in the Lord. We also saw them come under attack by the spiritual enemy. Prayer was a factor in helping them stand fast and firm in the Lord. At times, the "darts" thrown at them were "fiery" (Ephesians 6:16).

Richard's Visit to Eastern Europe

While working with Friendship International, Richard had the opportunity to once again be a world traveler! He accompanied a friend, Bob, on a three-week trip to Eastern Europe. Bob had a small faith organization called Reach and Teach Trust and shared our burden for reaching unreached Muslims around the world. The trip was not a "pleasure" trip and could not be taken without the help of many supporters, prayerfully and financially.

For over 40 years, we experienced God's provision for our needs. "Where God guides, He provides," someone has said. Hudson Taylor, missionary to China, said, "God's work, done in God's way, will not lack God's supply." We had lived by that. And God supplied the necessary funds for both Richard's and Bob's trip.

In Romans 15:18-20, Paul closes out his great epistle with "so that from Jerusalem and round about as far as Illyricum I have fully preached the gospel of Christ … I aspired to preach the gospel, not where Christ was already named, that I might not build upon another man's foundation …" Illyricum is modern-day Yugoslavia where Richard and Bob were planning to go! We prayed that they would also have an opportunity to preach there.

They first travelled to Austria and met with the Operation Mobilization team in Vienna before eventually travelling to Yugoslavia, a country of (at the time) 23 million people.

The first week in Yugoslavia, they went to Zagreb where they visited Muslim villages. Bob felt that in some of these areas, the people had never heard or been exposed to the Gospel. Therefore, this was a first-time visit into this area—an opportunity for a pioneer ministry! When unable to speak, they prayed over the entire village.

286

The second week, they returned to Austria. Richard remained in Austria while Bob travelled to Poland where he had two meetings. The last week they returned to Yugoslavia to the city of Osiek. There they spoke, on Muslim awareness, to several churches and a seminary.

We prayed that God would use the fruits of their trip to His glory and to advance His kingdom. Unfortunately, this was the last overseas trip Richard made as his health began to decline.

Continuing Education

In the fall of 1987, I was fortunate to be invited to attend a mission-focused course sponsored by Grace Community Church in Columbia: Perspectives. I felt the course enriched my life as I sat, listened, and pondered what I heard during the course. Spiritually, many things "came together" for me as a result. Although I had been engaged in a personal commitment to missions for 43 years at that point, by no means did I feel I knew it all. If I could start over, I would do many things differently. Such is the substance of experience, I guess.

Although it was a wonderful course, if I felt any lack at all, it was on the emphasis of the need for a Biblical culture. Study in the field of socio-ethnology was still somewhat "new" to us as Christians but seemed to be growing. My personal interest stemmed from the study I did while in Iran with Michigan State University. I felt if we could somehow further the Perspectives study by doing some group study/seminars on Biblical Culture, we would be providing not only a tool for transition to other cultures, but one useful in our ever-increasing international community here in the US. The final chapter in the textbook we used by Andrew Murray stated, "The missionary problem is a personal one." It seemed to me the very heart of the matter was the need to develop a Biblical culture.

Understanding another's culture should be the aim of both the missionary and the Christian. The process of enculturation is the means to the end of developing a Biblical culture. This "third culture" (neither ours nor theirs) would better equip Christians in ministering to the increasing number of internationals with whom we intermingled daily.

I was again fortunate to complete a similar course in the fall of 1988: Perspectives on the Modern Christian Missionary Movement. This course was from the Chesapeake Seminary in Maryland. For that course I worked on a paper, "How Will the Church Witness to Muslims in America" and was encouraged to put it into booklet form.

Also, in the fall of 1988, I was also fortunate to take a course at Columbia Seminary in South Carolina on Islam. Since I believed there is a need for American Christians to know how to be a witness to their international neighbors, courses and seminars such as this helped answer that need. We discovered that many Muslims were locating in the Carolinas.

My Mom's Last Days

Death is always an intruder, an interloper. We have no control over when it will overtake us. Thus, it was with Mom.

A couple we had known for many years were in the pastorate of Denbigh Baptist Church in Newport News on the Peninsula and had asked if I would be the speaker at a women's retreat. We were to have a planning session on Sunday night, February 26, 1989, so I had come to Portsmouth to spend the weekend. Mom was in the hospital. She had fallen some days before and broken her arm. The family had spent a lot of time with Mom, so I agreed to stay Saturday night. Sunday morning, I went to my sister Evelyn's to get some rest before leaving to return home to Columbia. Later in the afternoon, I went by the hospital to say goodbye. As I left, I said, "I'll see you again before too long, Mom." Little did I know that the next time I saw here, she would be "absent from the body, present with (her) Lord."

My youngest brother, Bennie, had been at the hospital until about 8:30 P.M. and like me, had told Mom he would see her "soon." Mom was alert, talked freely, and none could have guessed that in a little over an hour, she would be gone. Shortly after my brother left, the nurse came in to tidy up for the night. Just as the nurse was finishing, Mom calmly said to her, "Call the children; I am going." A sparrow was falling to the ground, but the Heavenly Father knew about it.

The nurse immediately made the call, and the three children and their spouses who were living in the area left for the hospital. They arrived just as Mom was leaving us. Evelyn cradled Mom's head in her arms and my brothers, and their wives, watched as Mom silently and without fear "crossed that river" and passed from life through the shadow of death and into life eternal. They bowed in a short time of prayer and thanksgiving, and then a hospital chaplain assistant dropped by, asking if she could help in any way. They thanked her for the offer, but said they were fine. That same Heavenly Father was watching over the rest of the family of sparrows who had not yet fallen, giving all of them the "peace that passes understanding."

Earlier, Mom had written out the desires for her funeral and they were carried out. She would have been surprised at the long line of people who came for the visitation and funeral. Maybe she did know about it (Hebrews 12:11)!

Desire to Return to "Bethany"

Toward the end of 1988, Richard and I had given consideration to returning to our cabin in Etowah to continue ministry there. We wrote to the Department Council of Friendship International requesting they prayerfully consider a request to open a new station in western North Carolina and allow us to relocate to our home there. (Our two-year agreement with them was set to end in December.) Unfortunately, they never acted on our request.

We felt we could be used there as an information/missions-education link and to speak in seminars and church meetings. We believed there was potential for involvement in missions, with churches, and in outreach to the growing area-wide international community. This type of ministry would also not require any travel for Richard.

During one trip to the area in August, we found groups of international people living in cities within one half to three hours from our home. A young Tibetan convert who we met who went to school in Greenville told us of a group there and the effort of some Christians to reach them. He felt most American Christians were unaware of how to present Christ to other cultures. We thought church people might be more interested in reaching out if they knew more about the need and how to meet it.

Financially, God had met every need and we had been able to pay the bills on time. However, money was a factor in our request to relocate. We had often been affected and/or limited financially by the tightness of funds compounded by the high cost of living in Maryland.

We did not feel that we would be leaving the D.C. area without representation. John and Michele were mature and capable junior missionaries. They had rapport with both the older and younger generation. Time and distance had kept us somewhat separated; our communication had often been by telephone. We would remain available to encourage them in any way they requested of us.

At that time, we had served as missionaries for 38 years. Richard would turn 63 in October, and I was going on 61 years of age. Although the normal retirement age is 65, retirement was not our goal. It was our hope to continue in ministry as long as God opened doors and kept us mentally and physically capable.

If our request had been approved, we had planned to establish an "office" in our home. We also desired to work on some writing.

Although our request through Friendship International was not approved, in March 1989 we decided to return to Etowah. Why were we going? How does one ever untangle the web of circumstances of God's leadings? We see something of how He operates in Luke 4:25-27 and Acts 8:25-30.

We strongly felt that there were an increasing number of international people moving into that area of the US. We felt churches had not been fully alerted to the mandate of reaching out to these strangers coming into our cities and villages and now living among us and proclaiming their message to any who would listen. We hoped to inform churches and perhaps teach them how to reach out to the internationals, as well as reach out ourselves.

I had hoped to do some writing about Islam and felt this would be helpful for the churches, both for information and direction in how to minister. Richard was also having some ongoing medical problems and had been traveling to North Carolina for checkups and was possibly facing surgery.

Thus, with both sadness and anticipation we left Columbia and Friendship International: sadness because they had meant a lot to us; anticipation for what God was going to do with them and us.

Leaving the known to search out friendship in the unknown is not easy. It leaves a void and a sense of sadness. In going to Columbia, we had "drunk from some fresh springs" and had some "new food for thought." Our lives were the richer for that brief stopover in our earthly pilgrimage.

In going to North Carolina, we faced again what we had faced so many times in our missionary lives: new challenges, new opportunities, new testings. We both welcomed and felt a bit apprehensive about what God had ahead for us. He had ALWAYS proved Himself to be our sufficiency; why should this be any exception? In Deuteronomy 8:2-3, there is a precious reminder:

> *"And you shall remember all the way which the*
> *Lord your God has led you in the wilderness these*
> *forty years, that He might humble you, testing*
> *you, to know what was in your heart, whether you*
> *would keep his commandments or not ... That He*
> *might make you understand that man does not*
> *live by bread alone ..."*

Re-Tire-Ment ... But Not From God's Purpose

"Then Job answered the Lord and said,
"I know that You can do all things,
And that no purpose of Yours can be thwarted.'" (Job 42:1-2)

From the poverty of Pakistan to the wealth of Iran and the greater wealth of the UAE, I look back on a life that had allowed me to sojourn while digging into a well, not of oil, but of faith.

Throughout the 45 years we served as missionaries, we watched God meet our needs in unusual and unique ways. We were reassured that where the Lord guides, He also provides! PRAISE!

Many people have elaborate plans for their "retirement." But what happens when missionaries "retire?" When I gave my heart to Christ to be a missionary, I assumed I would spend all my life on a foreign field, in one country. We never expected to live in three foreign countries. The future was so far off. We were looking for the return of Christ at any moment. The Gospel needed to be taken to those who had not heard, and we wanted to do just that.

And then we were "retired." God's paths do not always lead in a "straight" way, but Job said it best: "He knoweth the way that I take ..."

We believed God brought us to all the places we lived during "retirement" for His purposes; therefore, we trusted Him to open doors of opportunity and show us how to serve Him. And He did just that. While in town one day while we lived in Hertford, Richard met a man who was a journalist and worked for the electric company which published a small magazine. They published an article about us which brought some invitations to minister. Being near friends opened up other opportunities. It was both exciting and wonderful to feel again that our ministry was not over just because we were "retired."

Return to Bethany

We moved back to our cabin "Bethany" in Chimney Glen Estates near Etowah at the end of March 1989. Although the cabin was tiny, like Rehoboth in Genesis 26:22, there was room for friends and family to visit. Was it not at Bethany Jesus found rest (John 11)? And did He not say, "Come ye yourselves apart and rest awhile" (Mark 6:31)? Therefore, we offered an open invitation to any who wanted to come.

When my mom passed away, she not only left us a share of her little savings but had both brother Willie and Jack add their share. More help for us. I cleared our lot in Chimney Glen Estates of the wild vines and "wilderness" growth. When we were on a mission trip to Parkersburg, WV, we stayed in a home where the man was in charge of the Forestry Dept. He gave us a big bundle of "Christmas tree" seedlings. I used them to line both the upper and lower driveways and planted some around our side of the cabin. Most grew, a few died. By the time we moved from there, they were about 12-15 feet tall. I cleared the front and sides of our hill, leaving only the dogwoods, which bloomed before we left.

The man across the road had a lumber mill. I asked him to save the bark from the locust trees for me, and he cut it to make a "retaining wall" and we put it up along the bank that led to the house beyond ours. Locust tress are a hard wood and do not rot very quickly. That man thought they would last as long as the cabin lasted! Railroad ties were being sold at that time and we got some to make steps down the hill and another short retaining wall on the far side of the house. We soon found that being on a hill meant constant erosion! Different people helped us get all that taken care of—can't just now recall who; we had so many people who helped us. It seemed the Lord always had someone there who saw how much we needed help. Some of our churches and/or individual friends had also contributed funds along the way, not large sums, but a few dollars, making life more pleasant for us. Calvary Baptist in Michigan always opened the "Missionary Closet" when we were there; we replenished linens and bedding on several occasions.

Our top deck was about 30 feet from the ground. It had a railing, but nothing to keep a child from falling through. In fact, one weekend when I had promised to keep baby Cara, our grand-daughter, while her parents were at a conference, she kept wanting to go out the front door. That was scary. I told her if she touched the door one more time, Granny would smack her hands. She did and I did, but that act was not repeated by either of us!

One weekend Elizabeth came for a visit and, seeing the situation, promptly went to Lowe's and had delivered the balusters that reach from the railing to the lower floorboard, and I, in a most unique way, nailed them on! I found a thick piece of wood. I drove the long nails through until they hit that board, then with a hammer in hand and holding it by the very end, leaned over the railing as far as I could, and I drove the nails into the lower floor and then into the railing! I had a plumb line, but in the end, Richard found I was about ¼ to ½" off. I told him if anyone commented on it, I was going to hand them the hammer and tell them to try doing it!

Later, one of our neighbors, Tom, wanted to earn some extra money for one of his projects and I was working, so I had him put in the driveway deck and another small deck around the back side—can't recall what that was for, maybe birdwatching! We knew another very nice man who did carpentry work and hired him to enclose the screen part of the lower deck which the Storrs had added when the house was built, and he enclosed part for a storage area.

A Continuing Hospitality Ministry

From the very beginning when we returned to our cabin, it became a place to welcome friends and family. In the first twelve days after arriving, we had thirteen guests! Some stayed for meals or overnight, some for several nights.

Less than one week after we got there, we welcomed one family of five, who needed some love and someone with whom they could talk. The man recommitted his life to Christ before they left! After this family left on Saturday, we had some guests from the Presbyterian church we had visited come on Sunday afternoon and evening! Oh well, I thought, I still had Monday and Tuesday to prepare for a retreat where I was scheduled to be the speaker. I had planned to leave on Wednesday to make the 450+ mile trip to Portsmouth, Virginia. How ridiculous a thought; there were still so many details to take care of! I did manage to find a few minutes for study.

Busy? Yes! We were certainly not "retiring!" With only one main interest in life—serving Christ—the word was difficult to define. We knew it meant a new challenge to faith and trusting God. Where is God when retirement comes? Right where he was almost 40 years ago when we first took up the walk of faith!

That summer was our 40th wedding anniversary and we had the whole Thompson clan down for several days in August. Our little cabin was brim full of happiness, with all our children, grandchildren, and other guests. We were even gifted a VCR and TV with an accompanying antenna.

Our little cabin continued to be a delight and blessing! We constantly thanked God for that little home. By that first fall we had entertained in the neighborhood of 100 guests. Not only were we blessed, but others seemed to have been as well!

God Continues to Watch Over Us

I continue to be amazed at the way God has continued to watch over us! One such occasion occurred during a drive in October 1989.

Richard and I were on our way from Etowah to Portsmouth, Virginia for a weekend of meetings and reminiscing about our earlier years of ministry: singing, praying, and praising our Lord. It was a precious few moments as we discussed what we would say at the missionary conference at Cypress Chapel Church on Sunday morning. About 6:30 P.M. we stopped at a fast-food restaurant for supper and were back on the road by 7:00 P.M., expecting to be in Portsmouth by 9:30 P.M. We never made it to Portsmouth.

About a half hour after we ate, Richard said he felt sick. A few minutes later, he said it again. I suggested he pull off the road and get some fresh air. I thought he was doing that, but realizing we were too near the edge of an embankment and going much too fast, I called out, and at the same time, looked over to find Richard slumped over the wheel! We were traveling about 60 mph, and there had been heavy traffic, but at that instant, the four lane U.S. 58 was clear. I pushed Richard with my left hand so as to free the steering wheel and guide it with my right hand. We landed in a wide, grassy median after making a complete U-turn. Richard came to; other than bruises, neither of us were seriously hurt. The car sustained some damage.

At first no one stopped to help. Perhaps they assumed the accident was alcohol related. Eventually two young black men, driving separate cars, did stop and went to phone for help.

After what seemed an age, an ambulance and state police arrived, and Richard was taken to the Greensville County Hospital in Emporia, Virginia where he remained for several days. The hospital staff (including a doctor from India!) were unable to find any problem other than food poisoning. However, they recommended he undergo further testing at home. As for Richard, he felt all right, but tired easily and quickly after any activity. He said he felt like he did in 1981, when he was so ill. His strength slowly increased; the doctors never found a reason, other than food poisoning, for the blackout.

We were very grateful to those who stopped, as well as the Virginia state police, the hospital personnel, the ambulance service personnel, the people of Bloom Retirement Home where I stayed while Richard was in the hospital, as well as the auto salvage place in Lawrenceville who fixed our car. At a time like that, even if at no other time, people are grateful for the graciousness of public servants. We were so grateful, that Richard wrote a letter to the editor of the local paper in Emporia, Virginia to express our gratitude! He wrote, "May we thank you all on the behalf of all of us, who may sometimes appear ungrateful." A sentiment that is even more appropriate today!

Our travel was not a complete loss; I had been scheduled to speak at a ladies retreat at Denbigh Baptist Church. This was a follow-up of a Spring retreat with the same group that had as its theme, "Bloom where you are planted." The October retreat's theme was "What did you reap?" Someone came for me, and we had a blessed day! The Sunday morning service, for which we had been preparing, also was not neglected. Long-time friends came and got me, and again, God blessed.

Still, we could not help but ask the question, "Why, Lord?" All of us know we are not indispensable, but we had really looked forward to the missionary conference. Surely, our lives have some ironic twists! There was another part of this accident story: our son, David, had called as soon as he got the news. Apparently, there were two older men, both named Thompson, and in the same ward. The other man died just before David called. David was erroneously told his father had died! The nurse called me to the phones, and I was able to clear up that matter in a hurry. We rejoiced at God's goodness in sparing Richard yet another time. Praise!

Richard's Ministry

Richard enjoyed fellowship with a local pastor's group in our area and also ministered to some retired people who had sadness in their lives. This was a wonderful privilege for him to be the link in a chain of events which bound us closer together as the family of God. As Paul wrote, "Bear ye one another's burdens and so fulfill the law of Christ" (Gal 6:2).

Richard also provided a listening ear (and heart) for some of our surrounding neighbors we visited. Some were firm in their commitment to a different concept of God, of life, of Christ and what He came to do. We got to know others who were hurting from life's appointments for them: specifically, the loss of a mate. Richard became part of the volunteer hospice program at the local hospital and provided comfort and prayer for those in hospice care and their families. Although the circle of ministry may have been smaller, the needs were just as great!

Richard was blessed to participate in numerous mission conferences during our time in "retirement." This brought such joy to him and he counted that ministry a real privilege. He even was able to attend TEAM's 100th anniversary celebration in 1991 which was a time of blessing as God's people recounted what God had done. He enjoyed the celebration and fellowship with many old friends. While attending, Quereshi, a convert from Pakistan, got word his son had died. Along with other men, Richard ministered to him in this time of loss.

Richard was also blessed to be able to travel to India one last time in the fall of 1993 when he accompanied his brother, Wayne, to visit places they had lived as children.

A Return to Teaching

After we moved back to Etowah, I was able to get a job teaching at Faith Christian School in nearby Hendersonville, which helped a lot with the extra expenses. I wondered if young people were ever more in need than they were then. (And today!) This tiny Christian school could not boast great things, but we wanted to help train the next generation of pastors, teachers, and laymen who could be used as a ministry in local churches and as missionaries. These, and yes, even those who are educated in Christian schools but who do not yet know Christ—this, too, is part of the vineyard. The pay was small; the rewards were "out of this world!"

Is serving in a small Christian school in the mountains of North Carolina—with long hours, teaching six different English classes, at low pay and with little recognition—a ministry? I think you know the answer. If not, consider the incident below.

During my first-year teaching at Faith Christian School, I taught a young man named John who was repeating seventh grade. Earlier, his family had broken up and he neither knew where he belonged nor where he wanted to be. A minor discipline problem (talking constantly), John spent about as many hours outside the classroom as in. At the end of the year, he wrote to me:

> "I thank you very much for caring for me. I love you and I always will. You helped me when I was feeling down about failing the seventh grade. You was (sic) the main one that knew when people made fun of me it hurt. I will always cherish you. I love you with all my heart.   Love, John."

John's dad was very concerned about him, and I was happy when John chose to live with him. John was saved several years later in the summer of 1992.

My second year at Faith was easier than the first. Getting to understand the students and their backgrounds helped, as did knowing the curriculum better. What helped most was believing that I was where God wanted me. Loving notes from parents and students reassured me that God had placed me in that school. The notes told me an impact had been made.

Someone has said, "Anyone can count the seeds in an apple, but only God can count the apples in a seed." I prayed that God would be pleased to grant many "apples" in the lives of the students from the seed we were planting. The students were no different from students in secular schools: they were pulled by every kind of worldliness. Yet we had evidence God was at work in many lives. Churches need Sunday School teachers and other church workers; Christian schools are a good place to develop them. The world needs strong Christian families; our emphasis was on that too.

Enrollment at Faith Christian School grew and one year increased from 185 to over 225 students. With growth came growing pains! Our schedules and classrooms were almost as tight as our finances. The ministry with those wonderful young people kept me busy and sometimes too tired! But the Lord continued to enable and the knowledge that that is where He placed me brought me peace. I am still in touch, after all these years, with one of my former students from Faith who became a teacher!

In January 1993, I finally joined Richard in "retirement." As my 65th year approached, I realized I was struggling to keep up with the heavy load I had, and a foot problem was causing me a lot of discomfort. God had already worked out all the details: I met a new teacher who needed a job, and who could take over at Faith. My desire was to act on a Scriptural passage which had been speaking to me for some time: Titus 2:3-5 and 3:14. Our church had a Senior Citizens group and I had been asked to be president and wanted to use that Scripture as our theme.

My Continuing Education

One regret I had during our years as missionaries overseas was that, although I needed and wanted further education, I was able only to get half enough credits for a coveted MA degree. While teaching in the Iranzamin International School in Tehran, the school brought in professors so we could upgrade our education. I did some courses and was accepted into the graduate program of MSU. When we had to leave the country, I had that same privilege at Wheaton College, Illinois, but we were soon on the move again, this time to the UAE where there was no university nearby. I had taken a number of courses in Community colleges, but they do not count. The most honored time and part of my study was after we returned to the USA for retirement.

In 1991, while teaching at Faith Christian School, I saw an announcement for a program for teachers. A list of summer courses was listed. I could apply for a National Endowment for the Humanities (NEH) scholarship. It would cost me nothing, of which I had an abundance, if I were accepted. I applied, and spent the summer at Bryn Mawr College in Pennsylvania, living in the Sun Oil Company Mansion which had been willed to the school. By that time, nothing resembling an exquisite lifestyle was left. It was bare floors and walls, no fans or air conditioning, and the very architecture was totally out of style with the modern school buildings, but it was fun. There were fifteen of us taught by a University of Pennsylvania professor, Dr. Jim McDonnell, who did a great job.

On the first night, we had to introduce ourselves. I said I thought of myself as a "committed Christian" who based my rule and practice of faith on the Scriptures. There apparently was no other person in the group with the same doctrinal position. Of the seventeen of us (including the professor and his assistant), were two priests, one nun, and the rest were either of the Roman Catholic/Episcopalian persuasion, or had no spiritual attachments. When the seminar was over, I knew quite a bit more about Catholic influence than I had known before.

The intellectual tone was very high: degreed people from many Ivy League colleges and schools, people with worldly knowledge and wisdom far beyond my own. My advantage was my knowledge of Scripture. Our topic, "FROM THE DESERT TO THE CLOISTER: The Bible and Its Influence in the Shaping of Medieval Culture" tells you what we studied.

This seminar was one of the most exciting times of my life. So many wonderful things happened; people were open to almost everything I had to say. I can only believe God used it. We had to read, write in a daily journal, and give a presentation. Mine was the first, a background of how we got our Bible. In giving my presentation, I took up the last days of Christ's ministry, the early days of the church, and Paul's epistles and how they were sent around to be used in the churches. It was very well received. Other topics had to do with the early church fathers, allegory in

301

Scripture, and the actual study of some Scripture: Romans (very briefly), Job, Psalms, Song of Solomon, to name a few. Below is one of my journal entries written after hearing the presentation by the Orthodox priest attendee.

****

LOVE DIVINE—A Variation on the Theme of The Song of Songs

Made in the image of God am I
Earthbound now, toward Heav'n I fly
Kedar's tents I would leave behind
I want to live with the King

    Not comely, no beauty which He should desire
    A keeper of vineyards, midst the flock I lie
    Yet hearing His voice, my heart leaps for joy
    O where shall I find my Beloved?

Companions I meet as I take up my quest
Contended in grasses with flocks they all rest
But I seek to find this King of all Kings
In search of His love I go on.

    He's there, in the valley, a Lily midst thorn
    The rose of Sharon, but I am low-born
    He offers me fruit, so sweet to my taste
    In His banqueting hall I feel His embrace

I rest me in peace for I am accepted
No fault in me is, while in Love I'm perfected
By Him in Whose presence I live now each day
My place with the King I have found.

    The Shulamite becomes like a disinterested by-stander
    The King comes, but she is weary, and does not arise

and open to his knock. She is then made aware of a
difference in the relationship:

Oh, what is this coolness? My love once afire
For the King in His beauty grew less in desire
He called me into His garden to come
But sleep filled my eyes and I nodded

He slipped into the night, And I left alone
Knew oh, so completely, I could not go on
I searched 'til I found Him, this King of all Kings
My Beloved's desire filled my heart

He brought me into His garden to see
The flowers, the figs, the pruned vines and the trees
To stay 'til the cool of the day by His side
My Beloved is mine and I His

He sought me, He called me, to dwell by His side
The love we have found is far better than wine
But the myrrh and incense a harsh note has sounded
In the garden, midst spices, I found the design

In Love stronger than death, His peace now is mine
While vineyards of fruits around me abound
Protected by Grace, His favor so great
I cannot be silent, His Name I must praise!

M.V. Thompson, NEH Seminar
July 21, 1991

The seminar ended and we all left for home. One of my
new friends lived in Florida. She offered to take me to Etowah on
her way. We had a good visit as we took to the road.

Later I saw a request for any who had attended the seminars to write an article about what they learned. I wrote one and

it was printed in their publication for which I was paid $200.00. My first and only paid writing endeavor! This became my incitive for writing and wanted to publish my story.

Conferences and Celebrations

Richard and I were invited to speak at the Calvary Baptist Church (near Detroit, MI) missions conference in October 1993. We had remained members of that church and they were a large and wonderful supporter of ours since the early days in Pakistan. However, Richard had tickets to accompany his brother to India soon after the conference was scheduled to start. Therefore, we asked if I could substitute for him. The conference was a special blessing to me; I realized how much I had missed being a part of them.

Rethinking our years of ministry brought about a renewal of our sense of calling, which had not been removed from us. For the ladies' luncheon, where I was the speaker, I did a study in how women in the Scripture were witnesses. It was a great blessing to find about 170 times when something a woman did is mentioned, and then to highlight the way the woman was a good or bad testimony in what she said or did.

Most of us need reminders of the urgency of carrying out our Lord's command. We DO become weary in our "well-doing" and tend to become spiritually sluggish. What amazed me most was the ability to pick up on friendships and visit as though we had never been away. I was with many "old" (it's not so easy to say that anymore!) friends and we just picked up where we last left off. I also met many new people who became "instant" friends.

After leaving the conference, I left for the Detroit airport. When I went into one of the Ladies' rooms, I noticed a middle-aged woman sobbing. I took time to ask if I could help with whatever was hurting her. She told me her husband was having surgery in Des Moines and she had missed her flight, so she could not get there in time. I asked if I could pray with her—there was not time to do more; it was almost time for my flight—and she seemed grateful for that. I had continued to pray that if she did not know the Lord, someone else would come into her life to add a further message. It made me realize again how often we might be a "steppingstone" to faith!

I also found myself attending the 125th anniversary celebration of Deep Creek Baptist Church in August 1994 alone due to a scheduling conflict! Richard and I had signed up for a Larry Burkett seminar that was going to be held just over the mountain from our cabin. Our congressman at the time was also speaking and the subject was to be about finances and elderly people. Burkett was the founder of a Christian financial consulting group based in Atlanta, Georgia. I was familiar with his approach but wanted Richard to hear him. Therefore, Richard decided to attend the seminar and I went to the anniversary celebration in Portsmouth.

The celebration was wonderful in every way. In a day and time when many churches were losing ground, it was a joy to see the strides this church had made. The only odd thing I noted was the absence of memorabilia about "Preacher Taylor" and his ministry. There were many names listed as those who had gone out from the church, in full time ministry. In looking over the list, I found no name earlier than his ministry and most of those I recognized on the list were from his time and ministry. I trust it was an oversight; I KNOW for certain it was the Preacher's ministry which brought me to Christ and showed me the importance of passing on this Good News by becoming a missionary.

I was also blessed to be able to attend the Taylor (Mom's family) reunions in Harrelsville, North Carolina on several occasions. We would have "dinner on the grounds" and recount family history (some notables and no doubt some failures) on ground given by a great grandfather to build the church. In the old church on this very land, my mother made her profession of faith in Christ.

Thus, the fingers of God reached out across the centuries and some from each generation have known and served the same

Lord I know and serve. At one of these reunions, two young men, both lawyers and distant cousins, and I enjoyed getting to know each other. One of them and I shared our experiences in missions. Their father, a Chesapeake, Virginia judge recounted the family history. What will Heaven be like when we celebrate our grand reunion with members of the family of God?

In 2006, my sister Evelyn, brother Bennie and I decided the Williams family also needed to have a reunion and we started planning. Our older brother, Jack, and his family from Birmingham were to be the honored guests. Neither Jack nor his wife, both 84, were very well, but they wanted to make this "last" trip home. Exactly two weeks before the reunion, Jack went suddenly into the presence of the Lord. It saddened us so much that at first, we thought of canceling, but then decided it would be a celebration. About 75 of my family gathered, four generations. It was wonderful to celebrate as a family! Was Jack looking down on us, enjoying it with us? Only Heaven will reveal that (Hebrews 12:1).

Richard and I were also both blessed to be able to attend the Pakistani Fellowship Reunion in 2010, held in Zion, Illinois that year. Meeting longtime friends we knew back in the 1950s and 1960s was so wonderful! We had not been able to attend for several years, but the friendships remained warm. The missionaries were and are like family members. Although we were older, the strong bonds remained.

Re-tire-ment!

Although we officially retired from the missionary field in 1989, Richard and I managed to stay busy! We wondered—was there ever a time when people really "retired" as some appear to think of it? Having been a teacher and a career missionary, I myself "changed careers" during those years. In 1994, I had two milestones: my 66th birthday and I completed the study and practicum to become a Certified Nursing Assistant (CNA). I wrote at the time to friends that the only problem was that having seen an

Occupational Therapist at work, I thought that would be a great second career!

While doing my practicum, on several occasions I had to care for an old man. He was becoming severely contracted (drawn up) and to the point where he seemed to understand very little. When I had to move him, he would cry out, using strong profanities. I assumed it was painful for him. I would softly say to him, "Jesus loves you, Harry." Sometimes, I would sing "Jesus Loves Me" or "What a Friend We Have in Jesus" to him. In his condition, could he understand? Only God, Who is able to commune with the heart of man, knew the answer to that. My heart went out to him and to all those patients who became so dear to me.

Another of those patients was a 95-year-old lady, Ann. She had a clear mind, could quote Shakespeare, poetry and the Bible, but was crippled as a result of osteoporosis, arthritis and a debilitating stroke. She weighed only 63 pounds, but had always been tiny, she told me.

She knew what she wanted and insisted on having it done her way! I told her since she was the one paying, I would certainly try to do just that. Apparently, she had had some sort of reputation for firing a sitter "every other day" but I remained with her; I think our respect for each other was mutual (but every day, I expected that might end!) She required 24-hour a day care since she could not get out of bed without help.

Once when I went in, she was "jittery." It was a stormy day, and something in her affairs had gone wrong. She asked me to quote Philippians 4:6-7 and she also asked for Psalm 91, Psalm 103, Psalm 118 and some verses from Isaiah. I believed she did NOT have assurance of her salvation, and I trust I helped her receive that, on the basis of Scripture.

She knew the Scriptures but did not fully understand God's forgiveness could ONLY be accomplished through the shed blood of Christ, the Holy God for unholy people. We talked of how that is a mystery for which we must exercise faith. We don't fully understand it, but neither did we understand electricity. We just knew both work!

After we talked out that bit about electricity, she began to remember hymns she had learned as a child—so many of which refer plainly to "nothing but the blood of Jesus" can wash away sin and sins in our lives. She knew many hymns!

Another day it was the Trinity—how can God be 3 in 1: Father, Son and Holy Spirit? For that one, I told her there are many things I did not understand, and some are very simple, like how H_2O can be liquid (water), solid (ice) and steam, each of which is different, but each of which is made of the same thing. I thought I might have been fired after that, though she insisted that I helped her very much and was thankful I was there. It was a wonderful experience and I realized God may not have moved us on (we had decided to sell our cabin by this time) because He had some "unfinished business" for us there!

More "Retirement" Living

In August 1994, we made the decision to put our little log house on the market. We increasingly felt we could not do the required upkeep. Richard sometimes got dizzy when he climbed on the roof to get the leaves out of the gutter; I worked on the "landscape" and pulled weeds. Often, after working up and down the hill, I could barely walk because of the pain. Sometimes it seemed I worked in vain to make it nice, but it really was too big a job for an "old woman" like me! Therefore, we decided it was time to find a flat area and considered the eastern part of the state, which would also be nearer to family.

We sold the cabin in December 1994 to a couple who we did not know had even seen it! They were from Vermont and fell in love with it. She was an entrepreneur of sorts, had a little business and used the lower floor for her work. She reaped the harvest of peaches from the two trees I had planted and made and sold the jam, along with other fruits and her handiwork. We found a house in Hertford, North Carolina and moved the early part of January 1995.

Doug, Jim and Bob all came down to help us move. The night before we were to move, they loaded the truck, expecting to leave in the early morning. Richard thought they were going to put the bed in the last thing, next morning, but while he was in the bathroom, they quickly hauled it out! That was so funny! They then made the decision to "move on out" and left that night, driving part way. I don't know where they stopped, but somewhere along the way they stayed for a few hours.

When we moved to Hertford, we did so because we still did not feel comfortable facing the traffic in the "big" city area. We found a wonderfully constructed house, built by one of the finest builders around the area, and when we sold it, made a little money on it. Again, I "landscaped" it and the last time I was there and saw it, I was shocked how things had grown. Doug came during that time and helped us put up lattice work around a little shed and did some other things for us. Looking back now, I realize each of our boys have added their hand to what we did or have. For that I am extremely thankful!

Then, it was time to get closer to family. Elizabeth was coming each weekend, a 140-mile round trip, and we felt we needed to be closer to "home." Property was not moving fast in Hertford, but one day a Fuji blimp flew over the Perquimans River and saw the area. Eddie Wynne liked what he saw and came looking, saw our house and gave us what we were asking. Thus, in the middle of 1999 (the same year we celebrated our 50th wedding anniversary!) we found ourselves moving once again; this time to Suffolk, Virginia.

We found a two-year old duplex in a lovely, growing new development where there were hundreds of other new homes. It is a "multi-ethnic" neighborhood with mostly young parents and small children. A quick observation made us think most were probably not church goers. It seemed like God had led us to a brand-new mission field, right here in America!

At our ages, not so much happened as it did a decade or two ago, but God opened some doors to teach and speak of His Goodness. I taught a large Sunday School class in a local

Methodist Church and had opportunities to continue speaking at various conferences and retreats. I also took a part-time job at Ṣam's Club, passing out samples of food in 2002. It was a fun job, non-stressful and put a little change in our pocket! It also gave me an opportunity to speak about the Lord. I worked there for about two years. Richard was increasingly finding it difficult to get out but encouraged and prayed for me. His gait was becoming un-steady and he had other physical problems.

There was another way in which God was looking over us. We had managed to save a little money. After we moved to Suf-folk, we got to know a man who had a Christian financial com-pany. Many people had invested with him, so we went to talk with him. It was a good time, so he took our money and invested it. We got a very good return.

****

Had we gone into debt for our children's education, I don't know where we would be today. We did not have that option, or did not choose it if it was available, so our kids have had to pay off their own loans and work their way through school. We could not be prouder of what they have done for themselves. I wish we could have helped them more, but since we did not/could not, that is one of the MANY added blessing to owning my home to-day. Instead, our children have given to their Dad and me and made our life an easy time for us. For that, we thank them from the bottom of our heart for what they have done. I earnestly pray THEIR children will do the same for them if they someday need it.

Aunt Leny's Passing

In January 2010, there were some health concerns with my siblings. Of our parents' nine children, only three were then still living, all "older" (almost 85, 82, and 79, but not exactly el-derly—just "getting there"). Then my beloved sister, Evelyn or "Aunt Leny," 84, became ill and talked of the pain she was having.

Tests and X-rays showed nothing; "possibly something viral," the doctors said. We were more concerned about our younger brother who was facing emergency open heart surgery. He came through that with flying colors; my sister Evelyn did not.

On Good Friday, Evelyn was admitted to the hospital, diagnosed with pancreatic cancer which had spread to her liver and lungs. Jim, our M.D. son, arrived on Sunday, saw the hospital records and said, "Mom, she doesn't have weeks, only days." She died on Easter Monday. It was a terrible shock! To me, she was a "best friend"; to her children, grandchildren and three precious great grandchildren, she was a bright light; to our children, she was a "second mother." All the family grieved while expressing praise and thanks to God because of the assurance we will see her again. She had a deep faith in Christ and knew she was going to Heaven. She was such an "ordinary" person who had an "extraordinary" effect on many people. She would have been shocked had she seen an overflowing funeral chapel filled with people who had come to honor her in death. At her request, our sons Bob and David had her funeral, a wonderful celebration of her life, and our four sons sang a quartet number she loved, "It is Well With My Soul."

****

In the midst of life physical, few of us take the opportunity to spend time thinking about life eternal. We take on the attitude of "Someday ..." or "I'll face that when I come to it." Thus, it becomes one of Satan's best ploys in his art of deception and it is accomplished by our procrastination. We Christians get so busy we neglect spending time with God—in prayer or in fellowship. And yet, we would be shocked if anyone were to suggest wonderment that we expect or want to go to Heaven to be with God when we die. Of course, we want to go to Heaven! "Why?" I ask, if God is a stranger here on earth.

So often I have been consumed by what I felt I HAD to get done. But should not the priority of the child of God be a mindset

311

about his Father? To at least check in often at the "Home Office," and with the "Boss"? And isn't doing that learning to "practice the presence of God"?

And so, the mundane affairs can become a time for practicing the presence of God, of hearing His still small voice, and of letting God speak through what has to be done and then relying on Him for the help we need to do it. I have not finished, but I have learned some lessons and had some reminders.

∗∗∗∗∗∗∗∗∗∗∗

Why do vines have tentacles?" I wondered. Now I know. Jesus said, "I am the Vine, you are the branches..."

In John 15, Jesus was teaching about our relationship to Him and to each other. I learned branches are strengthened by their tentacles. They reach out and touch anything around them cling tenaciously to help hold up the branches. Wind does not easily blow over vines with strong tentacles. I see a picture of the ecclesia; the church's need to be "strong in the Lord and the power of His might. If we are not strong, we will not be able to stand.

"Let this mind be in you which was also in Christ Jesus ..." Paul wrote. "... rejoice, be made complete, be comforted, be like minded, live in peace and the God of love and peace shall be with you." (2 Corinthians 13:11)

We expect fruit from the vines. The heart of God must be delighted as He sees His people being "tentacles" for other believers and bringing forth fruit by their labors.

Sorrow With Hope

*"I would not have you be ignorant, brethren, concerning them which are asleep, that you do not sorrow, even as others which have no hope. For if we **believe** that Jesus died and rose again, even so them also which sleep in Jesus will God bring with him..." (1 Thessalonians 4)*

MARRIAGE IS ...
        Two lives
        Two families
        Two backgrounds
                Coming together to become one

It is ...
        Valleys and mountains
        Rough places and smooth
        Smallness and overwhelming magnitude
        The aesthetic and the practical
        The dream and the reality

Marriage is
        The dew and the rain
        The desert and the sand
        The lake and the ocean

It is a garden which must be tended if it is to produce anything worthwhile.

                ~ M.V. Thompson, 1981

****

The afternoon of August 27, 2013, I had to face the biggest challenge of my life. My husband and I had celebrated our 64th anniversary on August 16. We anticipated many more years, but in the early morning hours of November 8, 2013, he left earth for Heaven. During the ten weeks before he died, I watched as he slowly descended into "the valley of the shadow of death" without me. Thankfully, he did not have to go alone. In Psalm 23, there was a promise for each of us. "Thou art with me..." was the promise for him. I found my comfort in the promise I will "fear no evil." God was with each of us. These passages, written by the apostle Paul to the Thessalonians, have assured me we will one day see each other again:

"For the Lord himself shall descend from heaven, with a shout, with the voice of the archangel, and with the trump of God: and the dead in Christ shall rise first: then we which are alive and remain shall be caught up together with them in the clouds, to meet the Lord in the air: and so shall we ever be with the Lord" (1 Thessalonians 4:13-17)

One Thousand Memories

All was well when I left home that day, Tuesday, August 27, 2013. I would return to find my life forever dramatically altered. Although we had been through some difficult times in the past, none had so dramatically altered my life as did the events of that day.

It was the day to do my grocery shopping day and some other errands. As a rule, on those warm August days, I tried to get out early, but the morning drew on and I was delayed. After making sure my husband had his lunch set out, I finally left the house. He always enjoyed that hour of watching some special TV programs in the kitchen while he leisurely ate. He was fragile in his body, slightly disabled, a little unsteady on his feet, but sharp

314

mentally, loved keeping up with what was taking place in the world. I had no idea he would have any problems.

I expected to be gone about two hours. One of my errands was to check out a new hearing aid office where Richard was to have a test the next morning. He no longer felt comfortable driving. I had become our chauffeur. We often joked about my being directionally challenged. I always turned the wrong way while going over an unfamiliar route. He knew I could easily get turned around. He did not want me to cause him to miss his appointment.

I took care of the errands, found the hearing aid office, returned home, and parked the car in the garage. With both hands holding bags of groceries, I tried to open the door into the kitchen, but my hands were too full. I called out, got no answer, worked harder, was able to turn the knob and walked in to find my husband lying on the floor, wedged between the table and the kitchen sink, unable to move his left leg without a lot of pain. His left hand was hurting. He had fractured his wrist. I knew what all that probably meant. Falling is akin to the worst kind of nightmare for the elderly.

He had on socks, but no slippers. He had both a cane and a walker but had not brought them into the kitchen. While trying to get something off the counter, he had stood up by holding onto his chair, tried to turn around, then slipped and fell on our wood floor, toppling the chair over on him. He reached for the phone but was unable to dial. Both the telephone and cord were dangling down the side of the kitchen counter. The base was not close enough to reach.

He thought he had been lying there for about an hour and a half, praying that God would send me home quickly. I dropped the bags of groceries and picked up the chair. I knew better than to try to move him. I reached across him for the phone. By habit, my immediate reaction in that nanosecond was to call son Jim, a doctor in Illinois, but I knew there was nothing he could do. Calling him would only take up time while my beloved husband lay in pain. My better judgment took over. I dialed 911, then dialed son

315

Bob, the pastor, and asked him to call Jim and the other siblings. Jim could call back. He would be able to advise me if I needed any special instructions.

The EMS is near our home. The 911 operator took the message, and the men arrived within minutes. I knew they would take him to the emergency room, but while they assessed the situation and prepared to move him, I quickly tried to think what I should take with me. I would need his medical information and would have to locate his insurance cards. I would follow the ambulance in our car.

As I walked through the house to the bedroom, I lifted my hands in prayer. Like a tree losing its leaves in winter, thoughts rained down on me in those few minutes. I knew our life would never be the same. It would be dramatically changed, but I did not know what the future would hold. No one ever does. I am thankful I know Who holds my future.

The psalmist said, "In the multitude of my thoughts within me, Thy (God's) comforts delight my soul." (Psalm 94:19, KJV). I would not call it a "delight," but I did remember I had a Comforter (John 14). He was the same One in whom I had placed my confidence when I first trusted Christ.

On a few occasions when there had been a family emergency, I had sensed something was not right. Sometimes that is called a "sixth sense." This time was a different experience. There was no "warning bell" that went off that day. It was a terrible shock to find Richard in that condition. I had never before known a time when I wanted to pray, and the words did not come to convey my needs. In my feeling of aloneness, the screen was blank. To describe the thoughts invading my mind at this point is impossible. I just latched onto the promises of God. What God gave me during those first hours and days was simply to leave the matter to Him, to rest in His love. I had learned that from Zephaniah the biblical prophet who wrote of his faith.

Dr. Luciana Perez, an orthopedic specialist, just happened to be on duty when we arrived in the ER. It was another promise fulfilled, "My God shall supply all your needs...:" (Philippians

4:19). Dr Luciana had been delayed. Without the doctor's knowing why, it seemed God had kept him there for this moment so he could care for Richard. How many times have these "happenstance" incidents been arranged by God?

Richard was placed on the operating table and the doctor asked for the scissors. When he said he would have to cut off Richard's favorite silky blue shorts, Richard asked if he could remove them without cutting them. Richard loved those shorts. He had several other pairs, but Elizabeth had found these and their softness against his fragile skin made them his favorites. I had to keep them washed and dried after he went to bed so he could have them the next morning. The doctor assured him there would be time enough during his recovery to find new ones. The large pair of scissors seemed to know just where and how to be used by the cutter. It took only seconds to do the job.

With the shorts removed, Dr. Luciana told us the damage. His bones were very fragile. He had once been a strong man, climbing in the Himalayan foothills, but in recent years, osteoporosis, arthritis, and a crooked spine had left him "in pain, all the time," he once told me. The left hip was broken, the left hand fractured. The ambulance transported him to the hospital, several miles away. I followed in our car. It was a painful ride for him. He said he felt every bump in the road.

At the hospital, I was told he would have surgery the next day. I got back in touch with our children who made quick plans to come, and I returned home to sleep in our bed by myself, a rare thing for me. A new chapter in our life had begun. I could not immediately comprehend he would never again sleep there beside me.

All of the children arrived the next day. We thought the surgery would be the next morning or afternoon, but it was delayed until late that evening. By that time, all the children had spent time with their dad. I was thankful we were all together. We had dinner while he was in the operating room. The surgery went well, and Richard was placed in a room to recuperate. He was no longer in pain with his hip, but moving his hand still hurt.

About five days later, he was placed in the rehab section of the hospital. The children had returned to their jobs. I was left alone to entertain plans in my mind for changes we would need to make so I could take care of him at home. I knew that was what he would want if it could be done. He would want to sit in his recliner and relax. He would want to sit at his desk and take care of our bills, something he always did. He would want to listen to the radio and know what was going on in the world. He had been a keen observer of world news from the time I first knew him. In college, he had been an announcer on their radio station. I would need help with his care, of course. The first weeks were coupled with both expectation and concern.

There were the days when I had some hope. I watched to see if he was making progress, but it seemed to be two steps forward, one back. Sometimes he was slow, not willing to push himself. The rehab instructors wanted him to stand up straight and tall. Although he rarely complained, one day he said his back hurt too much to do the exercises. It was not a surprise to me. I had noticed him progressively becoming bent over. Jim had used the medical term to describe his condition, "severe kyphoscoliosis" and said he would not be able to stand fully erect, but the more erect he would stand, the better balance he would have. I knew injuries for the elderly do not heal quickly and tried not to expect too much.

As if in a gentle warning, Jim also told us that elderly patients often did not have the ability to recover after a trauma like my husband's. They do not have the physical resources younger people have. Their bodies have used up daily strength and are worn out. But for most of us, hope lies eternal in the heart. I trusted if it was God's will, our Dad would be the exception. Each day, I spent time in prayer, not knowing what the future held for him or for me. I could not permit the word widow to find a place in my thoughts.

After those first weeks, I was faced with the realization he would never again be able to come home to stay. We could only watch as the drama unfolded. My first lesson was a well-known proverb: "Life is fragile. Handle with care." We do not know what a day will bring for us.

Earlier in the summer, son David had recommended a devotional book, Ann Voskamp's *One Thousand Blessings*. Ann had been challenged to count her blessings and keep the record in a notebook. I read this book and made notes as I sat in the rehab with my husband. Ann had a busy life as she tried to meet the needs of her husband, their farm life and a large family of children. It brought back many memories of our life. I capitalized on her title for a book I was planning to write and thought of naming it *One Thousand Memories*. A long life like ours does not get through with less than that.

I was not unaware of blessings. We had them all the time, but what part of this incident could I call a blessing? I was not unaware of the small things that come wrapped from God's Hand of mercy. Over two millennia ago, Jeremiah wrote, "It is of the Lord's mercies we are not consumed, because His compassions fail not. They are new every morning. Great is Thy faithfulness" (Lamentations 3:22). I needed to remember and seek nourishment from that.

The rehab workers were wonderful. I don't think Richard wanted to do the rehab, but it was essential. At first, they had to push him, firmly reminding him he needed the workout. When they got to know him better, they discovered my husband had a dry wit and sense of humor. In one conversation, I told them about his life before we retired, how he trekked into tribal areas, sometimes walking as many as 25 miles in a day. They began to understand his now weakened condition and did not push him as hard. It was amazing therapy. I watched as they taught patients how to be self-reliant. They used so many different methods to exercise each part of his body.

Being retired missionaries, we occasionally think more quickly in our acquired language than in English. Richard would sometimes utter an Urdu word from the Pakistani language, like "*shabash*!" (well done) or "*bas*" (stop, or enough). I am not sure they appreciated this when he first used the words. It probably seemed like an affront. Soon, however, they were picking up on it and using it with him and we were all laughing. Even some of the other patients overheard and enjoyed the exchange.

There was a small, enclosed garden outside the rehab facility doors. I often took Richard in the wheelchair, and we sat outside in the fresh air. The weather was cooling, the leaves were falling, and it provided a break from being inside. We read from his devotional book, *Daily Bread*, and from the quarterly worldwide prayer guide for missions he used regularly. We had prayer for the needs around the world, something we sometimes forget when we ourselves are in need. It had been his daily ritual for years. In the garden was a dug-out area with a little bridge over it. We wondered if when the hospital was first built it might have been a pool, maybe a fishpond, but now, like so many good architectural ideas, it was neglected, possibly abandoned. We crossed over that little bridge many times as I pushed the wheelchair around the area.

It was like a reminder our lives had once been dug out of a place on earth for a special purpose. Each of us had been taken from a different area, then drawn together to be a bridge of service to God. We had served as missionaries in three countries of the world, as well as our own. Our days as a part of the "big name band" beating out the Gospel were over. What we could do now was small and different, but we still desired to serve. There were people who still needed that little bridge to help them cross over pools that had dried up in their lives.

I thought so often how our lives are encased in the unknown, hidden under the Hand of God. I thought about how most of us live from day to day, never anticipating these changes that could come. The same recurring thoughts I had that day when I walked into the bedroom to get the medical card for registering Richard kept coming back. I struggled with the question, "Is this how our life is going to end?" Could I hope Richard would have a measure of healing? I became acutely aware of how the future is withheld from us. I began to write a reflection, "The Unknown He Knows."

We had been in this rehab facility about a month. The number of days which Richard's insurance would pay were running out. We would need to make other arrangements. Since he needed further care, we were told he could be moved to a different facility where the rehab would continue, but not be so intensive. We moved him to a Bon Secours Nursing Facility which was nearby. It meant I could be with him and help care for him. The rehab staff had a little "graduation" ceremony for him and others who were being discharged the same day. They had become like close, loving friends.

I decided to save the expense of an ambulance or other carrier and drive him myself to the new facility. The staff at the new facility brought out a wheelchair, helped him into it, and got him into the room that had been prepared. It was a double room. Richard's first bed was just inside the door and another patient was in the bed next to the window.

David flew in from Chicago that night, rented a car and arrived late that first evening. He wanted to stay the night with his dad, so he just slept on the floor, breaking the rule, of course. It was a good move, but a cold floor and not much sleep for David. He found out the patient who was in the bed next to the window was leaving the next morning and jumped on the chance to ask if his dad could have that bed. It was agreed, and such a good idea. One of the first things he did the next day was to buy and put-up bird feeders, one right outside the window. His dad loved watching the birds. It was wonderful to have David's help for a few days before he had to get back home to his family.

Our children had been back and forth, keeping tabs on their dad's progress. I let them break the news to him that he would not be able to return home. It did not seem to surprise him. I was not sure if he would have liked to come back for a day to tend to his desk and care for the bills. He did not reply when I asked him. To my knowledge, he never asked to return home which, in retrospect, was a surprise to me. How many times are things left undone or in disorder after an accident like this? The compelling notion that we have tomorrow can be interrupted in a moment.

I could not have been more thankful that Elizabeth took over and found her dad's desk in good order, all the bills and payments up to date. I am not that meticulous. I depended on him for all of that and he was faithful, keeping good records. He kept me up to date, except for one thing. What he forgot to tell me was how to operate the thermostat in our house. He had always taken care of that. When the weather abruptly changed, I had to find the instruction book.

Since the new facility was near our home, I was able to go back and forth quickly and easily and spend much of the time at his bedside as well as care for things at home. My being there meant the nursing staff did not have to do some of the things for him that I could do. The rehab continued, but on a smaller scale. Again, we had a very good relationship with the staff. Working day in and day out with bedridden or wheelchair bound patients has to be a gift. There are menial chores they have to do, as well as random demands on them. The staff in these nursing homes deserve our thanks and we tried to give it.

Our children were wonderful. Elizabeth, who lives nearby, was in and out every time she had a free minute. She was more able than I to anticipate what he might need and saw to it he had anything and everything he might want or need to make him comfortable.

As the days passed, all of us began to realize what Jim had earlier told us was probably right. The "tunnel" with the proverbial "light at the end" seemed to be getting closer. We were all anxious to spend as much time as possible with our dad. Young business people in this fast communication age amaze me. Our four sons handled a lot of their work by the computer, or by phone, making it possible to continue their daily jobs while sitting by their dad's bed. Since all four sons live out of town, they decided to take turns and stagger their visits.

Doug tried to think of ways to keep his dad comfortable. We were all thinking the same thing: How many days are left and how can we spend them with him?

Jim had committed to be a part of a medical mission trip to Brazil and was also planning a trip up the Amazon River into the rain forest. As a young missionary, his dad had trekked in rugged mountainous areas in Pakistan and could foresee the dangers and problems. Jim knew if his dad took a turn for the worst, it would have been difficult if not impossible to get a message to him in Brazil. We all prayed for Jim's safety. He returned with lots of stories and pictures. Richard was still alert enough to ask questions and see the pictures on Jim's laptop.

Bob phoned his dad every morning. Richard called him "my *padri walla beta.*" In the Urdu language, that means my pastor son. His dad always added, "and my friend." Bob, senior pastor of a church in Hickory, North Carolina, and wife Linda were able to make quick trips, sometimes staying a couple of days, at other times, having to return the same day, or within 24 hours. Their coming was a help to me, made their Dad feel special and left no room for doubt about how much they loved him.

October 31 was a pivotal day for us. It was the ninth week since Richard fell. Once again, the insurance money was running out. We had to make other plans for where Richard would go next. He had a week left, but that could be extended for still another week if it was felt more rehab would help him. Bob had been with his dad and had seen his dad's workout in rehab that morning. After the routine was finished, his dad had walked from therapy to his room, the most he had been able to walk since he fell. We were thrilled. It was the most encouraging thing we had seen. He might be making some progress. If so, we wanted him to stay in this rehab for the rest of the time his insurance allowed.

It was also the day for the rehab staff to tell the family what they believed about Richard's progress. Most of our family were together at this meeting. The young lady who had worked with my husband in rehab was first. She told us how pleased she was about how well he had done in the morning workout. The

Director of Nursing believed my husband had plateaued and should be transferred to an Assisted Living facility. These two opinions left us in a state of confusion.

Bob was optimistic about Richard's recovery, but Jim reminded us patients with a body as weakened as his Dad's often do not survive for long. The osteoporosis, arthritic and spinal problems were what had initially precipitated his unsteady walk and probably added to or caused his fall. Fragile bones would not likely get stronger, Jim said, nor allow a lot of mobility. It was very prophetic. Jim's long-term dealing with medical problems and procedures helped us to understand why his dad should go into a long-term care facility, especially if we wanted him to have a private room.

We chose to check out an Assisted Living Facility near our daughter's home. She could more easily help me keep a check on him. With the final decision made to move him, Bob and Linda left for home in Hickory.

Churchland House is a private facility. Jim, Elizabeth, and I visited it the next morning and liked what we saw. We decided it was the best option. We wanted Richard to feel like he was sitting around in his own room, not in a "hospital" room. We looked forward to his move to Churchland House after that final week in rehab, although at the time we did not know it would not happen.

My Beloved's Last Days

When I went to the rehab facility on Saturday morning, November 2, the first thing he wanted was his handkerchief to wipe his eyes. It was on the bedside table, right beside him. I had been told to insist he needed to do things for himself, but I knew he did not find that easy. I picked it up and handed it to him. He extended both arms in a flailing motion, trying to take it. I put it in his hands and helped him wipe his eyes. It was a shock to see he could not coordinate his hands enough to take it from me. I began to be concerned. A definite change had taken place since Thursday when Bob saw him walk. It was the up and down

324

mobility that left such a big question in my mind. I remembered what I had written back in the first facility: "The Unknown He Knows." God alone knew his future.

On another occasion, Richard wanted to be put to bed for a nap, but the facility's policy was for patients to remain upright throughout the day. It was the only time I felt unhappy with their policy and felt they were not considering the patient's needs as much as they were just following policy.

As the days passed, I was moving in low gear, mechanically doing what I thought I was supposed to do or needed to do. I saw my husband becoming weaker and I desperately wanted him in the new facility where he could rest. I have very little recollection of anything special that happened those last days, nor who came and went, even of our children. I was on autopilot, trying to be upbeat while having silent grief. Perhaps it was that which had shut down my memory. I can find no notes I took. I needed the balm of Gilead but could find none. Part of me was also being taken away.

Backward glances are never a good idea unless we can learn something to give us light for the future. I did not know how quickly he would be gone from us, but I suspected his last earthly hours were few. It was now Wednesday, November 6. Elizabeth came in the afternoon. I decided to stay the night with him. He spent a restless night. He said very little, but when he did, his talk was garbled. I had to listen carefully to hear what he wanted to say. For the most part, he was asking for water. I sat beside his bed with my head on the covers, holding his hand, reminding him how much we all loved him. Sleep did not come to me.

He was nauseated during the next day. He ate almost nothing but whatever he took in, food or the Ensure drink, did not stay down. I called the kids to tell them about his condition. Bob had a very busy day, but as soon as he finished his last program with some young people doing their confirmation class, he and Linda left Hickory to come here. Elizabeth was teaching.

Richard was vomiting more often. I became more and more concerned. I remember some details, but they may not be in order. Bob and Linda arrived and offered to stay the night with him, but they had had a full day and long drive. I told them they needed to rest, that I thought I could manage, so they left for the motel. The nursing staff was in and out.

When a decision was made to move Richard to a private room in another part of the facility, I did not question it. We had earlier wanted a private room and were told there were none. I did not know why the change was taking place, except that he was to be moved to Churchland House the next day. The aide said he would be moved about midnight, after the next group of workers came in. Just a few minutes after that, the nurse came in to say they were moving him right then. The staff likely knew what I did not: death was imminent. He was in the last stages. He was awake when I told him he was being moved but did not ask any questions.

The restlessness and vomiting continued. I knew I needed help but could not get any staff in that unit to respond, perhaps because it was the time for the changing of the shift. I was having to wash out the emesis basin only to have it immediately filled again. I did not want to call Elizabeth because I knew she would have to report to school the next morning. Doug had come the day before but cannot drive at night. Jim and Anna and David were *en route* but would not be here for several hours. Bob was trying to get some rest. Finally, an orderly came by, but there was little he could do because he could not stay. I needed someone for emotional and spiritual support.

At 1:30 A.M., I called Bob at the motel and told him I needed him, he had to come and help me. He had had two hours sleep but came immediately. What happened next was likely the most thought-provoking part of this death experience for both of us. I have spent a lot of time thinking about that night.

Richard's vomiting slowed down. He was talking but it was garbled, and we could not understand him. At one point, he was stretching out his arms. Was he welcoming someone or just flailing? Then, he opened his eyes very wide and looked around, very obviously seeing someone or something we could not see. We wondered what he was seeing. Next was a bitter cry, several times, "I am such a terrible sinner!" He seemed in some kind of spiritual distress. We tried to comfort him with words of how much God loved him, how much we loved him. We repeated Scripture. Finally, I said, "Honey, just say, O God, forgive my sins!" I had to say it a couple of times and then he seemed to get the message and in a very repentant voice, repeated it. We prayed again and I think we tried to sing. He settled down and fell asleep. He seemed at peace. I wondered if his next breath would be the last. I kissed him and my heart released him to Heaven.

Soon it was morning. Around six o'clock, the Chicago group arrived, and the family began gathering, children, grand-children and even two great grandchildren were around his bed, singing, reading Scripture. David crawled in bed beside his dad and said, "Dad, we're all here, do you know who I am?" His dad said a clear "yes."

Was he waiting for them to say goodbye? It seemed so. He was ready to pass behind that thin veil that separates earth from Heaven. Jim with his knowledge of how the last moments usually go, thought he would last until about noon. Someone told me I should go home and take a nap. I did not want that, but I thought I needed a shower. Jim had been up all-night driving. We both left.

I came home, got my shower and was getting dressed when the phone rang. Elizabeth said, "Mom, you better come. I think Dad is going." Just as I started for the door the phone rang again. She said, "Dad's gone." It was about ten o'clock. He had simply stopped breathing, no gasping for breath, no fight. I arrived to find a very peaceful husband, looking like he was asleep, the battle over.

I will always have some regret that I was not by his side when he actually breathed his last on Friday morning. When Jim and I got back, we began to sing the favorite old hymns and cho-ruses we all loved. Bob as the pastoral leader read Scripture and prayed, then we all went our separate ways. We planned to meet that evening and discuss funeral arrangements.

I went back to my empty house, once again praying for whatever God had next for me. Isaiah 54 removed any doubt from me that I was a "widow." If Isaiah could metaphorically say Israel could look upon God as a "husband," I could also believe the promise that as a part of the body of Christ, I was a part of what John called "the bride of Christ." He was the Lover of my soul. I would have the help I needed, even in the moments of tears and loneliness. I believed there was still work on earth for me, and I wanted to do it.

Richard's was a unique funeral by all accounts. The chapel was filled, friends from the past and the present, including the dentist who had cared for us when the children were growing up. We had not seen him in years. Due to a prior appointment, he could not stay, but wanted us to know he remembered Richard. Each of the children spoke about what their Dad meant to them while growing up. They sang together a Christian song in Urdu, the language of Pakistan where they had lived as children. Jim prayed the Lord's Prayer in Urdu. Doug was the final speaker. He decided to use his telecommunications skill. He "phoned Heaven."

When Heaven could not find a George or a Richard or a Ratch Thompson, it seemed a little distressing. He was sure his Dad was there. Then, Doug remembered a nickname his dad once had. He asked for "Shortpants" Thompson. "Oh, yes," he pretended the operator said. "Shortpants" is here. It was a family story about when his dad got off the ship as a young child. He had returned to the US in his British boarding school outfit, short pants and knee length stockings. Some American kids had seen him and immediately called out, "Hi ya' Shortpants." Richard was so humiliated he tried to hide, but Shortpants became an overcomer. He no longer had to hide. His record of serving the Lord was written and he was now being welcomed home.

Here is what *"Padri walla beta"* Bob wrote about his dad's burial:

"Horton Veterans Cemetery is such an appropriate final resting place for my Dad. He would have been pleased at the dignity of the setting, Taps, the flag ceremony, the reading of his Navy service record by my brother David, the use of his own Bible by Jim (reading Psalm 19, the first passage he and my Mom memorized together), and the songs we chose – the Navy hymn, America the Beautiful, and In Christ There is No East or West – his father's favorite hymn. Aside from my casual dress, it was the part of the entire week where I felt most like a pastor as I laid my hand on the coffin for the prayer of committal. I used my great grandfather's service book, because Abraham Lincoln Shute (Dad's maternal grandfather) was a Methodist missionary, statesman, and author. I couldn't resist pointing out that the burial service in that service book includes the FULL text of Psalm 90!"

****

It is in the dark hours the child of God seeks for light—any small bit—something to keep our feet on the path and avoid a fall. I was well acquainted with death, funerals and Scripture, but during the hours of Richards' passing, the curtain dropping and the inability to see in the dark what I knew could be light on the other side held an indescribable wonder for me—what really is it like to die? There is no answer for only God knows the unknown.

THE UNKNOWN HE KNOWS
The unknown He knows ~
And that should be enough, but I am she who ponders.
We are those who wonder, who push to know the future
Unknown to us are the steps ahead of us, steps that have been planned,
Written in the Book from the beginning of life in the womb.
Who is this One Who knows it all?
He is the Eternal, all knowing, all seeing God of Eternity.
He knows what lies ahead, but we are bound by time.

Our eyes are dimmed by the dazzling lights of everyday affairs.
Time is not of the essence to Him Who knows Eternity.
If I believe He knows the unknown,
Can I be content with that?
If He knows the unknown and He knows my name
Can I rest with that as my only hope?
Am I able to trust the future into the Hands of the Creator God?
It was He Who told His people in the past, before they were
born,
He had a plan for them.
Will I trust and not be afraid, because the unknown He knows?
He Himself ordained that Eternal and Master plan.
He did it from the beginning.
He planned the seeds of birth and life.
Like the seed when it pushes a tiny leaf out of dry ground
Like lambs are birthed
Like the tiny cells of fish eggs in the ocean. They open as He
planned
And the sea spawns a whole new creation.
Like when an ugly worm wraps itself into a chrysalis
And a new kind of creativity emerges.
The Unknown He knows
It is He, not I, Who knows the way I should take.
I must learn to be content, to trust, to watch for His leading~
To pray, to wait until what is now a mystery is unveiled.
The Unknown He knows.
I must await the unfolding of His plans for me.
I made that first promise many decades long ago.
He has kept to His promises. He has led me in the past.
I ask again today that I will keep to my promise
to accept His will for all He planned for me, for us
That His design be fully complete when we meet Him face to
face.
Enduring light from the words of the prophet Habakkuk
has again reached out to me.

Over two millennia ago, the prophet was struggling with a prob-
lem
He was told an ancient maxim:
"The just shall live by his faith."
I want to live with that call to obedience.
I will trust this One Who knows the unknown to keep me con-
tent.
HE knows the times He has appointed for us
Like Zephaniah, another prophet of old,
"I will rest in His love" for me, for us, knowing well
The unknown He knows.
Who is this One Who knows what we do not, cannot know?
The Bible says He is Jesus Christ, the Creator and Sustainer of
the world.
Our tides, our winds, our sun, the moon and stars all act in
accordance with His plan.
Should I not do the same?
I read about Him in the New Testament, Colossians,
chapter one.
I know that one day I will praise Him that I waited
for His will.
(Psalm 139; Jeremiah 1:5; Habakkuk 2; Job 39:1; Jeremiah 12:3a;
Zephaniah 3:17)
Myrtle Virginia Thompson, 2013

The long night of illness had passed. It is in the long nights
of darkness the child of God must wait for light before taking the
next step. With my beloved now secure in the arms of the Everlasting God, all sin forgiven, finding healing, peace and rest, I was
alone, yet not alone. I had read what God said to Isaiah about Israel, comparing them to a bride, "The Lord thy Maker is thy husband." In Isaiah, Jeremiah and Revelation, God uses a figure of
speech and compares His people as a bride adorned for her husband. Paul said Christ died that the blessing of God might come
on the Gentiles. (Gal.3.) I was in a new relationship and considered a bride. As God had plans for Israel, so He had plans for me.

During the years since Richard passed, I have felt that loving relationship. I have seen God's words fulfilled. His presence has gone with me. He gave me new responsibilities, and opportunities to tell of His love. He has given me peace and protection. I have experienced the joy of the Lord as my strength and the comfort of the Holy Spirit. From the 1920s and my birth to the 2020s and the likelihood of my home-going It is the words of Holy Writ which taught me I was bought with a price that I might glorify God. There is no greater privilege than to be a part of the company that awaits His return to set up His Kingdom on earth.

May "Thy Kingdom come, Thy will be done on earth as it is in Heaven."

GUIDEPOSTS

I see the mist, the fog of the night
Come slowly rolling in
Soon covering my sight
Somewhere beyond, I know,
There is a cloudless sky
The moon and stars are shining
I will not ask this "Why?"

But mist has surrounded me; I cannot see my way
I long for the One who can lead me to day

Darkness so dark, clouds so heavy
No guideposts to lead me on
And I am weary

"Weeping may endure for the night, but joy cometh in the morning." (Psalm 30:5, KJV)

The fog will lift; the radiance will appear
My Shepherd knows my way
And He is near

Only a glimpse of Him I see in the night
But He points to the way
And He is my Light

The mist rolls on
The clouds pass away
And my burden is lifted
In the dawning of the day.

I Have Been Young and Now I Am Old

"God, you have taught me from my youth;
to this day I proclaim your wondrous deeds." (Psalm 71:17)

"I have been young and now I am old,
Yet I have not seen the righteous forsaken
Or his descendants begging bread." (Psalm 37:25)

Culture is said to be the totality of our experiences as we live our lives. When we move from one culture to another we become "enculturated" with new ideas, new foods, new surroundings. Because America is a multi-cultural country, young people today may have already experienced some of that when they interact with people here at home, choosing foods from other countries and accepting the dress of others.

None of that was a part of my early life, but it was a part of my husband's. He had been born of missionary parents and spent his early years in India. I would learn of other cultures when I went overseas as a missionary. God placed us in different countries, but He made us individually. We have individual tastes governed by our culture, but for most of us, He makes it possible to adapt. The joy of that is when we know Christ, we can accept each other. As His children we can be free of bondage and self-centeredness. That message became clear during my life in three foreign countries. We were able to adapt to the foods and dress of the people among whom we lived.

I look back on my childhood in a tiny house in a country village where life was simple. Little did I know God had plans for my future that would involve village life in other countries of the world, such as a remote village in Pakistan. True, our first home was a large house built by the British many years earlier, but when we actually moved into the village, I felt at ease with the way the villagers lived and free in sharing my faith, another bit of "preparedness."

My early years as a missionary might be compared to a quick trip on an airplane. We fly through the air at high speed and both distance and time pass quickly. My years were filled with child care, language study, overseeing the mission school and hospitality. Those first years were filled with excitement, inexperience, and anticipation. Soon the first five and a half years in Pakistan were over. We were going home for our first leave. I would see my family, friends, find again and celebrate the familiar culture I had left behind. What I did not realize was the familiar would be changed. Life never remains stagnant. Some old haunts were removed and some new places like shopping malls and McDonald's ten cent hamburgers were added. Even friends from the past had under-gone changes like I had, most of us now married with children.

At this time, likely the final chapter of my life, I find I want to write of these things, to leave a legacy which will tell my family and friends God is for real, a very present help in trouble. Most of the time our lives pass before us without any special consideration for tomorrow. It is when trials come, we find the need for help that is outside ourselves. It is at that low point many will call out to a God they had not known but somehow now think He can help them. Scripture reminds us God knew before He created us what would be our future. Trusting Him before that time will put us on the right path for peace and guidance.

"Do not be afraid of anything that you are going to suffer. Indeed, the devil will throw some of you into prison, that you may be tested, and you will face an ordeal for ten days. Remain faithful until death, and I will give you the crown of life."
(Revelation 2:10)

334

"For our struggle is not with flesh and blood but with the principalities, with the powers, with the world rulers of this present darkness, with the evil spirits in the heavens." (Ephesians 6:12)

Too Many Birthdays to Count

Many young children will refer to their birthday year with the reminder of "and a half." I feel sure I was one who did that. Now, like them, I can say I am ninety-three "and a half." I admit to loving birthdays, mine, or my children's. I think it is important to remember God gave us birth rights and we should be thankful for every year He gives us. It may have been one more thing my Mom and I shared. I have some old birthday memories I can't forget. Like the time my mom made me a surprise birthday cake for my sixth birthday and the time my dad gave my mom the money to purchase a part of roller skates for my twelfth birthday.

At age sixteen my sister and her friends wanted to plan a "coming out party" for me. By this time, I was a very committed Christian and wanted no part of a dance like others had. They planned a party with games for the celebration. We had so much fun it became the talk of the kids in high school for weeks.

There were many other celebrations but for my 90th birthday in 2018 my children planned the party, and I became acutely aware of how gracious God had blessed me with five very talented and gifted children. They had gotten together and planned each detail so all of them were involved. It was held in the social hall of the Centenary Methodist Church where I was teaching a Sunday School class of older adults. Everything was beautifully arranged, and the hall was full of people, including some out of own guests. I felt so honored, so blessed and so thankful for all God's blessings, family, friends, and years of happy times.

If it seems like my life has been concentrated on birthdays I have celebrated, that is only because I actually have loved growing old and remembering happy times. This year's advance into another year, my 93rd, has almost equaled my 90th. I have had cards, gifts and invitations to lunch or dinner. My pastor son put a notice on his daily email to his church people. At last count I had gotten many cards and emails wishing me a Happy Birthday.

I know I am growing old but mostly I don't *feel* old. My health is still good, despite problems with diminishing vision and hearing. I don't need a cane, a walker or prescription drugs. I do find days like yesterday leave my body reminding me it wasn't meant to last forever. I did both housework and yard work. By the time I got home from having dinner out with a friend, I was ready to call it a day.

I love what the psalmist tells us about sleep. He says God gives His beloved sleep (rest) and God neither slumbers nor sleeps. When we lived in one remote village in Pakistan and our dad was away on a trek I would read or say five verses to the children before we went to bed. The last one always was from Psalm 3, something like this, "I will both lay me down in peace and sleep for Thou Lord only makes us to dwell in safety." We trusted His watch care over us and were kept safe.

Now there are eight great grandchildren added to our Thompson "clan." What will growing up in the culture we have today be like for them? We seem to be stepping far away from the biblical teaching once more important for our welfare. Our laws of governance were based on a behavior of consideration for others. An egocentric world will leave a vacuum. Because of my loving family, I understand family life like I experienced it in the culture of Pakistan. There the elderly were cared for by the younger. I am blessed with being able to care for most of my needs and my children are always available to help when I can't.

God has blessed my life with meaningful times but that does not mean there have not been trials. We learn through our mistakes which God allows. The Andrae Crouch song, "Through It All" spells it out so beautifully. He sings of many anxious moments where he has learned that he must trust Jesus to get him through. It reflects my own feelings.

Even with some of my own sorrows and mistakes, I have come to trust Jesus to get me through. I know for sure I am one of God's children and I know where my life will be when that dark curtain of death drops. I will be home with my Savior Who has indeed led me all the way.

Until then, I continue to ask for ways He can still use me. Someone said, "God doesn't call the qualified, He qualifies the Called." Paul reminds us of God's strength made perfect in our weaknesses: "My grace is sufficient for you; my power is made perfect in weakness" (2 Corinthians 12:9).

God Still Has a Purpose for Me

I got out of bed and began the day's routine, made the bed, showered, dressed for the day, heated the kettle for a cup of instant coffee, then settled at the kitchen table for Bible reading and prayer. Both my husband and I from college days started with "No Bible, no breakfast." We later added the early cup of coffee for me and a cup of tea for him. Prayer begins with asking God to search my heart and then some quiet intercession, first for my family and for those who have asked for it.

Prayer became an important part of my life after I became a Christian. There were many times I prayed for God's provision and found Him faithful. He provided the means for me to attend college and even provided the small and seemingly trivial needs. He met our needs when going out as missionaries, not just for material needs but also putting people in our lives to help us at every step. He provided His loving watch care at every turn, sending someone when I needed help and seeing me through several health crises.

Having experienced God's faithful answer to my own needs and prayers, has led me to take seriously the request of others to pray for them. Richard and I routinely prayed for those we encountered during our missionary years. That routine continued long after we "retired." And for me, has never ceased. Today, wherever I meet someone who asks me to pray for them, I say, "Let's pray right now" and we do. Whether on a phone call or in the grocery store, I find that praying at that very moment ensures that the prayer is put in God's hands.

"Therefore, confess your sins to one another and pray for one another, that you may be healed. The fervent prayer of a righteous person is very powerful." (James 5:16)

Many prayer requests came from people I encountered while teaching. I was asked to teach Sunday School at a local church for a couples' class, even though I was not a member and had never taught men. The friend who invited me to teach insisted none of that would make a difference. And so, I agreed and have continued to teach there for the last fourteen years, and it has been a great blessing and privilege.

Unlike the students in most of my prior teaching experiences, we are a group of older adults who have grown together in faith and now a few younger ones are joining. We have stayed in touch with each other for encouragement and garnered money for missions and for individuals in ministry.

One day, a group of friends from church invited me for lunch in a nearby restaurant. Our conversation turned into something akin to a Bible study. Before we parted, we had decided to continue meeting, not a Bible study but a time to ask questions about the Bible. I sometimes find myself stymied by their questions. The Bible message is always new. The language is such that it is constantly updating itself revealing new truths or truths we had not noticed which are again relevant to our day. Even after 70 years I have to go back and search out answers which always apply to the circumstances.

Bible teaching and ministry with the elderly have become a part of my life. I began teaching a Bible study in a local assisted living facility as well as visiting and praying with individuals in others. It was at one of these where I met Candice who agreed to help me put my memories and stories in order for this book.

I discovered that there are many elderly residents who are quite depressed and lonely. Many times, their families have moved away and are not able to visit as often as they would wish. The residents feel the loss of spending time with family and friends. They miss being part of their community and church activities. Sometimes their inability to use modern technology to keep in touch adds to their isolation. Seeing their loneliness has made me realize how important a simple visit from someone can be. I would encourage readers to be attuned to the needs of these dear people and consider a ministry to the elderly, even if it is a simple and short visit or phone call so they understand they are not forgotten.

Our society also seems inclined to "write-off" the elderly and think they have nothing valuable to contribute. But Scripture teaches that wisdom comes with age. They have stories to tell and should be encouraged to share them with the younger generations. While some may think the stories out of date, they are full of experiences and lessons that are still relevant today.

What can the elderly contribute? Some think because they are bedridden or in a wheelchair, God no longer has a purpose for them. But those who are in a wheelchair can visit with other residents who might be feeling low or unable to leave their rooms. Even the bedridden can pray for their family, friends, or fellow nursing home residents who do not know Christ as their Lord and Savior. God has a purpose for us all. Even at my age, God still has a purpose for me!

Why Do I Write?

I was 85 when my beloved left us. What does a widow that age do to keep busy? I had spent the days caring for his needs and began trying my hand at writing. I have always found writing down my thoughts to be therapeutic. The apostle John confirms the importance of writing.

"I write these things to you so that you may know that you have eternal life, you who believe in the name of the Son of God." (1 John 5:13)

Writing helps keep my memory alive. Even so, I have a block of wood with a memo on it: "My mind not only wanders, but it also sometime leaves completely." Writing down my thoughts while I read helps me pay attention to what the Scripture is teaching me.

Long ago I found singing and writing are two good ways to share our faith. One day a man working for us as a cook asked if anything was wrong. I said "No, why do you ask?" He said I had not been singing!

"I will praise you among the peoples, LORD;
I will chant your praise among the nations." (Psalm 108:4)

Writing and keeping family and friends and churches informed has remained my responsibility. I had kept records, journals, notebooks, letters—all information about our lives, Richard's treks and our growing family. I did not have a typewriter during those first few years of our missionary life. Everything written was done by hand. Moses had to carve in stone what he wrote so I guess paper and ink were a great improvement. Then came the computer technology. Recently when my computer gave out and had to be replaced it was like the loss of a good friend. Today's technology is incredible, many ways to keep in touch but I fear social media could outclass or obviate written memos like mine.

In both Galatians and Corinthians, Paul writes about our gifts for ministry. I believe one of my gifts was writing. After Richard's passing, I began writing and sending articles for the Opinion page of the *Suffolk News Herald*, a small newspaper which dates back to the 1860s and has a wide distribution area. In my articles I want readers to see the Biblical relevance to our times today. I sign my name, my "writing qualifications" and my age.

I have the freedom to incorporate Scripture in my articles. Since the "advent" of COVID 19—from which we have not yet seen its ending—I was reminded and hoped to remind others we can trust God's guidance in the dark circumstances. I took the lesson from Paul's adventure in Acts 27.

The ship in which Paul was traveling was facing a violent storm. The mariners were not able to control it. The turbulence had blown the ship off course and into "uncharted waters" that almost ended the lives of 276 people before they landed on Malta (Acts 27,2 8.) The seamen had tried to "chart the waters" as they sailed from territory they knew well but were thrown off course by the wind. God was rerouting Paul's journey and because of this, the people on the island where they landed would get the Gospel.

Like that ship, COVID-19, has changed our course and the ways we interact and worship. But this situation has not been without lessons to learn. God is still in control and has allowed us to discover new and innovative ways to share the Gospel.

****

Friends continue to drop by. During the pandemic we sat six feet apart in the garage with the door open and visited. My problems with vision and hearing do not limit my joy with those who come to me. I am still able to share the Good News teaching the Bible in Sunday School and in a small class. I pass out copies of what I write, asking God to give the readers insight into what life with God can be like. In the still uncharted waters of our times, we need a younger generation to continue the message Jesus left with us, "I will come again..." I don't know if my strong feelings about that time are because of my age or because we are near the fulfillment of Scripture given us. I know only I want to be found in Him, faithful until He calls my name.

My Earthly Sojourn Included Children

I have now been in the same city, the same house since 1999. We were exceedingly blessed with five children who stay in close touch. They got into their chosen careers by working hard and each has excelled. They are daily remembered in prayer. It is to them I owe so many blessings of my life.

Elizabeth, the oldest, lives nearby and keeps a close check on me, helps with any needs I have. She and David just celebrated their 50th wedding anniversary. They spent ten years as missionaries in Belgium, then returned to work in the US. Elizabeth went into education, teaching History, French and the Humanities. She has 2 MA degrees and has had several honors for her work. She is now a professor in the Community College. They have 2 daughters and 2 grandchildren in Iowa where she visits and stays in close touch using facetime.

Doug started his career with a small independent telephone company when the Bell Telephone system broke up. Over the years through mergers and acquisitions, he survived them all and spent most of his career in telecommunications and IT as a Complex Systems IT Project Manager having earned his Project Management Professional certification in 2002. After 47 years of continuous service, he retired in 2020. He married Renee shortly after starting work and they raised 3 children. After the kids grew older, she worked in the telecom field as well and eventually started a very successful business providing professional services to telecommunications and IT Communication system providers, which she continues to do today They now live in south central Pennsylvania where they enjoy spending time with their 4 grandchildren.

Jim skipped through school rarely bringing home a book but always seeming to know the subject. In high school his teacher told me she thought he had a photographic memory. He finished Wheaton college and wanted to go to medical school. We had no money for that. He worked on building a shed for a businessman and then married his daughter Vivian. They had 3 children. He graduated from Loyola Medical College with a clinical career in academic Internal Medicine and Emergency Medicine. He now works in Denver as a Physician Informaticist and our family's "personal and private" physician when we need his medical expertise. He takes great delight in having playtime with his two grandchildren.

Bob, our third son seemed to have been born for the ministry. At an early age he scolded himself with the rebuke, *"bob um!"* He earned his doctorate in theology but just prefers "Pastor Bob" as a title. With Linda as a gracious, loving partner he has led a large flock in Corinth Reformed Church in Hickory NC. He can identify with his parishioners because he has had so many of their same situations. They have 3 children and 2 grandchildren but must make the trip to Hawaii to see their son and his family with one grandson. The church airs their Sunday morning traditional worship on YouTube and I can hear what he is teaching. He followed the train of his scholarly great grandfather and is a resource person for any Bible knowledge I need.

Our youngest son David is a businessman. We celebrated his birth the day before Bob's 7th birthday. David went with us to Iran and finished his education in the US and graduated from Averett University in Virginia. He and Rayanne had 3 children when they were led to adopt "parentless" little ones. They added 2 Russian orphans and then had another son; for a total of six children. His entrepreneurial spirit has shown him to not be afraid of challenges. He is now starting his 8th business helping the elderly, like his mom. It will provide lighting products that reduce fall risks, cut sundowning in half, and improve mood for the elderly and third shift workers. I have only praise for this and pray fervently for his success.

All during my sojourn I have planted gardens. During my sojourn the garden of my life has had both sweet and bitter herbs. They blended to bring fulfillment. The Psalmist said it so beautifully, "O taste and see that the Lord is good. Blessed is the one who trusts in Him." Psalm 34:8

Eternity means there is a future sojourn for everyone. Jesus said He was going away to prepare a place for all who love Him and I do. I expect to sojourn in that heavenly realm John wrote about in his Book, the Revelation.

Afterword

I had the unique privilege of spending my life in villages around the world and also had the opportunity to visit in palaces. It was the *calling of God* which put me in those places. Many years later, I would pen the thought, "I Know That I Was in His Plan," as I hummed the tune of "Danny Boy". Here is what I wrote:

"I think Scripture has made clear for me the incredible thought that I was in the mind of God before I was born: Job 10, Isaiah 43, Psalm 139 and Jeremiah 1:5. I was reminded of the people God used in the Old and New Testament: Moses, Joseph, Esther, King David, Paul and the Disciples. I believe He gave life and had/has a plan for each person born, and we are happiest when we know God's will for our lives. So great is His LOVE for us."

"I KNOW THAT I WAS IN HIS PLAN"
Oh, Wondrous Shepherd, I am just a wand'ring sheep.
You came to live, and die for all mankind
You saw me long before I knew you as my God.
You chose my way, for I was in Your Plan!

Oh Wondrous Love, far greater than my words can tell,
when I remember, what You've done for me
You took a wand'ring sheep and have redeemed my soul,
and with your Love, You set my spirit free!

Oh, Love of God, so pure, so free, so wonderful;
oh, Precious Blood, 'twas shed on Calvary~
I never can, by human wisdom understand,
yet this I know, that I was in Your Plan!

This Precious Shepherd came from Heav'n to give me life;
He lived on earth, and showed me how to die
He came a babe and walked the roads of Galilee,
He lived a man, and brought me victory.

Oh, Praise His Name! This Shepherd lives forever!
He's there for us, and longs to hear our prayer
He sees our needs and satisfies our heart's desire;
though wayward sheep, yet we are in His Plan!

This Very God, the One Who gave His life for all,
will intercede, as long as earth shall stand;
And when someday, we see Him face to face at last,
It will be then--we'll understand His Plan.

Oh, Wondrous Shepherd, I am still a wand'ring sheep!
Take Thou my life, and make it all Thine own
None other can compare among the gods of men,
'twas Calvary where all Thy love was shown.

That plan of Thine, which brought salvation full and free,
will stand through time, and all Eternity
For God's Great Grace, that purchased and redeemed my
soul,
has proved to me, that I was in His plan.

Those wonderful days live on in my journals, copied down
with how I lived them and when I go back and read about my life,
I see the strengths and the weaknesses, the blessings and the dis-
appointments, the joys and the sadness, but overall is the "atmos-
phere" like a covering that the God of Eternity was present and in
the lives of all those God brought into my life.

I have been blessed with one thousand blessings and
more.

Myrtle V. Thompson